The Elements of Blogging

Becoming a blogger takes practice, hard work, and, ultimately, a passion for the craft. Whether you plan to blog on politics or parenting, *The Elements of Blogging* is designed to give you the skills and strategies to get started, to sustain your work, and to seek out a robust audience. This book is loaded with practical advice on important topics such as determining a niche, finding the best stories, and blogging effectively and ethically. It features examples from both amateur and professional bloggers that show the techniques for building an argument, finding a voice, crafting a headline, and establishing a brand.

Key features:

- Real-world applicability. This book includes thumbnail profiles of bloggers and their sites, which illuminate key skills you will need to become an effective blogger
- Interactivity. Each chapter features discussion points and exercises intended to get you to think about, reflect on, and apply the contents of each chapter
- Creativity. While this book dives into software and plug-ins for bloggers, its main goal is to cover how to write blogs on myriad topics: news, opinion, travel, politics, art, and more.

Mark Leccese is an associate professor of Journalism at Emerson College. He has worked in print and online journalism for 35 years as a reporter, editor, and blogger. For several years, he was the media criticism blogger for *The Boston Globe* and WBUR-FM, a National Public Radio affiliate. His work has appeared in the *Columbia Journalism Review, Quill, Journalism & Mass Communication Quarterly, Commonwealth, America, The Boston Globe, Boston Phoenix*, and *Boston Magazine*.

Jerry Lanson is the author/co-author of *Writing for Others, Writing for Ourselves; Writing and Reporting the News*; and *News in a New Century*. He currently blogs for *The Huffington Post* and has posted several hundred blogs over the past five or six years on five different blogs. He was the first chair of the Department of Journalism at Emerson College (1999–2005) and has taught full-time on the faculties of NYU, Boston University, and Syracuse University.

The Elements of Blogging

Expanding the Conversation of Journalism

Mark Leccese and
Jerry Lanson

Focal Press
Taylor & Francis Group

NEW YORK AND LONDON

First published 2016
by Focal Press
70 Blanchard Road, Suite 402, Burlington, MA 01803

and by Focal Press
2 Park Square, Milton Park, Abingdon, Oxon OX14 4RN

Focal Press is an imprint of the Taylor & Francis Group, an informa business

Notices
Knowledge and best practice in this field are constantly changing. As new research and experience broaden our understanding, changes in research methods, professional practices, or medical treatment may become necessary.

Practitioners and researchers must always rely on their own experience and knowledge in evaluating and using any information, methods, compounds, or experiments described herein. In using such information or methods, they should be mindful of their own safety and the safety of others, including parties for whom they have a professional responsibility.

Product or corporate names may be trademarks or registered trademarks, and are used only for identification and explanation without intent to infringe.

Library of Congress Cataloging in Publication Data
Leccese, Mark.
  The elements of blogging: expanding the conversation of journalism/authored by Mark Leccese and Jerry Lanson.
  pages cm
  1. Blogs. 2. Online journalism. 3. Authorship—Study and teaching.
  I. Lanson, Jerry. II. Title.
  TK5105.8884.L43 2015
  302.23'14—dc23
  2015003366

ISBN: 978-1-138-02153-2 (hbk)
ISBN: 978-1-138-02154-9 (pbk)
ISBN: 978-1-315-77769-6 (ebk)

Typeset in Berling and Futura
by Florence Production Ltd, Stoodleigh, Devon, UK

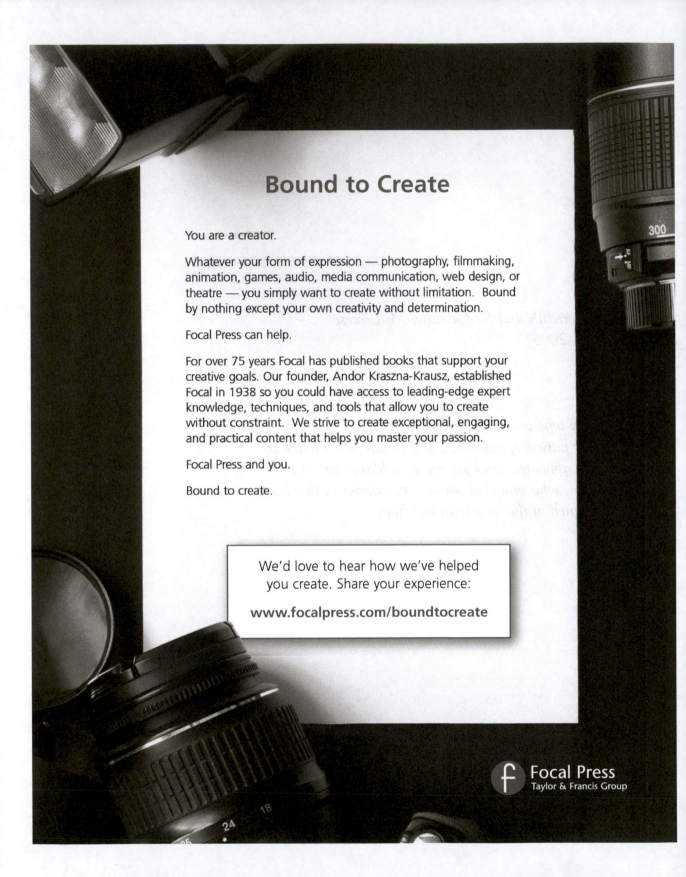

Contents

viii

Introduction

In the same way you do not have to be a professional driver to drive, you no longer have to be a professional publisher to publish . . . News can break into the public consciousness without the traditional press weighing in.

—Clay Shirky, *Here Comes Everybody*

So you want to be a blogger?

No problem. There's plenty of room at the table: this table circles the globe.

A year after his 2008 book, Shirky, one of the leading thinkers of the Digital Revolution, reminded a TED (Technology, Entertainment, Design) Talk audience we are in an age in which "consumers are now producers." Seven years later, this once revolutionary idea is so commonplace as to be almost pedestrian. Remarkable.

"The moment we're living through," Shirky told his audience—and the 1.4 million people who have viewed the talk online—has seen "the largest increase in expressive capability in human history."

Join the conversation. But accept the responsibility and expect the hard work it takes to do so well. Like anyone else, you can break news, comment on news, share news, tell stories, offer insight. Pull up any of an ever-growing list of free programs on your computer, and you can be your own publisher this afternoon; blog software is that easy and that ubiquitous.

There is, however, one small obstacle. Well, maybe not so small. When you hang out your shingle that reads "Blogger," you can expect a whole lot of competition. In 1999, one researcher tallied the number of blogs on the Internet and came up with 23. Twelve years later, the company NM Incite was tracking *181 million* blogs worldwide when it gave up counting. In April 2013, the marketing blogger Eric Pangburn looked through company press releases and found the reported number of bloggers using Tumblr, WordPress, LiveJournal, Weebly, and Blogster totaled 240 million—and he couldn't find any data on the number of users from the popular platforms Blogger, Blogsome, and Posterous, which host tens of millions more.

All of these bloggers are straining to be heard or seen or read. Drawing readers, viewers, or listeners to your new blog—and sustaining its focus and quality—is going to be a lot harder than getting it up and running.

This book is designed to help you with all three, to give you skills and strategies to get started, to sustain your work, and to seek out a robust audience.

We'd like to urge you from the outset to enter your new blogging enterprise with the right mindset. Come to blogging with a desire to share a passion or area of expertise, not an expectation to strike it rich (very few do). Or, to use an historical analogy, keep in mind that a lot more gold prospectors who moved to California and Alaska in the nineteenth century found great new homesteads instead of the mother lode.

Blogging, too, allows you to build not only a homestead, but your own neighborhood, occasionally as quickly as those mining towns sprouted up but typically much more slowly. It's a way of connecting with old friends and finding new ones, tapping into existing communities and assembling your own. Blogging offers much more. It can help you gather your thoughts. It can improve your skills and your ease as a researcher, reporter, writer, and storyteller. And it's great fun.

If you're good and smart and persistent, it also can—can, but not necessarily will—become a way of making a living or supplementing one. We'd advise, however, that you don't start with that expectation, and that, even if it's your ultimate goal, you keep your day job until your blog starts attracting audience and, ultimately, ads. We'd also advise you that, dreams aside, you probably shouldn't set your sights too high, especially for that first blog post. Let's face it: it's not going to go viral. Readers won't rush to leave comments. You're not going to get an invitation to *The View*. Not yet anyway.

Like most things, becoming a successful blogger takes practice, hard work, and craft. It demands finding a niche, developing a strategy, using media and social media well, and finding a compelling voice and something fresh to say. It requires patience, persistence and a bit of luck to draw that first ad, a bit of recognition or, ever so occasionally, a book contract. Success in blogging typically follows the tortoise, not the hare. It means moving forward, slowly and steadily, learning, experimenting, engaging others, and, to whatever extent you like, playing around with words and images as you go.

One early and prolific blogger is Barry Ritholtz, chief investment officer of Ritholtz Wealth Management, who began his blog, *The Big Picture*, in 2003. Nearly 12 years later, on September 27, 2014, he wrote an entry under the headline "What I've learned after 30,000 posts." And no, that number is not a typo. Here is a bit of what he learned. We suspect you will learn something quite similar.

> After more than a decade of getting up before the crack of dawn to write a daily journal about all things financial, here is what I've learned:
>
> **Writing is a good way to figure out what you think.**
> The act of putting pen to paper, or in my case, spilling pixels on a screen, requires thought . . . Often, I have no idea what I thought about a subject until I begin to write about it. Once you research an idea, you begin to develop a perspective. Writing about anything in public, often in real time, has helped fashion my views . . .
>
> **Writing is a good way to become a better writer (so is reading).**
> When I started the blog, one goal was to become a better writer. After more than a dozen years spending an hour a day writing—and another hour a day reading outstanding writing from others—your skills begin to improve. It is an old joke that it only takes a decade or so to become an overnight sensation.

As you get started with your blog, this book is meant to offer a mix of practical advice and inspiration. Look at it and use it as a blogger's guide, not a career guide. We hope it will give you the tools to blog well, effectively, and ethically, to find and build a niche that brings you followers and satisfaction. One author of this book, Jerry Lanson, has made a few dollars blogging. The other author, Mark Leccese, has declined to accept pay from the outlets that have published his blogs because he is a media critic and wants to avoid any appearance of a conflict of interest. Both of us came to blogging after significant careers as journalists. Neither of us have retired from our primary careers as journalism professors. We've kept those day jobs, and it's a good thing. We're not famous. Our words don't go viral, though sometimes they're well read.

Still, we blog. We do so because we love to tell stories and craft what we hope are well-conceived and supported opinions, because we have a passion and some expertise for the subjects we share with others, because we love to communicate something with (we hope) substance and style, because we enjoy the give-and-take with our audiences. So will you.

On the pages that follow, we'll also be sharing the experiences and stories of other bloggers, amateur and professional, all of whom we've asked to share their insights. You'll get tips on how to determine the best niche, where to find stories, how to write them, how to choose a platform or plug-in, how to build a brand, how to craft headlines that draw an audience, and how to find a voice that makes your writing distinctive (and more importantly, truly yours). Above all, perhaps, you'll learn of the triumphs and tribulations of being your own publisher, calling your own shots. This role is at the heart of the new world of consumer as producer. With it comes the joy and the responsibility to communicate with an audience not once in a while, not only when the spirit moves you, but on a consistent basis. It's a discipline that builds thinking and writing muscles alike, just as Ritholtz says.

Both of us have taken satisfaction from giving readers insight and information they might not have gotten from their customary news outlets. We've tried in our work to draw connections between events and ideas in the news and, sometimes, simply tried to make those in our audience smile. We have contributed to the conversation that is the blogosphere, shared perspectives, and perhaps given readers new insights on politics, the media, culture, travel, family life, and more.

To blog regularly is to learn about the world and yourself, to meet new acquaintances, and to share exchanges with your audience. It's an opportunity that plays a significant role in setting the twenty-first-century agenda.

In the end, your ability to embrace that sense of sharing stories and of entering a community's conversation as your own boss will do more to propel you toward bigger success than anything else.

Turn the page. Join us on the blogger's journey, an adventure that at times can take you across continents and to new insights without stirring from your keyboard—and we surely encourage you to do such stirring with regularity.

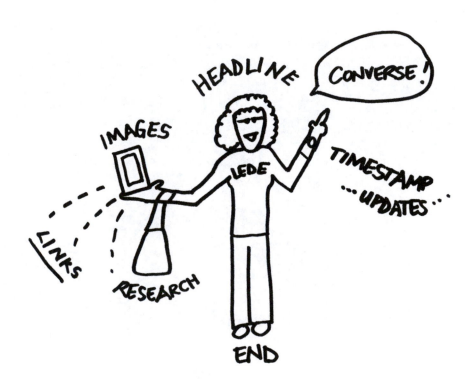

Anatomy of a Blog Post

What makes an effective blog post is an audience. But to get there, you'll need an original, focused topic; a clear headline that draws ever-fickle readers in; good pictures or graphics; tight writing; links to other media; a bit of personality; and the opportunity for others to talk with you or talk back at you.

Blogging has its similarities to traditional journalism. What makes it different is a little more voice and a lot more of a level playing field with readers. In some ways, in fact, it has filled the void of everyman journalism, as mainstream publications become more expensive and more written for and by elites. In contrast, the blogosphere is meant for the writer and reader to converse in ways traditional journalism never achieved, but at the same time for that writer to bring something new—a perspective, facts, expertise—to the discussion.

Let's dissect the elements of an effective blog post. One of this book's authors, Mark Leccese, wrote this post, which is about the first 48 hours of media coverage of the one of the biggest news stories of 2010—the BP offshore rig oil spill disaster in the Gulf of Mexico.

2

Gatekeeper **4**

Mark Leccese watches Boston and the people who report on it

< Back to front page **1**

Text size ▬ ▬

2 ## Confusion, secrecy and lies blight oil spill coverage

5 **6**

Posted by Mark Leccese May 28, 2010 11:51 AM

Print | Comments (9)

f Share 85 Tweet 2 in Share 0 g +1 0 ◄ ShareThis 186 E-mail

3 Media coverage of the "top kill" on the ruptured oil well in the Gulf Of Mexico over the past 48 hours has been, to put it kindly, bewildering. Without access to the site, journalists have had to depend on their sources — primarily BP and U.S. Coast Guard Admiral Thad Allen — and those sources were either inaccessible for long stretches of the day, issued oblique statements, or just lied.

7

This morning's lead story in the New York Times summed up Thursday's coverage.

> BP officials, who along with government officials created the impression early in the day that the strategy was working, disclosed later that they had stopped pumping the night before when engineers saw that too much of the drilling fluid was escaping along with the oil.

The confusion started Thursday morning at 7 when the Los Angeles Times website (in a story taken down from the site that night) "'Top kill' stops gulf oil leak, official says."

> Engineers have stopped the flow of oil and gas into the Gulf of Mexico from a gushing BP well, the federal government's top oil-spill commander, U.S. Coast Guard Adm. Thad Allen, said Thursday morning.

8 The story spread quickly throughout social networking sites and was the top story on the Google News aggregator, which ranks stories partly based on links and hits. It seems Americans wanted to believe the LA Times story.

But it wasn't true. Or maybe it was true for a moment, or not completely untrue, or a misunderstanding. It depended on how reporters interpreted a quote given to a local radio station by the government's top man on the scene, Adm. Allen: "They've stopped the hydrocarbons from coming up. They've been able to stabilize the well head, they are pumping mud down it."

The New Orleans Times Picayune, in a story posted at 8:15 a.m., read Allen's quote differently than the local radio station and the LA Times.

9
> An attempt to kill the runaway Deepwater Horizon well spilling oil into the Gulf of Mexico is going according to plan so far, leaving the coast guard admiral in charge of managing the spill "cautiously optimistic" but unwilling to say the well is capped.

The main page of the BP website — where the company would be expected to proclaim the oil spill had been stopped if it had — displayed only a terse three-sentence statement it did not change throughout the day.

11
> **Update on Gulf of Mexico Oil Spill** — "Top kill" operations continued over the night and are ongoing. There are no significant events to report at this time. BP will provide updates on progress as appropriate.

3

All day Thursday, news organizations reported some variant of a story that went something like this: "Efforts to stop the oil leak are going well so far but it will be hours but we know for sure."

Then, at 5 p.m., the New York Times reported that what the public had been led to believe was the essence of the "top kill" strategy, pumping drilling fluid into the oil well, had been stopped by BP 16 hours ago.

> BP temporarily stopped pumping drilling fluid into its stricken oil well in the Gulf of Mexico late Wednesday night after engineers saw that too much of the fluid was escaping along with the leaking crude oil.

12 Lisa Desjardins of CNN tweeted at 6:15 "#OilSpill more: BP says it stopped pumping mud into well 16 hours ago, but will pump again soon. Waited until end of business day to tell us," and then, a few minutes later, "Why did BP/response team wait 16 hrs to reveal it suspended Top Kill to reassess? Did Coast Guard commandant know? #oilspill."

Adm. Allen was wrong when he said Thursday morning "they are pumping mud down it."

On the 8 p.m. CNN news cast, Rick Sanchez summed it up when he said to the two offshore drilling experts he was about to interview: "I'm really confused. I was reporting on this very set three hours ago that it looked like things were going pretty well."

One of the experts, Ed Overton of Louisiana State University, said he guessed "they ran out of mud." That, he said, was "a wild guess on my part but it's probably pretty close."

And that's the how Thursday's media coverage went: The lack of accurate and timely information from BP and confusing information from the government reduced experts to making wild guesses and journalists to building stories from scraps of vague and sometimes statements from their sources.

13 The most informed speculation was at the website The Oil Drum (which crashed Friday morning), where dozens and dozens of anonymous posters, including many who said they had extensive experience in offshore drilling, watched the grainy underwater video stream provided by BP and offered theories on what was happening. The posters did not think it was going well.

As all this was happening, the government announced that this is the biggest oil spill — several times worse than the preliminary estimates by BP and the government — in American history.

And there were reliable reports that BP and local law enforcement officials were blocking photographers and reporters from documenting the effects of the oil spill. Mac McClelland of Mother Jones wrote a grimly amusing first-person account of being turned away from Louisiana's Elmer's Island. Newsweek reported "news photographers are complaining that their efforts to document the slow-motion disaster in the Gulf of Mexico are being thwarted by local and federal officials — working with BP — who are blocking access to the sites where the effects of the spill are most visible."

I got an e-mail from Lloyd Nelson, a reporter who works for the The Daily Comet in Lafourche Parish, Louisiana, a few minutes ago. **14**

10

> I've been on Fourchon Beach and Grand Ise Beach to see the brown oil wash upon the shore. It looks like a very thick brownie mix.
>
> The trips to the beach have been heavily monitored by the parish government, supposedly at the request of BP. I've tried to verify that with BP, but their unified command center is only unified in avoiding answering any question a reporter might have. It's frustrating.
>
> Media has been regulated to two trips per day to Fourchon Beach. The trips, 9 a.m. and 2 p.m., last approximately 15 minutes and are always under the supervision of a sheriff's deputy and a parish official.

4

> And trying to get the cleanup crews, the guys raking oily sand into clumps and throwing it into a clear plastic bag, to talk is futile. BP apparently said that's a no go. Those guys won't even admit that they're raking oily sand, let alone give a name for a photo cutline.

15 This morning, Adm. Allen said on the ABC News program "Good Morning America" that "they have been able to stop the hyrocrabons from coming up the well bore."

That's the same thing he said yesterday morning.

Quickly, The New York Times posted this:

> By injecting solid objects overnight as well as heavy drilling fluid into the stricken well leaking oil into the Gulf of Mexico, engineers appeared to have stemmed the flow of oil, Adm. Thad W. Allen of the Coast Guard, the leader of the government effort, said on Friday morning. But he stressed that the next 12 to 18 hours would be "very critical" in permanently stanching what is already the worst oil spill in United States history.

5

The BP website, of course, was giving nothing away by mid-day Friday.

> **Update on Gulf of Mexico Oil Spill** — Operations on the top kill procedure continue. Heavy drilling fluids were pumped under pressure into the BOP starting May 26 at 1300CDT, and top kill operations continue through 2400CDT on May 27. It is estimated that the full top kill procedure could extend for another 24 to 48 hours.

16 When reporters can't see and confirm for themselves what's happening, all they can do is report what their sources tell them. And when the sources conceal, give out inaccurate statement and lie, the public is left in the dark.

17   **18**

1. Collect your research and collect your thoughts. Too many bloggers just fire up their blogging software, write, and hit the "Publish" button. Their posts are rarely worth reading.

Writing is a process. It begins with your choice of a topic. Next, you need to gather information. The phone calls you make, the interviews you conduct, the documents you read, and the situations you observe are all part of this information gathering. Along the way, you have to organize and clarify your thoughts. Take something as simple as a restaurant review. You need to collect information: What's on the menu? What's the signature dish? How is the food prepared? What are the prices? Who are the clientele? Once you know this, you also need to collect your thoughts. What do you want to say? Even if you are writing about memories of your senior prom, you'll need to sit for a while and think through your experience before you start to write.

We'll talk much more about finding a focus, organizing, and writing a blog post in Chapter 2, "Two Models: The Reporter Blogger vs. The Op-Ed Blogger."

6

2. Write a crisp, clear headline. The sign on a storefront is important. It tells you what the store sells. The headline on a blog post is more important, because it not only tells you what the post is about, but also has to be interesting enough to convince you to read further.

We have devoted Chapter 6, "Why Headlines Matter," to headline writing. Headlines are that important. On top of a blog, a headline serves two purposes: it draws the reader into the post and contains keywords that Google and other search engines will look for. Making your blog as visible to Google as it can be is called search engine optimization, known in short as SEO, and a good blog headline combines cleverness, usefulness, and smart SEO.

The headline on Mark's piece was, "Confusion, secrecy and lies blight oil spill coverage." In writing, Mark was careful to include the words "oil spill," since he knew that would be a common search term as the disaster continued. Since the blog post is about the media's coverage of the oil spill, he wanted the word "coverage" in the headline, too. Then, trying to lure both readers and search engines, Mark chose three nouns—"confusion," "secrecy," and "lies"—to build the headline. With these keywords, readers would know instantly what the blog post is about. And because of the way search engines work, anyone punching "oil spill coverage" or "oil spill lies" would be much more likely to find a link to Mark's blog post.

3. The lede. If you've been trained in writing ledes for print news stories or broadcast news stories or press releases, you've got an excellent foundation for writing the first paragraphs of blog posts. But (isn't there always a but?) the first paragraph in a blog post differs in some important ways from a traditional new lede.

A blog post lede is more conversational. News ledes strive for an anonymous voice, but, as a blogger, you *want* a distinctive voice. In the first paragraph of the example, Mark used conversational phrases he would have hesitated to use in a news story: "media coverage . . . over the past 48 hours has been, to put it mildly, bewildering" and "those sources were inaccessible for long stretches of the day, issued oblique statements, or just plain lied."

Try to get "to put it mildly" or "just plain lied" past a news editor. Good luck. Notice, though, that the main point of the blog post is in the first paragraph: media coverage has been "bewildering" because reporters have had little access to sources.

If the first paragraph is a little different from a news lede, it is *very* different from a term paper first paragraph. If you start a blog post the way you start a term paper—with a long paragraph in which the main point doesn't come until the final sentence—you'll drive the reader away.

If your first sentence doesn't engage the reader and tell the reader what the post is about, the reader needs only to tap the mouse to leave your blog behind and head off to somewhere more interesting on the Internet.

4. Give the page a standing design and headline. In newspaper design, a "standing head" is a graphic element that identifies a recurring feature. A blog should have a standing head—a distinctive look that makes it recognizable when a reader lands on your page. Your blog needs to stand out from the hundreds of millions of other blogs on the Web.

We'll talk about the look of the whole blog in Chapter 3, "Getting Started." But remember that a reader's eyes go to the top of a web page first. That piece of real estate needs to communicate.

7

Professional designers at *The Boston Globe* designed the standing head in this example. The designers converted a photograph of Mark to what is called a "hedcut," made famous by the *Wall Street Journal* and created by designer and illustrator Kevin Sprouls. Sprouls uses a pencil, a technical fountain pen, and an eraser—each hedcut takes him hours. (He describes how he does it here: www.sprouls.com/blog/2012/01/sprouls-method-the-hedcut/.) You can achieve a very similar effect in Photoshop by stippling and hatching an image, and there are inexpensive mobile apps that can make a hedcut. Your photo at the top of your blog—or anywhere easily visible on the page—helps establish your personality. You are more than text on a screen; you're a person.

We'll talk more in Chapter 3, "Getting Started," about choosing a name for your blog.

5. Use a time stamp. A bit of trivia for you: the word "blog" is an ugly portmanteau of "web log." And a log is written in reverse chronological order—the newest entry will always be on top. So it is with a blog; it's one of the things that makes a blog a blog and not, say, a website. Your most recent blog post will always be on top of your blog.

The time stamp tells the reader the date, year, and time you published each blog post. For as long as you leave your blog online (even if you haven't posted to it in ages), it will be visible to search engines. When readers come across something you wrote, they'll want to know when it was written. The time stamp is particularly important when you're blogging about the news, or sports, or even the weather.

In most blog software, time stamps can be changed. It is possible to publish a post on Monday with a time stamp that falsely tells the reader it was posted last Wednesday. You'll note the "falsely" in the previous sentence. Changing a time stamp is unethical.

6. Offer share buttons. The row of icons at the top of this blog post are share buttons. They are one of the best ways to build readership to your blog. If your blogging software doesn't include share buttons automatically, you may need to add a plug-in—share button plug-ins are common, often free, and easy to install.

The share buttons allow the reader, with one click, to share your blog post via email, or on any number of social media sites, including Facebook, Twitter, Tumblr, Pinterest, or Reddit.

8

Most of your readers won't come to your blog directly; they'll find it either through a search engine or social media. Make sure to include share buttons on your blog.

7. Use images to help tell the story. No one wants to land on a web page and see a dense, gray, intimidating block of text. Just as the standing head, with its title and art, is part of the design of the page, so too are images. In fact, those images often help tell the story or become the main vehicle for telling the story. We live in a visual world. The more on-point images are, the more they enhance and complement what you've written, the more likely readers are to stay with your words. When you start thinking and planning a blog post, you should always think what images you can use to supplement or help explain the text. (We'll have a lot more to say about images in Chapter 7, "Beyond Words.")

Mark didn't choose a particularly evocative photo for this blog post—it's a photo of the destroyed wellhead spewing crude oil into the Gulf of Mexico. But his trade-off was that he wanted to be timely while the news was still fresh. So he chose the most evocative image he could find in 10 minutes.

A word of warning about images: *do not use photos or infographics you download from the Internet.* The vast majority of them are protected by copyright, and while lawyers for the copyright owner won't always track you down, it's wise not to take the chance. Violating copyright is illegal.

You have several options:

- If you are blogging for an organization or a company, you can use any images or infographics to which the company has purchased the copyright. Since Mark's blog was published by the website of *The Boston Globe*, he could use any images or infographics that had been purchased by the *Globe*.
- Join Creative Commons (us.creativecommons.org), a not-for-profit membership organization whose purpose is to expand the amount of creative work—including images—that are in the public domain and thus legal for anyone to use.
- If you're an independent blogger, take your own photos and make your own infographics (there are a number of useful websites that will create customized visualizations of your data). That way, you'll

9

not only stay on the right side of the law, but you'll have more fun and produce more of your own work.

8. Think carefully about links. Millions and millions of blogs posts on the Internet contain no links at all, just text. They may as well be screenshots of a typewritten page. What makes the Internet different from all other media is hypertext—the ability to click on a word and be taken to another place on the World Wide Web. The whole foundation of the Web, in fact, is hypertext—hypertext is the "h" in "http."

What makes the World Wide Web different from all other media is hyperlinks, the (usually) underlined words that, with a mouse click or a tap, take us to a specific page on another website. Readers who grew up in an online world may not grasp how revolutionary—and how useful—hyperlinks are.

You're reading a magazine article that mentions Madagascar, and you realize you are not entirely sure where on this big blue earth Madagascar actually is. You touch the word "Madagascar" on the magazine page, and—presto!—an atlas appears in your hands open to the map of Southeast Africa, and there sits the island of Madagascar.

Hyperlinks serve two important purposes for a blogger: they direct the reader to further information on the topic you are writing about, and they allow the reader to see where you got the information you used to build your blog post. A hypertext link on a blog serves a similar purpose as attribution—the assigning of a fact or set of facts to a source using "so-and-so said" or "according to so-and-so"—in a mainstream media news story.

Let's say you are writing a post about the population of people aged 65 in the U.S. doubling by 2050. Where, the reader wonders, did you get that piece of information? You got it from reading a story in the *New York Times* about a report issued by the United States Census Bureau. You could link to the *New York Times* story, which is a secondary source, but why not link to the *primary source*, the Census Bureau report? It'll take you 15 seconds and one Google query to find the web page with the full Census Bureau report. By linking to the primary source, you are doing your reader a service—you are directing the curious reader to the original, in-depth source of the information.

Be creative with your links. Don't always choose the first result you get on a topic from a Google search. Few things are more disappointing

10

to a blog reader than to click on a link and be taken to Wikipedia. "I can look something up on Wikipedia myself," the reader grumbles.

If you are writing about St. Francis de Sales, the patron saint of journalists and writers, you could link to the Wikipedia entry. But your reader might learn more if you dug around in your Google search results for web pages more informative, more interesting, and sometimes more *fun* than Wikipedia. You could link to the St. Francis de Sales page on the website *The Catholic Encyclopedia*. You could link to the home page of St. Francis de Sales' most famous book, *Introduction to the Devout Life*. There is even a Pinterest page for St. Francis de Sales—wouldn't your reader enjoy perusing that rather than yet another tedious Wikipedia entry?

You can also use links in your blog posts to direct your reader to differing opinions on a topic. In a blog post about a new government proposal for funding for universities in the UK, you could link to editorial writers or bloggers who both support and oppose the proposal. Again, you would be doing your reader a service.

Here's some basic advice about using links in your blog posts:

- **Link to your sources**. Use links to add credibility to your posts by allowing the reader to examine your sources. If you are writing a blog post about filigree jewelry, link to the website or a blog where you learned about filigree jewelry, or to a website that has particularly fine examples. Again, try not to link to Wikipedia— your readers can find the Wikipedia entry on "filigree jewelry," or any other topic, in five seconds. Do some searching to give your readers something informative they can't easily find for themselves.
- **Link to other bloggers**. Sometimes this is called "link love," and the idea is that if you link to other bloggers and help draw attention to their blogs, they'll return the favor and link to *your* blog—which will help *you* draw more readers. You're trying to create a community with your blog, right? Links to other bloggers also make *your* blog more valuable to readers because your readers know they can come to your blog for not just your writing but for the research you've done. There is also some evidence Google's search engine takes links into account in its ranking of websites in a search, which is another good reason to link to sources and other bloggers.

11

- **When linking to a blog post, link to the specific post and not just the blog.** If you want to link to a blog post about filigree jewelry your friend Ashley just wrote, click on the headline of that post and use that URL for your link (it's called a permalink). If you just link to www.ashleyblog.com, next week or the week after, when Ashley has written several new blog posts, her post about filigree jewelry will be at the bottom of the page and your reader—the one who clicked your link—will be confused. The permalink to Ashley's post about filigree jewelry will look something like this: www.ashleyblog.com/2014/07/23/filigree.html. When readers click on that link, they'll be taken to a page with Ashley's filigree jewelry post—which is where you wanted to send them.
- **Link to yourself.** Once you've been writing a blog for a while and you've got a few dozen posts (or more), there's nothing wrong with linking in a new post to one of your previous posts. You've built a body of work, and if you can make a point more clearly by directing the reader to a previous post of yours, do it.
- **Check all your links.** Before you publish your post, as part of your proofreading, click on every link you have included in the post and make sure it goes where you intended it to go. You may have made a mistake when you cut and pasted the link, and you do not want to promise the reader something you don't deliver.

9. Use blockquotes. You'll often want to quote from sources you've used in your research. When you want to use a direct quote that is longer than three lines or 30 words, use a blockquote. The blockquote function operates differently in different brands of blogging software, but it usually will indent the quotation on both sides and add a shaded background.

In the example from Mark's blog, rather than paraphrasing the lede in that day's *New York Times*, he quoted it. It is often useful to give your readers the exact words of the sources rather than paraphrasing. It adds credibility. It lets your readers read what you have read. Mark's role, as a media criticism blogger, was not to report the news, but to comment on how it was covered. To do so effectively, it was important for him to give verbatim examples of that coverage.

Note that a blockquote differs from a pullquote. A pullquote is a quotation—either from a source or the writer—copied ("pulled") from the story and placed in a larger font as a graphic element. It breaks up a solid chunk of text with some white space. A blockquote is *part of the text*, but it can serve the same graphic function: it breaks up a column of text and gives the eye a little relief.

Putting text in a blockquote is as simple as changing text from roman to bold. Almost all blog software has a blockquote button in the ribbon above the text entry box. WordPress, for example, uses an icon of a large open-quotation mark—just define the text you want to be a blockquote and click on the button. If you want to dig into HTML and write your own blockquote tags, you can give them various interesting looks. Most content management systems have a standard look, and that standard look (as in the example) works just fine for most blogs.

10. Long blockquotes are not only OK, they are helpful to the reader. In the last section of the example, there are two long blockquotes—the first is seven lines and the second is six lines.

Some bloggers may be hesitant to use longer quotes in their work. They may believe that since it is their blog post, the writing needs to be theirs. Quoting from primary sources can help the reader better understand the topic of your post and what you're trying to say. And setting the long quote in blockquote form typographically breaks up the text and makes it more appealing to the reader.

11. Choose standard typefaces. Just because your software has simple functions that allow you to do all kinds of different things with type doesn't mean you have to. In fact, the rules of typesetting—and typesetting is what you are doing when you create a blog post for publication—are venerable and pretty much fixed.

- *Never* **underline a word or group of words**. On the Web and in blogs, hypertext links appear as underlined words. Underlining a word that isn't a hypertext link will confuse the reader.
- **Use bold and italics sparingly**. The reader is slowed down and annoyed by overuse of bold and italic. In a list like this one, for example, bold can be used to emphasize each instruction in a bulleted list. Italic can be used when you really want to emphasize something, such as the word *never* above. Use bold when you are quoting if the bolded words are in the original; in the example

13

from Mark's blog, the first seven words in the blockquote are set in boldface because that is how they appeared on the BP web page being quoted.

- **Don't write in ALL CAPS**. This guideline could be restated as: DON'T SHOUT AT THE READER.

- **Use proportional, not fixed-width, fonts**. Fixed-width fonts, such as Courier and Monaco, give each character the same width, as typewriters did. They are difficult to read. Proportional fonts, such as the typeface used for this book, assign different width to each letter and allow characters to be spaced more efficiently. Proportional fonts are much easier to read.

- **Keep this in mind**. Serif fonts work best for text larger than 9 point; sans serif fonts work well for headlines. A serif is a tiny line at the end of a horizontal or vertical stroke in a letter. A sans serif font does not have these tiny lines. Serif fonts are generally considered easier to read. Many designers believe the serifs "guide" the eye through the letters and words. But not all designers agree, and some argue that proportional sans serif fonts are easier to read on a computer screen.

14

12. Expand your research to social media. It's so easy to punch a search term into Google, click on some links in the first few pages, and consider your research done. Not so fast—how can you possibly ignore Twitter, Facebook, Tumblr, YouTube, or even Pinterest (it's one of the 10 most popular social media sites in the English-speaking world)?

In the example, Mark includes tweets in his discussion of the breaking news coverage of the BP oil spill. Whatever you are blogging about—news, travel, music, parenting—make sure your research includes social media sites. It'll take some time. These sites are easy to search but you'll have to scroll through a lot of verbiage before you find information, either in a post or a link, that will be valuable to your blog post.

The free Twitter search website topsy.com has a database of more than 500 billion tweets dating back to the early days of Twitter. Twitter itself, at the twitter.com website, offers a highly useful "Advanced Search" function that allows you to search words, phrases, specific accounts, and places by location. Facebook is easy to search—the search bar is at the top of the page. To limit a Google search to just blogs, go to www.google.com/blogsearch.

13. Go beyond the usual websites and find where the experts gather. This example, for the first 19 paragraphs, talks about the coverage of the oil spill by large media organizations, and the 19th paragraph serves as a summary for the first part of the blog post.

In the 20th paragraph, the example transitions with the introduction of an obscure blog that Mark discovered in his research, called "The Oil Drum." It was a blog about oil drilling frequented by people who worked in the oil drilling business, including many who had worked on offshore oil rigs similar to the BP rig in the Gulf of Mexico that exploded. Throughout the first 48 hours of the disaster, many former (and current) offshore oil rig workers posted to the blog. Needless to say, their assessments, while sometimes bafflingly technical, were far more sophisticated than what was being reported in major media outlets.

Blogs, message boards, and websites where experts meet to talk about their fields are all over the Internet. Find them. If you're writing a blog about playing the bass guitar, do a Google search for something specific having to do with the bass guitar. A Google search for a particular model of electric bass—"Fender Jaco Pastorius Jazz Bass"—returns, on the first page, a thread in a discussion board called www.talkbass.com. You won't find more expertise on the bass anywhere else on the Web, and, since it is a discussion board, you can jump in and ask questions.

14. Blogging can demand reporting, too. Opinion pieces are stronger when the blogger is a reporter, too, and gathers facts that aren't readily available with a Google search. Give your readers information they can't easily get for themselves.

In the example, Mark sent a quick email to a former student, Lloyd Nelson III, who was working at a daily newspaper in Louisiana, and asked him what he was seeing and hearing—and Mark was careful to let Lloyd know that whatever he responded would be on the record and for use in Mark's blog. That's important. Never use someone's words in a blog post if you don't have the person's permission. All you need to do, when you contact someone, is to identify yourself as a reporter and writer who publishes a blog.

15. Keep it updated. Mark wrote this post in the late afternoon and evening, intending to post it on his blog first thing in the morning, so

15

that it would be fresh all day and have the whole day to attract the most readers possible. By morning, there were a few new developments in the story—and new media coverage—so Mark updated his post with new information before he published it.

16. Write an appropriate ending. Unlike a basic news story or a press release, a blog post needs a satisfying ending. Writing good endings can be tough—we've all sat frustrated in front of a blank screen, as the minutes seem to crawl by, writing and then deleting ending after ending.

In part, the ending you write depends on what kind of blog post you've written.

An opinion post should end strong, with a "takeaway." This is where you drive home the point of your post as clearly and concisely as you can. What do you want your reader to take away from your post? What is it you want the reader to remember about what you had to say?

A blog post that's more of a narrative or more like a feature story can end by circling back to where it began. If you are blogging on a trip, for example—the subject of Chapter 9, "On the Road Again: The Travel Blog"—and began your post about visiting Gaeta, Italy, with a description of your first look at the imposing Montagna Spaccata (Split Mountain), it would be effective, when finishing your post, to circle back to your last view of Montagna Spaccata.

17. Always include a link to your Twitter account. There is no better way to attract readers to your blog than with social media. And there are few better ways to build a Twitter following than to include your Twitter account in every post you write. We'll talk much more about this in Chapter 12, "Building Your Blogging Brand."

As your blog audience grows, the number of your Twitter followers will grow along with it, and you'll build a community around your blog.

18. Expect comments on your blog post. Few features of blogging stir more controversy than the anonymous comments under blog posts and articles. If you've ever read such comments, you know many comments can be not only rude, but appalling. Blogging software provides a "disable comments" option—hunt around for it. It's there. Some bloggers and news organizations have gone so far as to ban anonymous comments.

16

Huffingtonpost.com is the largest website (and blog home) that has banned anonymous comments. "One glance at our comment section or the comment sections of other sites demonstrates what we're all up against," wrote Huffington Post Media Group Managing Editor Jimmy Soni in August 2013 in explaining the site's policy. "Trolls have grown more vicious, more aggressive, and more ingenious. As a result, comment sections can degenerate into some of the darkest places on the Internet." Soni ended his blog post by saying, "Our hope is that this decision will lead to more of the robust conversations that we love having on HuffPost."

That said, few things will do more to create a community around your blog than an open comments section. We'll talk more about this in Chapter 5, "Striking up a Conversation." But for now the authors want to make it clear we believe you should click the "disable comments" button only in rare circumstances, and that you, in our view, should welcome even anonymous comments on your blog posts.

The best blogs are conversations. Participate in the comments section. And don't despair if you don't get any comments at all—or comments from only friends and family—as you publish your first few dozen blog posts. It takes time, effort, and frequent updating of your blog to attract the kind of readers who'll comment and participate in a conversation.

17

DISCUSSION

1. Is the headline on this blog post effective? Does it tell what the blog post is about and draw the reader into reading the post? Why or why not? Come up with ideas for different headlines that are no longer than 10 words.

2. Is the image effective? Does it add to the text? What would have been a better image? (Consider what images might have been available at the time.)

3. How is the main point of the blog post, which the writer makes in the first paragraph, reinforced and proven in the rest of the post?

4. Do you agree with the statement in the final paragraph of the post? Why or why not?

EXERCISES

Choose five blog posts from the past week by bloggers who write about similar topics (politics or hockey, for example). Click on every link in each post and write down where the link takes you. Out of all the links in the five blog posts, choose the *three* links that you thought were the most helpful, useful, or interesting. Describe *why* each of those three links was helpful, useful, or interesting.

18

Two Models

The Reporter Blogger vs.
The Op-Ed Blogger

What Kind of Blogger Do You Want to Be?

Are bloggers journalists? That debate has stirred considerable passion over the years. But turn the question around and there is no debate: nearly all professional journalists today write or edit blogs. It's part of the job description.

Certainly, many serious bloggers do independent reporting, consult and link to primary sources, verify facts, and maintain high ethical standards, just as professional journalists do.

Other bloggers prefer to write opinion pieces. Using a blog to establish context, they provide fresh and clear viewpoints, contributing valuable arguments. Even amateurish bloggers do add to societal conversation and, at least to some extent, information.

Before you set up your blog and start posting your work, it helps to figure out what kind of blogger you want to be.

Remember the novel *Moby Dick?* Herman Melville's peg-legged Captain Ahab, who hunted the oceans for the white whale who took his leg, would go below deck and "refer to piles of old log-books beside him, wherein were set down the seasons and places in which, on various former voyages of various ships, sperm whales had been captured or seen."

Had Ahab had the capacity and desire to share his ship's logs with the world, he'd have been a blogger. In keeping his ship's log—a record of where he had been and what he had seen, heard, and learned on his journeys—Ahab was a particular kind of journalist: he was a *reporter*.

A reporter gathers facts, decides how to organize and write up those facts in an effective, useful, and engaging way, and disseminates his or her account to an audience. If that is the kind of blogger you choose to be, you will be a reporter, whether you work at a big professional news organization or on your screened-in front porch.

"The journalism of the future is going to blur across economic sources, across styles of work, across the divide between professional and amateur," Michael Schudson, a sociologist of journalism and professor at Columbia University's Journalism School, said in a 2010 speech.

Think of the reporter-blogger as a modern-day equivalent of the town crier, telling fellow citizens the news. That news needs to be carefully vetted, accurate, and either documented or attributed to respected people, or sources, who have the knowledge to pass it on.

Here's a story by Adam Gaffin, a citizen-journalist who runs a news blog and website called *Universal Hub* that covers the neighborhoods of Boston:

Doug Bennett is running again after all—for sheriff

<u>Doug Bennett</u>, who has made two unsuccessful tries for a seat on the City Council, today announced he's setting his sights a bit wider—on Suffolk County Sheriff, a job that involves running the two jails that serve Boston, Chelsea, Revere and Winthrop.

Bennett, a Dorchester resident, is running as a Democrat this year for the six-year term to replace Andrea Cabral, now state secretary of public safety. Steven Tompkins, a former Cabral aide, is current acting sheriff.

Bennett's name is underlined because it links to his website. This post is also accompanied by a YouTube video on which Bennett announces his candidacy. The post is short and simple. But it conveys the news: Doug Bennett is running for office yet again despite two past defeats. And it uses a link and multimedia so the reader with time and interest can go deeper.

There's a second kind of blogger, someone who analyzes and comments on events and other news. This blogger, an "opinion blogger," is somewhat akin to the old-time pamphleteer. Opinion bloggers base their views on information, too. It can be gathered by the bloggers themselves or based on materials found elsewhere and shared as links in a blogger's piece. But opinion bloggers go beyond gathering material. They draw conclusions from it. They take a stand and exhort people to act or react.

Howard Cohen, a pop music critic for the *Miami Herald*, started writing a blog about the TV show *American Idol* in 2005. Here's his blog post telling readers what he thinks about the show on the eve of the last episode of its 11th season.

> *American Idol* closes its 11th season with the usual fanfare tonight. Ryan Seacrest will tease out the results to the bleeding last second—7 minutes after the two-hour mark because it is just impossible for *Idol* to not overstay its welcome or endless need of self-promotion in a season crying for any good news. A record 100 million votes . . . Seacrest will gush, as if a fraction of that number equates to actual viewers.
>
> The wrong winner will be crowned, according to at least half of the people on the Twitterverse. Jennifer Lopez will take her leave from the judge's panel most accounts say. *Idol* will be back in January for a 12th season. And for a 13th and for however long it keeps beating shows in its time slot. The whole machine will grind back to business. But does anyone really care?

23

In traditional newspaper journalism, opinion pieces are known as "op-eds." Most newspapers have an editorial page, in which the newspaper, in earnest prose, takes a position on an issue of the day. Editorials are not signed because they are meant to be read as the opinion of the newspaper.

But on the page opposite the editorial page (hence the term "op-ed"), newspapers run bylined opinion columns. These writers comment on the issues of the day, too, but they speak for themselves, not the news organization. Op-ed columnists and contributors attract readers with their views and also their style and personality. They don't just badger readers with their views; they connect with them.

Put another way, traditional op-ed writers have a voice. Traditional reporters have a different, more restrained, voice. In blogging, voice matters regardless of the style or topic (see Chapter 4, "Writing as Rap," page 65). Engaging readers matters, something we'll discuss later.

For now, just keep this in mind: voice isn't something writers put on like a pair of rain boots or a colorful scarf. It is, in a sense, something writers are, or become, when they listen closely to the cadence and style of their own words.

How to Blog Effectively

All blog writing has its baseline rules, regardless of type. Here are our dandy dozen. Stick them in your smartphone, your egg crate, or however you cart things around. Refer to them frequently.

We'll elaborate on these throughout the book.

1. Keep the focus of each post narrow.
   - Don't try to say too much; stay on point.

2. Write short headlines that summarize and sell.
   - Headlines draw the reader into the post. They must be clear. They can be clever, too.

3. Write in chunks: keep your paragraphs short.
   - Reading off computer screens takes about 25 percent longer than reading from paper.

4. Write in the active voice: Subject → Verb → Object.
   - Verbs power sentences.

5. Mix post lengths and styles.
   - Give the reader choices.

6. Write regularly.
   - Try to post something at least weekly.

7. Be yourself.
   - Blogging is a conversation. No one talks long to a blowhard or phony.

8. Provide links.
   - Share your sources and other interesting stuff with the reader.

9. Put breaks between paragraphs.
   - Give the reader white space, subheds, and bulleted lists to make reading easier.

10. Don't overdo boldface or italics or other font styles.
    - It hurts the reader's eyes.

11. Include visual cues.
    - Photos, slide shows, and video add pizzazz.

12. Copyedit and proofread.
    - Sloppy writing has no credibility.

Establishing a Focus

Before you sit down to write a blog post, know what you want to say. That's how the pros do it.

That doesn't mean you can't sit down and write a disorganized jumble of things you know or think about a topic. It doesn't mean you can't write a first draft so rough you'd be embarrassed to show it to your dog. Both can be helpful in figuring out what you want to say. But do those things *before* you sit down to write your actual blog post.

Every good piece of writing, from a quick note to your roommate to a cinder-block-sized novel, has one focus, one overarching thing it wants to say. It may be small, and it may have sweep. It may be "wash the dishes!" or it may be "human motives are irrational."

Many bloggers commit the offense against good writing of wandering from topic to topic in the same blog post. When a writer wanders, the reader can't follow and stops bothering to try. Keep your focus narrow. Write about one topic—how to make a lemon poppyseed scone, what to pack for a music festival, or where to find a farmer's market—and one topic only.

One of the best ways to narrow your topic and develop a clear focus is to imagine a friend asking, "So, what are you writing about?" and answering in one sentence. You don't even have to imagine: write a one-sentence email or a text to a friend that begins, "I'm writing a blog post about . . ." and finish the sentence. Think of it as a *focus statement*—a single, simple statement of what you want your blog post to say.

Remember learning about outlines when you were a kid in school? You have your Roman numerals as main topics (I, II, III), then capital letters as sub-topics (A, B, C), with Arabic numeral for sub-sub-topics

25

(1, 2, 3), and lower-case letters (a, b, c) for sub-sub-sub-topics, and so on.

Forget all that. You *do* need to outline anything you're going to write that's longer than a few paragraphs. But you don't need all the apparatus of formal outlines. What you need are directions—the same kind of directions you'd get if you were in a new city and stopped a native to ask where you can find the nearest pub. You need just enough information to know how to get where you're going.

You may want to write a blog post about what to bring to an outdoor music festival. That might be your focus statement: "What to bring to a day-long outdoor music festival." No, wait. Let's liven this up. New focus statement: "The seven essentials to bring to a day-long, outdoor music festival."

Now you know your outline needs seven items. This is sometimes called a "jot outline." Just jot down enough information to get you from the start to the end of your piece of writing.

Lede: what to bring to for a day at an outdoor music fest—seven things. (For now, this will do. In writing, you'll want to liven it a bit. Maybe, "You've been there, arrived, psyched, for a day of outdoor music and it starts to pour. Or the sun scorches. Or you can't see the stage for the glare. Here are seven things to remember before leaving home.")

> *Water*—sealed container
> *Wallet*—just cash and ID, leave rest home
> *Snacks*—prepackaged in case you can't bring food in (energy bars)
> *Sunscreen*—max strength
> *Lip balm*—wind/sun will chap lips
> *Sunglasses*—cheap ones b/c you might lose them
> *Poncho*—lightweight. Can double as a ground cloth

Once you've got a focus and you know the overall shape of your blog post, start writing for real. One last tip: as you write, look forward and not backward. What you want to do in your first draft is make words into sentences, sentences into paragraphs, and paragraphs into an engaging and informative piece of writing. Write what you have to say from start to finish. Then, when you've reached the end, you can go back and begin to rewrite for clarity, precision, and conciseness.

FUNGAI MACHIRORI

"The mission is to tell as many stories as we can"

There is much that is personal and practical in the remarkable blog *Her Zimbabwe* (http://herzimbabwe.co.zw/), from a piece in early 2015 on reusable menstrual pads to another on "Unsilencing Depression." There's nothing trivial. But then, everyday life for women in this struggling African nation is very different than it is for women in developed Western nations.

Fungai Machirori

Begun by Fungai Machirori in 2012 "to harness the potential of digital media to share and tell Zimbabwean women's stories," the blog and its writers are voices of substance, style, and courage in a politically unsettled land. After an introduction from a former student, Nadine Hoffman, deputy director of the International Women's Media Foundation, Machirori talked to the authors about her mission as a blogger and what she hoped to accomplish:

How was the vision of Her Zimbabwe born?

I was studying towards a master's degree in International Development and my dissertation centered on Zimbabwean women's organizing. Over the years of political and economic upheaval, we have seen widespread migration of Zimbabweans to countries across the world, including South Africa, the United Kingdom, the United States, and Australia. As such, social relations and cohesion have become somewhat fragmented. I wanted to study this fragmentation and understand if there were points of commonality that still existed among Zimbabwean women organizing in the diaspora, and those organizing locally in Zimbabwe.

One of the recommendations I put forward was that there was need to explore the role that digital media could play in collapsing the geographical space between Zimbabwean women. I also fully understood that the use of digital media could potentially create its own hierarchy of access—Zimbabwe has a quite low Internet penetration rate of about 30 percent of the entire population, whereas many in the diaspora enjoy unlimited access. All the same, I realized that I could keep my interrogation at a purely theoretical or academic level, or I could attempt to put it into practice. Also, I didn't want to write a dissertation that no one would implement. So I took the onus upon myself to effect my own recommendations.

That's how the vision was born, although it has changed somewhat along the way. In the initial stages, *Her Zimbabwe* was more or less an experiment and we took in all kinds of content, some of which was not as cogent and analytical as we now attempt to be on the platform. Now, *Her Zimbabwe* is more about encouraging and cultivating thought leadership and provocative discussion. It is also about documenting the stories that often go undocumented, because ask anyone in the West what they know about Zimbabwe and the usual responses will be, "Robert Mugabe, AIDS, and hunger." Of course, these issues and personalities are quite real. But they are reductive and incomplete. So we are really trying to fill in the other parts of our experience.

What in your mind is the blog's overall mission?
I think I have already alluded to it. But I would say our mission, above and beyond engaging Zimbabweans and the broader world in conversation and thought, is to ensure that 100 years from now, when to whomever it is that we shall leave this earth looks for information on Zimbabwe, they shall find our work there too. We want there to be alternative narratives and counter-narratives, diversity and nuance about our experience. Perhaps this has more to do with our vision, but the mission is to tell as many stories as we can.

The site seems as much a place of community as it does a place of news. Do you think of it that way too?
Yes, I think many of those who write for us feel a sense of having found community. There aren't many spaces for Zimbabweans to write about themselves, and even more limited space for women to write about their lived realities. So many of the writers are people I know personally, people we've invested some time with getting to know and understand, and also people who know each other through their work, which converges on our site. They are definitely part of a community.

Whom do you have in mind when you post to the site?
Admittedly, the discourse is not what one would call "basic," for want of a better word. But we also don't write work that is convoluted and hard to comprehend. We introduce complex topics through accessible language and anecdotes. So our content is really for anyone who would like to challenge themselves to think more variedly and to expose themselves to new ideas. But of course by nature of our platform, our content is only accessible via the Internet. Additionally, the content is largely for an audience conversant in English, although we do intend to introduce more vernacular content as we go along.

The blog takes on some intimate and personal subjects but gives its advice in the context of stories. Is this something you and your writers work to do?
We don't really work on it. Things seem to just come that way for most of them. Most are bloggers anyway, so this is the conversational style that I suppose they naturally use. Our editing is more around angling and building themes within work.

How difficult is it to maintain a strong voice of independence in a country without a strong tradition of press freedom?
We've never had anyone approach us on our work, so we've never had to deal with any of it. We have brought up questions about the country's leadership and different political figures within this space, but no one has ever threatened and intimidated us.

What are your goals for the future?
We would like to be a stable entity, with a decent staff complement and a growing editorial team. We just want to tell as many stories as we possibly can.

The Basics of Reporting and Writing a News Blog

Being a Reporter

Anything happening that's important or interesting to you can be the subject of a news blog. You could go to the county commissioners' meeting every week, take careful notes, and write a report that you post on your blog for anyone in the county (and the world, for that matter) to read. You could do the same for your local school committee. This is what is sometimes called "accountability journalism," where the journalist acts as a watchdog of government. It's needed at every level of government, especially as the so-called legacy or traditional media shrink.

But everyday life includes a lot more than government—and is often a good bit more interesting. So find your own niche. Love Little League? Become the authoritative voice about the teams and players in your town, mixing words with action photos and video shot with a mobile phone camera. It's that easy. Love public art? Start a blog showing, and giving the story behind, the murals, installations, and graffiti around your community. Love locally grown food? Take readers on a weekly tour of where to find the freshest and tell them who is preparing it well, and how.

Reporting does have its rules, though. If you decide to start a reporter blog, you should follow them, just as if you were reporting for a traditional publication. Here are some of the basics:

29

Always identify yourself. Whether you are talking to someone on a street corner or calling the mayor, always say upfront that you are a reporter. "Hi, I'm Barbara and I write a blog about public transit in the city. May I ask you a few questions?" It is unethical to publish quotations or even to paraphrase what someone told you if you haven't told that person you are gathering information. Once you identify yourself and make it clear that anything your interview subject says may be published, everything in your interview is "on the record." You can use it without permission or review.

Have the tools you need. Even in this cellphone-centric era, carry paper to write on and keep more than one pen or pencil on you. If you are going to record or shoot photos, make sure the battery in your mobile phone or your audio recorder is charged. If you're going to take notes on a laptop, do the same.

Ask permission to tape. You may want to record an interview as well as take notes. Most mobile phones allow you to do this easily. If you do want to record, always ask permission. Many states make it illegal to record a phone conversation unless both parties know it is being recorded. So it is not only ethical, but wise, to ask permission.

Plan your interviews in advance. Interviewing takes practice. It's more than a conversation. Your job is to gather information. You'll succeed if you do three things: (1) know what information you want; (2) do some advance research so you know something about the topic you're covering; and (3) listen closely once the interview begins. There are two broad categories of questions. Some elicit facts: How many kids are in the league? What kinds of vegetables do you grow in July? When is the next meeting? These are called "closed-ended" questions. Others elicit insight: How do you balance the need for quantity and quality? Why do you believe public art has exploded in this city? How do you go about planning a good urban garden? These are "open-ended" questions. Whichever approach fits your interview, always be ready to follow up and dig deeper if an answer surprises you.

Take careful and accurate notes. Don't write everything down. Taking notes for a story isn't that different from taking notes as a student: you write down the most important stuff. Listen for statements that sum up or punctuate a situation and write them verbatim in your notebook. They may serve as quotes later. If you take notes slowly and a person speaks too quickly, it's OK to say, "hold on for a second, I want to write down what you just said," or "could you repeat that?" Develop your own shorthand for key facts. Again, you're not a stenographer. Only write down what matters. Finished with the interview? Go over your notes immediately to make sure you can read them and don't have other questions. Do so while your memory is fresh.

Verify information. Remember, you're a reporter now. That means recognizing the difference between information and rumor. It's not good enough to quote someone who heard from someone else that two people were injured when a car skidded into a storefront on Main Street. A bystander can tell you what he or she saw. Police give the authoritative account of what happened. Blogs built on misinformation don't hold readers long.

Attribute information. Always let your readers know where your information came from. In attributing information to a person, write "so-and-so said," placing that attribution either at the start of a quote or paraphrase, or, following a comma, after the first sentence of a quote. Or place it at the end, following a comma. But tell your readers exactly who said what. When your information comes from a written source, you can either quote the source or, better yet, link to it if it is online.

If you quote someone, use that person's exact words. If something is in quotation marks, it should represent the precise words someone used. Listen for sharp, succinct, and colorful quotes. And quote people in complete sentences or phrases. It is, "'This storm will be a wild one with big gusts up to 60 miles an hour,' meteorologist Lashonna Travis said." It is not, "This storm will be a 'wild one' with 'big gusts' up to 60 miles an hour, meteorologist Lashonna Travis said."

Don't allow yourself to be manipulated. Reporters pride themselves on their independence. It's all right to blog for Jettlin's Menswear, as long as you are upfront with readers that you are in the business of marketing for the store. Reporters write for an audience, not a client.

31

They don't show people what they write before it runs. They don't promote their friends. They don't change quotes or stories because people want to look better. Reporters also don't let people tell them after an interview it really was "off the record." Establish "ground rules" up front. Once you tell someone you are a reporter working on a story, that individual can't tell you later that what they've already told you was "off the record." That would mean you couldn't use it. If someone tells you in advance, "I want to be off the record," your best answer is to decline. Your task is to gather information. What good is information you can't use?

Organizing and Writing Your Reporter Blog Post

In his book *A Writer Teaches Writing*, Pulitzer Prize-winning journalist and writing teacher Donald Murray explains writing as a process with three steps: *Collect, Order, Clarify*. Following these steps, a writer should answer these three questions when writing:

1. What do I have to say?
2. What's the most effective way to say it?
3. Have I said what I wanted to say?

Imagine, for a moment, that you are writing a note to your roommates asking them to clean up the dirty dishes in the sink.

First, you have to decide what it is you want to communicate. Do you want them to wash the pots and pans, or just the dishes? Do you want them to put away the clean dishes on the bottom shelf of the cabinet or the middle shelf?

Then you decide how to say it. Do you want the note to be curt and bossy, or do you want it to be friendly but prodding? Do you want to excoriate them for always leaving dirty dishes in the sink, or do you just want to suggest that the apartment would be a more pleasant place if this particular batch of dirty dishes were cleaned and put away?

Once you've written your note, you look it over. Does it have the voice and tone you want? Is it clear about what you want your roommates to do?

In writing news stories or blog posts, Murray's *Collect* phase is your reporting: writing down what you see and hear, conducting interviews, making phone calls, looking over documents, searching the Internet for background information. Good writing builds off content.

When you sit down to write, think about *Order*: What form will this story take? What information in my notes is the most important (and what do I leave out)? What does the reader need to know to understand what I have learned in my reporting?

The last stage is *Clarify*. Don't click the "Post" button as you type the final word. Instead, step away from the computer for a bit. Clear your head. Then go back and reread what you've written to make sure that it is clear, focused, and clean (no typos). Read your work aloud. It's the best way to catch errors and awkward sentences. Finally, set aside time to revise. Trim unnecessary words. Add a good example. Eliminate a sentence or paragraph that's off point. Good writers draft and then revise. The latter too often gets ignored. Even if you have only 10 minutes, use the time well.

Keep this in mind: if you're writing news, it's usually best to get to the point quickly. Then elaborate on the main point before providing smaller details or introducing secondary themes. If you've studied the basics of news writing, this may sound familiar. It is the basis of what's long been known as the *inverted pyramid*. This short, sharp, and direct writing form can be even more essential in writing for the web than in newspapers.

Consider this. The average web page or blog user stays on the page *for less than a minute*. Mobile phone users stay on web pages for even less time. The inverted pyramid format allows you to make the focus of your blog post instantly clear and to organize the information that follows in descending order of importance. Here's an example from the Associated Press:

COLUMBIA, S.C.—A surprise snow swept across parts of Tennessee, Georgia and South Carolina on Saturday, falling on pumpkins and power lines.

It was the earliest snow on record in the Columbia area by eight days, according to the National Weather Service.

The wet flakes in South Carolina collected on trees and sent branches still full of leaves crashing down on power lines. Utilities reported a peak of about 20,000 power outages as the snow tapered off before noon Saturday.

The weather service said around 2 inches of snow fell in some areas of Greenville, which is in the northwest part of the state. The band continued south dumping a couple of inches of snow all the way to Lexington County, just west of Columbia.

Forecasters expected the snow to mix in with rain as low pressure moved through the state, but the low was more powerful than expected, and the snow fell to the surface before it could melt, weather service meteorologist Chris Liscinsky said.

"It was the complete changeover to snow that was quite unusual for this time of year," Liscinsky said.

The snow caused few problems on roads. The high in Columbia was 84 on Wednesday and 69 on Friday, so the pavement was too warm for the snow to stick.

Troopers did close a part of Interstate 20 in western Lexington County for a few minutes because several 18-wheelers got stuck in the slush trying to make it up a small hill. They were pulled to the side until the burst of snow stopped, Highway Patrol Cpl. Sonny Collins said.

Most of the snow was gone by the afternoon, leaving behind a cold, windy, bitter day in the 40s. Highs in Columbia will be back in the 70s by midweek, forecasters said.

The Lede

The first paragraph of your post is known as the *lede*, pronounced *leed*. (The odd spelling is a bit of journalism jargon that keeps the name for a first paragraph from being confused with *lead*, which can be pronounced *led*.) The lede summarizes your story's main point. It's built around the most newsworthy fact or facts. Here are some tips in writing one:

Convey the news. Of all the information you have collected, choose the key facts that sum up the story to tell the reader what happened.

Keep it short. Try to keep your first paragraph to a single sentence no longer than 25 words. You should be able to read it aloud in one breath.

Write in the active voice. Use a subject → verb → object construction.

Put the news in context. Use a short second sentence or a single phrase in the first to alert readers to related essential to understanding what's new—the news—in a lede. This related information is called context. It must be limited to what's really important. Many stories don't need context in the lede.

Here is that Universal Hub lede again, its context in boldface:

> Doug Bennett, **who has made two unsuccessful tries for a seat on the City Council**, today announced he's setting his sights a bit wider—on Suffolk County Sheriff, a job that involves running the two jails that serve Boston, Chelsea, Revere and Winthrop.

In writing a lede, the first step is always to find the news. To do so, imagine your mother asking you, "What are you working on?" Tell her in one sentence. That's likely your lede or close to it.

Here is an example that fits within that 25-word guideline:

> A large wave capsized a fishing boat off the coast of Northern California Saturday, leaving four of the five people aboard dead, authorities said.

The Body

A news blog post needs unity. Everything in it should expand on, amplify, and add information to the facts in the lede. Why? Because, as we said earlier, blog posts need a tight focus. Each post should be built around a single, dominant idea. The lede summarizes it. What follows should answer the questions the lede provokes in readers. As you write further, it helps to think like a reader: What would you want to know next?

Let's try an example.

If someone told you that there had just been a car accident at Elm and Main streets, what would you want to know next? "Anyone hurt?" you might ask. Then, "What happened?" Then you'd ask about the details—who was involved? (You'd want names, since you live nearby.)

If you think like a reader, organizing your blog post will come easily.

A few other tips:

Be Quick to Expand on the Main Points Your Lede Raises

Let's say the lede says, *A bicyclist suffered skinned knees and needed several stitches yesterday when a car skidded into him on black ice at the intersection of Elm and Main streets.*

What's next? Who was the bicyclist, right? And what happened to him?

Levon Williams, 27, of 89 Justine Court was knocked to the ground and rushed to nearby Mercy Hospital, but X-rays showed no broken bones.

And then?

The car's driver, Anita Johnson, 63, of 14 Tremont Boulevard, was not cited by police.

These sentences answer reader demand, raised by the first sentence. (Reporters give the age and address of those identified in such stories because there could be multiple Levon Williams and Anita Johnsons in the same neighborhood.)

Each New Idea Earns Its Own Paragraph

Keep paragraphs short. In news, one- and two-sentence paragraphs are the most effective way to communicate. The paragraph indentations and the spaces between the paragraphs leave what graphic designers call "white space." Readers, coming upon your blog, won't be intimidated by big gray blocks of type. They'll also have an easier time digesting the news. So Williams and Johnson are identified in separate paragraphs above.

Quotes from Your Subjects, or Sources, Enliven Your Writing

Used sparingly, voices of those involved in a story help punctuate the reporter's voice and add veracity, a sense of being there.

> "It was terrifying," Johnson said. "Suddenly my car had a mind of its own and I couldn't do a thing about it."

In a blog post, you can use short quotes like this or longer quotes that you can set off from the rest of the text using the "blockquote" function described in Chapter 1.

Gathering material for the police news blog of wickedlocal.com, a website that covers the Boston suburb of Brookline, reporter Jim Morrison came upon an unusual police report. He took notes, then interviewed the town resident who had called the police, and wrote his story. In this case, he used a different kind of news lede—a "delayed" lede in which the first paragraph is meant to entice the reader and the subsequent paragraph gives the news.

Two Addington Road residents had an unusual home invasion last week.

Didi Coyle was standing with a neighbor in her driveway at just after 6 p.m. on a Sunday evening when she watched a turkey fly through the window in her family room where her husband, Tom Szydlowski, and their deaf cocker spaniel, Lily, were quietly watching television.

The turkey crashed through the aluminium screen, the storm window, and an 1890s plate glass window, covering the floor with broken glass, and just a few drops of blood. Lily started barking and pursuing the turkey, and was quickly scooped up and placed behind a closed door in another room, according to Coyle.

Coyle and her neighbor, Jan Remien, scrambled to find and call the Brookline Police Department's non-emergency number, and soon an officer was on the scene.

"The officer, I think his last name was Sullivan, was very nice," said Coyle.

According to Coyle, Szydlowski and the officer were standing in the family room when the turkey flew over the 6-foot, 1-inch Szydlowski's head and into the bathroom. The officer shooed the turkey into the adjoining laundry room and closed the door. Then he opened the window in the bathroom, opened the door to the laundry room, and closed the bathroom door.

The turkey flew out the window and fled the scene on foot. No charges were filed.

Blogging Your Opinions

Notes Rebecca Blood, who began her blog *Rebecca's Pocket* in 1999 when there were only a hundred or so blogs on the Internet: "Write about what you love. A weblog is the place for strong opinions, whether about politics, music, social issues, gardening, or your profession. The more engaged you are with your subject, the more interesting your writing will be."

On her blog's "About" page, Blood describes her blog as "devoted to highlighting whatever catches my attention, and I'm interested in lots of things."

Back in 2006, the Pew Internet & American Life Project reported that 12 million Americans had a blog. Pew surveyed bloggers and asked them, among other questions, what they blogged about. More than a third answered that they blogged about their personal lives and experiences. The next most popular topic for bloggers was politics. If you're not ardent about politics, no problem—you undoubtedly have strong opinions that you want to share about some other topics.

We've talked about the writing process as *Collect*, *Order*, and *Clarify*. The opinion blogger, too, has to *collect*, but in this case in a couple of ways. The first is to collect a list of ideas: the notepad app of most mobile phones is a good place to keep a list (if you're old-fashioned, a small, pocket-sized pad works, too). Next, you, as opinion writer, have to collect your thoughts, to think about what you want to write about and why. This may be prompted by "string" you've gathered—weblinks to reported pieces and editorials you've filed away, original reports, polls or studies you've saved, or other bits and pieces of information. Or you may now need to collect information to help support your argument.

Whatever the exact order, you, as an opinion writer, have to not only decide what argument you want to make, but how and why. What information backs up your viewpoint? What do you have to say that 10 people haven't said before you? Are you offering a fresh take or perspective?

This is important because, as with all journalism, originality matters. Opinion blogs have been referred to as a vast echo chamber of people with the same opinion on a topic, all writing their own blog posts. By all means, have your own opinions. But you'll draw readers by synthesizing and analyzing existing information in interesting ways. A good opinion piece doesn't just say, "I believe such and such." It shows the reader why and advances the argument in a unique and distinctive way. That takes not only practice. It takes homework—research to find information.

You have to know something about the subject you're writing about because you'll have readers who know the subject well.

We recommend gathering your research in a text file that will serve as your notebook when you begin to write. Don't just take notes. Keep the web address of the web page where you found the information, so you can link to it in your blog post. This is a form of attribution in blogging that helps establish your credibility.

Now you're ready to write. Well, almost. First, go back one step. Sit and think some more about how the information you've gathered supports your opinion. Make a quick outline of the structure of your blog post.

Below are the first three paragraphs of a blog post written by Mark Leccese about CNN reporting information from a diary kept by the murdered U.S. Ambassador to Libya, J. Christopher Stevens. It was found by a reporter in the wreckage of the U.S. Consulate in Benghazi.

> Journalism ethics have been much discussed, taught, argued about and codified. I can understand why, but I've always believed the first word in the phrase "journalism ethics" matters far less than the second. If you want to be an ethical journalist, be an ethical human being.
>
> The editors and producers at CNN failed to live up to a universal ethical principle, respect for families of the dead, when the network used information from the diary of the murdered Ambassador Christopher Stevens it had found in wreckage of the U.S. Consulate in Benghazi.
>
> And they violated professional ethics at the same time by using information from a personal document in their broadcasts. The professional (and, by the way, legal) distinction here is simple: If CNN had found a draft of a diplomatic cable written by Ambassador Stevens to the State Department, that would be a government document. His diary—and even CNN called it a "diary"—is a private document.

Mark kept the notes he made while researching this blog post (he always keeps his notes) and the quick outline he made of what he wanted to say. You'll find a shortened version of his notes and outline below. Remember, when we talk about an outline, we're not talking the kind of outline your eighth-grade English teacher required, with Roman numerals and capital letters and small letters—just a series of main points that helps you organize thoughts as you write.

— CNN ethical failure

— Gov't doc vs. private diary

— Clip from Wednesday AC 360
http://ac360.blogs.cnn.com/2012/09/19/amb-chris-stevens-worried-about-al-qaeda-hit-list/

— change Fri—clip from Fri AC 360
http://www.cnn.com/video/data/2.0/video/bestoftv/2012/09/22/ac-stevens-security-concerns.cnn.html

— WSJ story—family did not want diary made public
http://online.wsj.com/article/SB10000872396390443890304578012473529847226.html?mod=djkeyword

— AP story—CNN promised family
http://www.washingtonpost.com/national/cnn-posts-report-of-diary-of-slain-ambassador-stevens-us-state-dept-says-family-had-objected/2012/09/22/15ae33b6-0514-11e2-9132-f2750cd65f97_story.html

— CNN statement —
http://cnnpressroom.blogs.cnn.com/2012/09/22/cnn-statement-about-ambassador-stevens-journal/

— Why CNN statement wrong—key points

Mark's outline starts with opinion, moves to research so he can explain to his readers (with links to the stories) what happened, and ends with opinion. The research is essential to this blog post—a blogger needs to *show* the reader what he or she is giving an opinion about.

Mark did so by providing these underlined links to his online sources:

> The way CNN <u>initially reported</u> the information it found in Ambassador Stevens' private diary was misleading, to say the least. On Wednesday night's "Anderson Cooper 360," CNN reported information it said it got from "a source familiar with Ambassador Stevens' thinking." The phrase occurs at about 1:20 of <u>this video</u>.
>
> By Friday night's "Anderson Cooper 360," the network, facing heated criticism, <u>admitted the source was Stevens' personal diary</u>.

If your post needs information that is missing, do more research. You've got to anchor your argument.

It sounds like a lot of work, but it shouldn't take that long—and we say "shouldn't" in two senses of the word: it *won't* take long, and you *can't let it* take that long. One of the most important aspects of successful opinion bloggers is speed. Bloggers must post while the topic is still fresh, and the news cycle in the twenty-first century is lightning fast.

Tips for Writing a Strong Opinion Blog Post

State your main point in the first sentence. Or, if you don't do it in the first sentence, do it in the second or third. Readers come to your blog because they want to know what you think. Tell them.

Make your main point with specifics. Let's say you're writing a blog post lamenting how cable television news has changed for the worse since its inception and that you believe CNN is to blame. You might write a first sentence that reads:

CNN has been a major force in American journalism.

True enough. But what's new here? And *how* has it been a "major force in American journalism?" A better opening to your blog post would be:

CNN, the first television channel to broadcast news 24 hours a day, changed American journalism by delivering news as it happened. That was then.

Take a strong position without being obnoxious about it. Many bloggers, alone at their computers, hurl insult and invective across the Internet. But you're not going to persuade people by shouting at them and hectoring them. Nor do you want to be tepid. Make a strong point, then back it up. That CNN blog might continue like this:

Today CNN too often traffics in rumor to fill airtime and the American public suffers the consequences. That was all too evident in a string of false pronouncements this week about the Boston Marathon bombings.

Use your research to back up and demonstrate your main point. Your research can be facts you gathered reporting. It also can be information learned from living your life. So you might write:

First the network joined other news outlets in speculating that the suspect in the bombing was a young college student who had disappeared about a month earlier. He was not. Then reporter John King brought word the bombings allegedly were the work of a "dark-skinned male," the kind of stereotypical and utterly useless language that anyone who has lived in Boston for a while knows to be something of a bomb in its own right. In any case, once again, the network was wrong.

In the example above, the blogger would link to both examples cited. In blogging on a more local story, the writer might rely on personal experience in building an argument. Consider a blog post arguing that a stop sign is needed at the intersection near where you live. You'll know plenty about the issue without consulting a library database. Personal expertise counts, too.

You have to engage readers if you want to inform them. Even though a blog is a journal, it's not like a personal journal you may keep under lock and key—the point of a blog is to communicate with others.

41

The burden is on you, the writer, to draw the readers into your blog with good, clean, clear writing. You want readers to respond. That won't happen unless they read to the end.

Go ahead, use the first person pronoun. The word "I" is frowned upon in most journalistic writing. Not in the blogosphere. Blog readers want to know the blogger, to make a connection. The best and most widely read bloggers have personalities that come through in their writing.

What matters in an opinion blog is the opinion, not fancy writing. Make your point simple (which is different from simplistic) and clear. Avoid overuse of adjectives and adverbs; the sturdiest writing relies on nouns and verbs.

Use anecdotes, analogies, and examples to illustrate your points for the reader. Opinion writing can get lost in abstractions; anecdotes bring people into your argument, people who are acting. Example and analogy can help make a complex point simpler to understand. You could write that a year of tuition, room, and board at a private college is an onerous expense for students and their families. Or you could write that a stack of dollar bills equal to a year of tuition, room, and board at a private college would be two stories high or could feed a family of four for more than five years. Just make sure your analogies are accurate.

End with something for your reader to take away. Finish your blog post with a thought, a suggestion, a call to action, or even a simple summary of the opinion you have just expressed. Circling back to where you began can help leave readers with a sense of emphasis, too. You want your blog post to stay in the reader's mind well after the reader has walked away from the computer.

Here are the first and the last paragraphs of a blog post written by author Jerry Lanson in the wake of the mass murder in Newtown, Connecticut:

First paragraph: Vice President Joe Biden hasn't yet issued his report. The earth scattered on Newtown's graves has barely settled. But it seems just about everyone in Washington—the press, politicians, perhaps the president—already is backpedaling on a serious attempt to ban assault rifles.

Last paragraph: But Washington, I suspect, will not be moved by words or reason alone. Martin Luther King Jr., whose birthday and life we will celebrate this week, understood well the importance of non-violent protest in the face of sometimes violent oppression. What better time than now to heed his teachings and make plans to fill the lawns of the National Mall in Washington with a "Million Parent March?" What better time than now to ignore the handicapping of insular and insulated politicians and pundits alike? What better time than now to truly pressure Congress to take away those guns—assault rifles—that no self-respecting sportsman would be seen carrying in the first place. The mass killings need to stop, before they get even worse.

Go back and reread what you've written. We'll say the same thing we said about publishing a news blog post: don't type the final period in your post and then click the "Post" button. Walk away from your computer, and, when you return, ask yourself these questions. Do you have a strong main point at the start of your post? Do you use examples and information as evidence to back up your main point? Do all the sentences make grammatical sense? Look for missing words (a problem that bedevils one of the authors) and typos. If you have the time, ask someone to proofread your post before you send it out across the World Wide Web.

43

Then post and get ready for the comments to pour in.

DISCUSSION

1. Which blogger do you consider more valuable to the public—a reporter blogger or an opinion blogger? Why? Or do you believe they both provide an equal service to readers?

2. When do you click on the links in stories you read? Why?

3. How might the links and the multimedia in the first story example (see page 22) change the way readers engage it?

4. What opinion blogs do you read? How do you choose them?

EXERCISE

This is a three-part exercise:

1. Cover a speech or a meeting at which an environmental issue is discussed. Write a news blog post about the event, giving at least three links to sites that will help the reader gain a deeper understanding of the issue.

2. Write an opinion blog post about the same issue, again including at least three links (different from the links in the news post) to the places you got your information.

3. Write a short, personal reflection (or blog post) about how your approach and thinking differed as you wrote the news post and the opinion post.

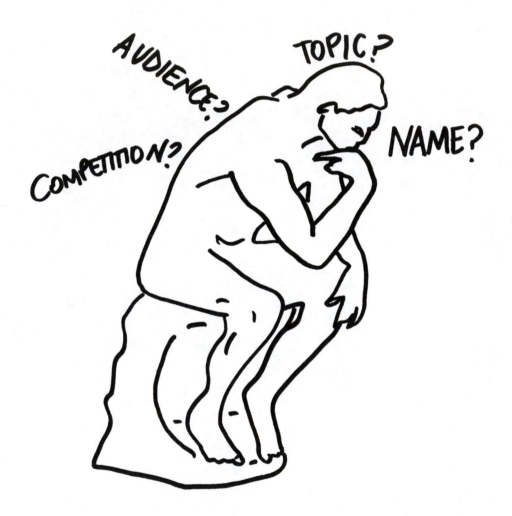

Getting Started

Nulla dies sine linea—Not a day without a line
—Horace, 65–68 BC

In 1999, there were 23 blogs on the Internet, and in 2000 the word "blog" appeared in the *New York Times* exactly once.

By 2011, the company NM Incite was tracking 181 million blogs worldwide before it stopped counting. In the Introduction to this book, we gather data and estimate that in 2014, there are at least 240 million blogs worldwide.

Rebecca Blood, one of the first bloggers, wrote in a September 2000 post that by keeping a blog, a writer becomes more assured. A blogger, she wrote, "by virtue of simply writing down whatever is on his mind, will be confronted with his own thoughts and opinions. Blogging every day, he will become a more confident writer."

Join in, but understand that by doing so, you need to plant yourself in front of your keyboard and write. Heed the advice of Roman poet Horace: "Not a day without a line." You don't have to post every day, but you should write every day, even if only a few lines.

Even before that, however, blogging means finding a topic, honing its focus, scouting the competition, and building an idea file. This chapter will give you tips on how to start your blog with determination, with purpose, and with a plan.

Choosing a Blog Topic

Christopher O'Leary had been working as a reporter covering finance and investment, first as a staff writer in Manhattan and then as a freelancer in western Massachusetts when he decided to start a blog. "It was meant, basically, as a way to let off steam," he says.

A book about presidential gravesites he'd been working on in his spare time had stalled. He wanted "to write something that was fun, that I could dash off over a cup of coffee." A passionate fan of pop and rock music, O'Leary, browsing the Web, came upon a blog by the British music writer Ian MacDonald discussing every song that had ever hit No. 1 on the British charts.

That gave him his idea: Why not do the same for a single popular musician? But which one? "I wanted someone who had a career that spanned decades and that had a lot of variety," O'Leary said. He settled on the protean and prolific David Bowie, even though, he admits, "I wasn't even a big fan."

O'Leary's goal: to write a blog that would go song by song, in chronological order, through Bowie's 40-year career. "I had a listener's perspective," he recalls, realizing that wasn't enough. "So I learned to read music, I studied music theory, and I learned to play the guitar so I could understand the songs better."

He began the blog—called *Pushing Ahead of the Dame* (bowie songs.wordpress.com)—in the summer of 2009; five years later, he had written more than 500 posts and had a book contract. The book, *Rebel Rebel*, is two volumes.

O'Leary had found an unfilled niche and stuck with the subject until he became recognized as an expert. A lot of bloggers lack that kind of staying power.

Before you start a blog, ask yourself these questions:

- **Am I ready to spend a lot of time on this topic?** O'Leary says he spends about 20 hours a week on his blog. Blogs take a lot more work than you think. Your topic should be something that not only interests you, but about which you are eager to learn more. Or it should be a topic about which you are already an expert (be honest with yourself) and believe you have valuable information or points of view to contribute to a discussion.

- **Can I get an unlimited number of posts out of this topic?** No matter how much a topic interests you and no matter how much you already know about a topic, you may quickly—*surprisingly quickly*—feel as though you've run out of things to say. Pick a topic that will provide you with a wealth of material, and be prepared to put in the time researching it.

- **How committed am I to posting to my blog regularly?** Anyone can fire up some blogging software and, in 15 minutes, have a blog up on the Internet for all to see. The Internet is littered with such efforts—blogs with a handful of posts, begun with good intentions and abandoned. There's no sin in that, of course (and there are such things as short-term blogs), but if you're reading this book you're already somewhat serious about blogging. A blog updated once a month, or even several times a month, will attract very few readers, at least until you're established and perhaps have emerged as a hub for bloggers writing on similar themes.

- **When during the course of each week will I set aside time for blogging?** You have to treat blogging as a job or as something for which you will make time. Consider the parallel of learning a musical instrument. To play it well takes daily practice, a routine—held sacred—to improve your skills. Blogging is no different. Author Mark Leccese spent several years as a freelancer writing about books. He learned that every author he interviewed had a writing routine: a set time to write each day, usually with a set number of words to produce in that time. Be professional about your blog.

- **Can I effectively illustrate my blog?** We live in a visual world today, and blogs that can rely on photos or graphics to help tell their story have a better chance of enduring. Rule of thumb: every blog post should have at least one image. It could be a photo, it could be a simple chart, it could be a drawing—any image that *adds meaning* to your blog post. Some blog posts will be nothing but images, as we'll discuss in Chapter 7, "Beyond Words." But always keep in mind one very important warning: Do not use images in your blog to which someone else holds the copyright. Either create the images yourself or use images that are free of copyright restriction.

49

The Sauce Bauce and *Corona Del Mar Today*

When Mark assigns students to choose a blog topic, some struggle and some know right away what they want to blog about. Tom Carroll, a volleyball player and a guy who seems to always be smiling, got right to work writing about buffalo wings. He became (using the current slang for someone awesome) the Sauce Bauce.

Why wings? "I really wanted to find the best buffalo wings in Boston," he said. "I love buffalo wings, and knowing I was going to be in Boston for the next few years, I wanted to find the place where I could definitively go for the best wings."

With each post, Carroll took a photo of the restaurant where he tucked into some wings and included it with the post, and at the bottom of each post he gave each eatery two rankings: "Overall Rating" on a scale of 1 to 10, and "Wing-Sesh Rating," which ran from A to F (more slang: a *sesh* is a *session*).

His posts were lively, detailed, and fun. "The reason I went with a light-hearted and humorous voice was simple: food is fun. Why would someone want to read a serious food blog? People eat to relax; they should be relaxed and having a good time when they read about food, too."

Carroll followed all the steps to write a good blog: He was prepared to spend time researching his blog (given the topic, wouldn't you be?). He knew there were dozens and dozens of places in Boston that serve wings. He was committed himself to his topic, and, even with his busy schedule of classes, an internship, and volleyball practices and games, he just *knew* he could make time for some wing sessions.

Amy Senk works 40 hours a week—and sometimes more—as a blogger. A former newspaper reporter, Senk decided in 2009 to start a local news blog for Corona Del Mar, the seacoast town in Southern California where she lives.

Some days she puts in 12 hours reporting, writing, and posting local news to her blog, *Corona Del Mar Today* (www.coronadelmartoday.com). Other days, she pre-schedules stories she has already written or edited to appear on her blog at intervals, which keeps the blog fresh and keeps readers coming back.

"In the beginning," Senk says, "I was very covert and only about four or five people knew what I was doing. I was finding my voice.

It was more bloggy and I didn't know about various community meetings and so forth. But people began to hear about it from friends, and now it's a must-read . . . I [am] very organic and very local, very word-of-mouth."

Senk works like a reporter. She regularly checks the agendas of government boards and commissions, checks the police log, keeps in touch with local business leaders and the local PTA.

"I also get tips and news releases, and I check regularly the city's online new business license page," she says. "Mostly, my ideas come from living in this town and driving through it. I will notice a business has closed, or a man leading horses down the highway, or construction signs posted. My kids will come home and tell me about a major food fight at school. I kind of always am looking for news."

Tom Carroll is a college student who loves wings; Amy Senk is an experienced reporter and a mother who loves the community in which she and her family live. They both found blog topics about which they wanted to learn more and which would provide them with an almost endless amount of material for posts.

FERNANDA ROSA

"Everything that comes from blogging is a surprise"

When Fernanda Rosa travels abroad, she says she is as likely as not to have strangers cook a meal or throw a party for her. But then they're not really strangers. They are fans of one of her two blogs, written in her native Portuguese though the Brazilian-born Rosa has lived for nearly two decades in and around the California city of Davis.

Rosa has blogged regularly since 2000, when the Brazilian blogosphere "was like maybe 10 people." For the last decade, she's primarily written a food blog titled *Chucrute com Salsicha*, the name of a recipe she found of her mom's. But she still maintains her original blog, *The Chatterbox*, which, she says, remains a photographic and written chronicle of her life—a diary of sorts.

Fernanda Rosa

We caught up with Rosa, 53, by telephone at her home.

You've blogged for a long time. What drew you to blogging in those early days?

I have to communicate. That's part of who I am. Also I live in an English-speaking country and I have to practice my Portuguese . . . [At first, the blogosphere] was like a small group. You would write something. People would react to it . . . It was a community. I would visit other blogs. Other blogs would visit me . . . We were connecting.

In 2001, there was a boom and people started discovering the blogs. I got interviewed a lot because I was one of the first ones. Then it went ballistic and everybody had a blog.

How has the blogosphere changed over the years?

Now the competition is fierce. The regional blogs are not so popular anymore. People would rather go to a specific topic. My food blog was very popular. It was famous for awhile . . . Now the people are stable. They come because they want recipes.

How have you evolved as a blogger?

It has changed a lot. Sometimes I'll go to the archives to check the facts. I'll say, "What did I do that year?" . . . When I go to the archives, it's very clear to me how I've evolved as a writer, a person. Now I'm more self-conscious about what I write. Before, I'd say anything. I'd write about the weather, what I did, what I watched on TV.

My food blog is more like a hobby . . . On the food blog, I can express myself better. I think it was better for me. I cook mostly with the ingredients I find here. Where I live, in this area, they have lots of tomatoes. So I say I live in Tomato Land. When I started posting recipes of tomatoes, people would go crazy. Tomatoes are my trademark . . . We also have orchards of almonds. This area I live in is heaven for agriculture so it's the best place to be for a food blog.

Of course, I write faster, too . . . One big thing that helped me was migrating from a camera to an iPhone. All my pictures now are taken on an iPhone. I have this system of taking them and cutting them and getting them online, which is just a snap . . . I've adjusted to my lack of time and it's working pretty well. Sometimes I don't post anything for a week and that's fine . . . Before I would get very stressed out.

Who are your readers?

All kinds of people who speak Portuguese—in the United States, in Europe, in Brazil. For my first blog, the readers were mostly Brazilians. They were fascinated by the lifestyle in California. At the time, I didn't work. I would just sit every morning and write about my thoughts, everything I experienced, dialogues with other people, things that happened to me. The blogosphere was small, but I would get 500 hits.

With my food blog, a lot of people were from Portugal. It opened my horizons to a lot of things. I got a job in 2005. [Now] I prepare everything on a Sunday afternoon so I have the posts ready . . . I compile a lot of tweets and make a post for my blog.

A lot of people don't even go to the blog anymore. They just read it through their RSS reader. Before, I would go to my counter every day to see where they came from . . . Now I don't care anymore. Still, the food blog gets like 2,000 hits a day.

You've met readers around the world?

People want to meet me every time I go to Brazil. They want to have a gathering. Now I don't do that anymore. But a lot of them became my friends. The most interesting thing to me is that I went to Belgium and I met a reader there. I went to Portugal and I met a reader there. Sometimes readers cook me meals . . . It makes me self-conscious . . . When I went to Portugal, they were so excited to meet me, it was really, "Oh my gosh!" . . . I have had people taking pictures of my house. It was really strange.

Have you ever sought to make money as a blogger?

I chose not to do it because I feel self-conscious to make money off of a blog. For years, I got many offers. But they were all lame. I feel it would betray my readers. My blog is about me and my life and my food and my family. It's very personal. It has all the recipes, but it has pictures of my life . . . Sometimes I write little things about my life. It wouldn't feel right if I started writing about products.

My husband is sort of like, "Why don't you want to make money?" but I have a job and I don't think it's worth it.

What advice would you have for today's new bloggers?

Do it because you like it, because it's fun. Find your niche, a subject you love. But I personally don't expect anything from it. I do it because I like it, which is maybe why I survived all these years. Everything that comes from blogging is a surprise . . . Besides, if I don't blog, what else am I going to do? I don't garden. I'm not an athlete. I don't run a marathon. Blogging is something that feeds my creativity. I need to have the call for the photography and the creative things I do. You have to have that in your life. Everyone has a hobby, and I blog.

Naming Your Blog

It can be difficult to choose a name. Think carefully. Avoid cute—blog readers have been cuted to death. Make the name descriptive and, if you can, active.

Tom Carroll called his blog *Wings Over Boston*, a play on words that gives the name some impact but still makes it clear the blog is about wings and Boston. Amy Senk named her blog as if it were a newspaper: *Corona Del Mar Today*.

Here are the names of the technology blogs at some of the United States' largest newspapers:

- *Bits* (*New York Times*)
- *The Switch* (*Washington Post*)
- *Digits* (*Wall Street Journal*)
- *Technology Live* (*USA Today*)
- *Tech Now* (*Los Angeles Times*)
- *SiliconBeat* (*San Jose Mercury News*)
- *TechKnow Bytes* (*Denver Post*)
- *Silicon Island* (*Newsday*)

Then there are the major online-only tech blogs, whose names may hold no resonance for you but do in the tech world:

- *Mashable*
- *Gizmodo*
- *GigaOM*
- *Engadget*
- *The Verge*
- *TechCrunch*
- *Ars Technica*
- *ReadWrite*
- *9to5Mac*

54

Journalism tradition has long given the name "gatekeeping" to those in the newsroom who vet the quality and value of information that flows to the public. Mark and his editors decided *Gatekeeper* would make it instantly obvious to the reader that he or she is looking at a blog about journalism. Note, too, that the blog doesn't just have a name; it has a line underneath the name that explains the subject of the blog in 11 words: "Mark Leccese watches Boston and the people who report on it."

When Christopher O'Leary sat down to begin his blog on every song David Bowie has ever recorded, he took about 10 minutes to come up with the name *Pushing Ahead of the Dame*. It's an obscure play on words. There's a Bowie song about a drag queen with the lyric "she's known in the darkest clubs for pushing ahead of the dames," and Bowie was sometimes known in the British rock press as "The Dame." And so *Pushing Ahead of the Dame* meant keeping one step ahead of Bowie. It was clever. But, says O'Leary, "I've come to regret the name as it's a bit of an ungainly title . . . It should've just been *Bowiesongs*," he says, "which is how many people refer to it anyhow."

Checking out the Competition

If you wanted to be a really good dancer, you'd carefully watch other dancers perform, right? If you wanted to be a really good bass player, you'd spend some time listening to the bass players on your favorite recording and trying to figure out what they're doing.

The same holds true for writing blogs—for all writing, in fact. The jazz trumpet player Clark Terry always told his students that learning to play jazz is a three-step process: Imitation, Assimilation, Innovation.

Let's apply that to writing. You need to read abundantly and widely if you want to write well. All of us, as we develop as writers, find models, writers we admire. We imitate them (taking care not to copy). As we imitate, we absorb, and, finally, we go beyond imitation to create our own voice.

If improving your writing is one reason to check out the competition as a blogger, another is to keep up to date on what's happening in your topic area and to keep an eye on the competition.

55

Before you begin blogging, search the Web for other blogs on the same or similar topics about which you plan to write. Assimilate yourself into the subject. This is a big step: it can help you position your blog. So compile as complete a list as you can.

To make following your favorite blogs easier, set up an RSS reader. The best ones, most of which are available for desktop and mobile and are either inexpensive or free, are Feedly, NewsBlur, NetNews Wire, and The Old Reader.

RSS stands for Real Simple Syndication, and once you set up an RSS reader, it will "feed" every new post on the blogs you follow into your RSS app; instead of visiting a dozen or more blogs every day, you only need to open your RSS app to read everything those blogs have published.

Pretty much every blog and website has the capability to subscribe to an RSS feed, although on many pages the RSS feed can be a little hard to find. When you go to a blog you want to include in your RSS reader, look for this icon or a box that will look something like it.

Sometimes simply clicking on the icon will add the feed from that blog to your RSS readers, and sometimes you need to copy the feed's URL (which will read something like this: http://feeds.feedburner.com/websitename). On some blogs, and especially news websites, there is no RSS icon. If so, search the page for the letters "RSS." On the home page of nytimes.com, for example, the link for RSS is at the bottom of the page in a tiny font. But once you find it and click on it, you can choose from more than 100 RSS feeds on various topics.

Coming up with Ideas for Posts

We all read things that interest us, hear things at parties, observe things as we ride the subway or bus or walk to school. The first step in finding good ideas is to be curious, to ask someone, "What's going on?" If you see a crowd gathered in the park, find out why. If you notice that cool wings place you went to last week is now shuttered, ask questions.

Being a good blogger, like being a good reporter, starts with being interested and by gathering string—snippets of information of interest to you—on your phone, in a notebook, on a tablet, or, when all else fails, on a napkin.

Jerry Lanson spent six months in France, trying to overcome challenges of language and culture. As he did so, he turned these experiences into blog material that told English-speaking visitors something about the culture and where they could enjoy it away from the most predictable—and crowded—tourist sites.

When, for example, a French theater audience reacted with a loud "shhh" and "*sortie*" ("leave") after a cellphone went off mid-movie, he wrote that reaction down in a notebook he always carries in his pocket. When his language teacher told him about a bookstore with more than 100,000 titles, struggling to survive in a tiny mountain town, he drove there. And when he noticed a passing reference to a medieval ruin on a plateau that few tourists visit, he went there, hiked it, and compared it to another ruin that draws 1.5 million visitors a year.

Lanson chronicled these and other experiences in a blog called France in the Slow Lane (www.slowlanetravel.com).

Some blogs lend themselves more to such old-fashioned skills— listening, watching, and asking—than others. But no blog in the twenty-first century should rely on these skills alone. Today, we can keep up with the world from our own little corner of it by using some great technological tools that can bring the world to our tablet, phone, or desktop. The trick is to use them well.

RSS feeds are just one such tool.

If you have a tablet computer (or a mobile phone), you can use "personal magazine" apps, which are much like RSS feeds but with a much more attractive and visual interface. Try Flipboard, Zite, Pulse, or News 360—they're all free, so you might as well download them all, try them, and decide which ones you like best.

If you are not on Twitter and Facebook, you need to get an account and you need to get one now. The Pew Research Center reported in April 2014 that 73 percent of all Americans who use the Internet use social media networking sites. And the younger you are, the more likely you are to use Twitter and Facebook. Among Internet users 65 and older, about half use social networking sites. Among Internet users 18 to 29, almost 90 percent do.

We understand you may find these social media sites annoying and vapid. You are, for the most part, absolutely right. But Twitter and Facebook are absolutely essential for keeping up with not only what is going on in the news but also with what is being published in blogs, on the websites of magazines, and at off-beat news aggregators (think of them as "news highlighters"), such as gawker.com and fark.com. In other words, Twitter is a useful tool for coming up with ideas.

Lars Willnat and David Weaver, professors at the University of Indiana School of Journalism, surveyed more than 1,000 journalists online in late 2013. Their 2014 report, titled "The American Journalist in the Digital Age," found Twitter is the single most used social media tool among journalists. More than half of journalists in the study said they use Twitter. A quarter of the journalists said they also read blogs by other journalists.

Today, 80 percent use Twitter regularly to follow breaking news and 73 percent use it to check out what other news organizations are doing. But 60 percent of journalists also use Twitter to "find ideas for stories," and 56 percent use it to "find additional information."

The key to Twitter is that you need to "curate" the list of the people and news organizations you follow. Follow too many Twitter accounts and you'll just be overwhelmed; follow too few and you'll miss a lot of good stuff. After a while, you'll know which Twitter users in your area link to or file interesting material. Don't feel obligated to stick with the others.

Try this experiment: Follow 10 or 20 new accounts for a week or so to find out if they're worth following. Check Twitter at least daily. Of those 10 or 20 new accounts, unfollow the ones that aren't useful to you. Do the same next week, and again the week after. By doing so, you'll refine your list without expanding it indefinitely.

Mark keeps his Twitter account manageable by following no more than 250 (give or take a few) people, and he regularly deletes tweeters who become annoying or no longer useful. That gives him room to follow new tweeters who post interesting stuff.

Once you've set up Twitter to your liking, you'll find ideas easier to come by.

Scrolling through his Twitter timeline one day a few years ago, Mark noticed a tweet from a group called Public Policy Polling (@ppppolis) announcing the results of its annual "News Trust Poll." The tweet included a link to the poll results, and Mark studied the poll, chose a topic for his blog from among the polling data, and wrote a blog post titled "Older viewers distrust TV News—except Fox News." Another time, he read a tweet from his hometown newspaper's police log that a resident had called the police to complain about seeing a coyote in the neighborhood. Mark went back and read through the local paper's police logs for the past month and discovered that citizens of his town (which borders the City of Boston on three sides) had called police to report seeing not only a coyote, but foxes. One man called police to tell them his wife and two children were "trapped" in the courtyard of their apartment building by three wild turkeys.

Mark wrote up a blog post about the media's coverage of wild animals in the Boston suburbs.

To cast a wider net when you go fishing for ideas, try the two powerful blog search engines Google Blogs Search (www.google.com/blogsearch) and Technorati's search (technorati.com).

Technorati, by the way, is the source on the Internet of pretty much everything you may want to know at any given time about which blogs are hot, which topics are hot on the blogs, and what's being written on tens of thousands of blogs across the world.

Remember: if you do all that we suggested above, or even if you only do some of it, make sure to leave time for gathering string, collecting scraps of information or thoughts that can evolve into blog posts. You can do this by taking a walk (Jerry noticed that condoms are sold in dispensing machines outside most French pharmacies), by driving through town (he also noticed jarring speed bumps had been installed at the entrance of villages throughout the south of France to slow down drivers), or by sitting in a café (he did a photo blog on all who passed a Montpelier café in one hour). Or you can wander through the blogs you check, the news sites you read, the Twitter timelines you examine, and sometimes begin to see patterns before your competitors do. Both require a keen interest in what's new and what's changed.

Building an Audience

In Chapter 12, we will talk extensively and specifically about ways to build an audience for your blog and a "brand" for yourself and your work. For the purposes of this chapter, let's talk about how you can manage *just your blog and your writing* to build an audience.

- **Push out—but not too far—from the topic of your blog.** It's OK if you wander a little distance away from your blog topic from time to time. The reader will not only accept it, but will find it interesting. The reader, actually, may even be grateful for it. If your blog is about athletic shoes (and there is plenty of material for a daily blog on athletic shoes), a post now and then on shin splints in runners or the importance of good cleats on a football boot may draw new readers and still be useful to your current ones.
- **Write well, and leave time to revise drafts before you post.** This is our most emphatically obvious piece of advice. It's like advising a basketball player to score more points to be successful. But if you read many blogs, even those published by major media organizations, you'll see how often this advice is ignored. They're filled with typos and punctuation errors. *Never* write directly into the "new post" window of your blogging software and hit "publish." Serious writers do not publish their first drafts. Write a draft of your post in whatever word processing software you use. Put the URLs for the links you will use at the end of the paragraphs containing the link for easy access. Rewrite your post until you are satisfied with it, and only then copy and paste it (along with link, images, and whatever other media you have) into your blogging software. Then proofread, reading your writing aloud

59

(it catches many more mistakes). Finally, check to make sure all your links work.

- **Vary the lengths of your posts.** There is nothing wrong with a 150-word post if that is all you need to say about something, and there is nothing wrong with a 1,500-word post if you research and write it well enough to keep the reader interested all the way through. Not every subject needs to be written about at length. Some blogging software (WordPress, for example) allows you to make a post out of a quote, or an audio file, or to post a "status"— a very brief sentence or two. Mixing up the length of your posts also makes your blog more visually appealing.

- **Keep an "Ideas File."** As you read and as you go about your daily life, stray pieces of information, observations, images, and so on will cross your path, and the writer in you will think, "Hmm. Interesting. I might be able to get a blog post out of that." Make a folder on your computer called "Blog Post Ideas" or "Stray Ideas." (Mark calls his "Rogue Ideas;" Jerry, "Ideas File.")

- **Be patient.** The Count of Flanders, a cleric in the court of Phillippe of Alsace in the twelfth century, wrote a small book of what he claimed were peasants' proverbs. *Rome ne s'est pas faite en un jour*, wrote the Count: *Rome wasn't built in a day*. It's a hackneyed old expression indeed, but one that has lasted a millennium because it is true. The same is true of building a blog audience.

Christopher O'Leary, the blogger we met earlier in the chapter who has spent five years writing blog posts (more than 500 and still counting) about every song David Bowie has ever recorded, said his blog has "a slowly building readership."

Who were his readers when he began the blog? "I don't know," he said. "Just people searching for songs or lyrics."

Tom Ewing, a blogger in the United Kingdom (UK), has been working for years on a blog that reviews every UK No. 1 hit single, in order, starting with Al Martino's 1952 smash "Here in My Heart" (http://freakytrigger.co.uk/popular/).

Several years ago, Ewing discovered O'Leary's blog and linked to it on his own blog. This brought it to the attention of the UK newspaper the *Guardian* and its website, which named O'Leary's blog the "blog of the week" and wrote about it. Not long afterward, *Time* magazine singled out O'Leary's work as one of its Best Blogs of 2011.

Now his blog draws as many as 1,500 readers a day, and his readership's still growing. "Twitter was another big thing," said O'Leary, whose Twitter account is @bowiesongs. "That's brought me a lot of readers."

"The readership has been good," he said. "I've got a good group of commenters."

His patience also earned him the knowledge and recognition needed to write a book.

Writing a Time-Limited Blog

Headed to Modena and Bologna in northern Italy for a couple of weeks to tour the Ferrari, Lamborghini, Maserati, Pagani, and Ducati factories and museums? Packing up for a summer music festival? Whetting your appetite for Restaurant Week in your city?

Write a time-limited blog. Not every blog needs to be kept going and kept fresh with new posts for months and years. Time-limited blogs—some last no longer than a few hours—have become a staple of journalism and communication.

Think of a news organization live-blogging the Oscars or a ballgame (the British news organization the *Guardian* is particularly good at informative and amusing live blogs). Think of a specialty publication publishing a blog for the duration of a trade show. Think of friends of yours blogging every day about their trips to Dubrovnik.

As you can see from the examples above, there are two kinds of time-limited blogs: live blogs, which can last from a few hours to a day, and short-term blogs, to which a blogger will post daily (and more) for at least a few days but less than, say, a month.

Here are some tips on writing both kinds of blogs:

- **Conduct your background reporting and research well before you start the blog.** You don't want to be gathering background information on the fly. You want to have it ready to go when you begin your short-term blog. Gather facts, images, and whatever else you think will make your blog more informative, interesting, and fun. Keep that material in a word processing document and (for images and other multimedia) in a folder in your desktop for easy access.

61

- **Announce when your live blog or short-term blog will begin on several platforms less than a week before it starts.** Don't announce your blog too far in advance. Readers forget. When you do announce your short-term blog on social media, make sure to include the day (and time, if it is a live blog) it will begin and the day it will end. That alerts readers to what time commitment they'll need to keep up with your blog.
- **Announce your short-term blog after you publish your first post, and make sure to include a link to the blog.** The best places to announce the start of your blog are Twitter, Facebook, and, if you have one, another blog you are writing. Tweet about your blog—with a link—every day you are writing it. Nothing works better than Twitter to drive traffic to your blog.

DISCUSSION

1. In small groups, build a list of the relative strengths of traditional reporting vs. blogging. Discuss whether there are particular situations in which one works better than the other.

2. Consider what blogs you like to read. What draws you to them? Why do you keep going back? Is it the topic, the design, the writer, the photography, the style, the content? What do you think makes it a good blog?

EXERCISE

Draw up a list of three blogs you would like to write.

1. Use social media to identify three blogs on the topic that you find interesting.

2. Read these for an hour each. Ask yourself:

    (a) Does the blog have a tight focus?

    (b) Does the blogger vary length?

    (c) Does the blogger use multimedia?

    (d) Do the blogs seem crisp and well edited?

3. Consider whether these blogs help you further narrow and focus your blog.

4. Come up with a list of five specific ideas you might write about if you were to start your blog.

Writing as Rap

Around dinner time in the Lanson household, Jerry and his 7-year-old granddaughter Devon stand around the dining room table most nights and get ready to fire up the beat. They pull out knives, forks, and spoons; stand around the dining room table; and, with glasses, salt shakers, salad dressing bottles, chair rungs, and walls as their instruments, begin to work rhythms with different syncopations. Soon they're clinking and clacking, singing a little scat, playing off each other, and having fun with sound.

Making jazz, they call it.

Words, too, can be both jazzy and rhythmic. They've got pace and tempo, cadence and rhyme. They swoop and tumble, sizzle with the sounds of sibilance (think *s* sounds), and, sometimes, stop short. You want to be a blogger? Then don't be so darned earnest. Be your fun self. Make up words occasionally. And try firing up the beat.

Listen up here if you want to say
What's on your mind this very day
Hear the cadence of your words
Even if they are most absurd.
Be-bop, lop-bomb, boobie-do, sham-dom.
Time to shed the funk of grammar school rules.
Time to strip the vanity of big voice fools.

Chee-bob, wee-bob, sobble-zop, clah
Clicky-dah, shumba, blah, blah, blah.
No more need for pompous fuddy
Keep your message clear, don't let it get muddy.
Listen to it, listen to it, read it aloud.
If you're gonna jive, you can't be cowed.
Shoobie-do, bah-schwab, let your voice sing
Bop-a-loop, bob-a-lop, give your message zing.

Jerry wrote these words on a fall Friday morning subway ride to work. He was being silly, trying to loosen up . . . and getting ready to write his first draft of this chapter.

The Beauty of Free Writing

You're absolutely right. There's good reason Jerry and Mark blog instead of writing poetry.

That said, playing with words and their sounds, silly as it seems, has real purpose. It can help you cast aside the demons of writer's block and, over the years, make sense of that elusive quality called voice that mystifies most beginners, causing them to overreach. Free writing can scale away the encrusted cadences of cliché, shed the empty calories of multisyllabic words that plod rather than gallop. And it can help you relax.

So from time to time, just let your words cascade. Riff a little. Write a little rap, as the title of this chapter suggests.

Jerry started playing with free writing when he was about 30. He was a young college professor, searching for some way to crash through his writer's block and publish rather than perish. Following the published advice of author Peter Elbow, he began writing fast for a few minutes first thing each morning, never lifting his fingers from the keyboard. Jerry described his approach with this analogy in his book *Writing for Others, Writing for Ourselves*:

At the gym, it takes a steady regimen to develop muscles . . . But the first step, often the toughest, is getting out of bed and getting in the car. It's too dark. It's too cold. There's too much ice caked on the windshield. Why not roll over and hit the snooze button? . . .

Free-writing gets you to the gym and gets you through the stretching exercises. It primes you to develop more serious writing muscles.

And that's all it does. It's not meant to produce coherence. It's not meant to craft quality. It's meant to free you from self-judgment and self-doubt, to get the writer in you moving.

Free writing takes little time. Sit down with a pad of paper or an iPad and accelerate. Write as fast as you can for 10 minutes, max. The rules are simple. You can't stop. You can't correct. You can't pause to think. Just keep writing, even if it's gibberish. Shape doesn't matter. Form doesn't count. Forget design (though it's OK to rhyme). The one rule? Let things rip.

When you're done, read what you wrote aloud. Then throw it out and start again fresh the next day.

Once again: this is like stretching at the gym. The heavy lifting of writing, carefully crafted, comes later. Right now, you just want to get your fingers—and your mind—loose.

Finding the Space, and Place, You Think Best

Where you write matters. We're talking location here, not whether you're a Mac or PC kind of person. To put it another way, some of the great thoughts of our time will not be conceived at a keyboard.

We know this statement contradicts much of the advice you'll read out there. Most well-respected writers will tell you it's essential to write every day, at the same time, for a set number of hours. The marvelous nonfiction author John McPhee tied himself to his chair while a student at Princeton to force himself to stick with his task.

We're not dismissing this advice. We're amending it. Writing does take discipline and structure. But when you get hopelessly stuck, it's not worth having an aneurysm glowering at your computer screen.

Where do you think best? Seriously. Where do you think best? Odds are it's not a keyboard. And odds are the place you think best is where you'll best break down problems as you craft and draft. Spend more time there.

Jerry, for a couple of decades, has been asking participants in writing groups he's coached where they think best. The answers typically follow one of these patterns:

- *Moving* (biking, jogging, walking, driving, exercising)
- *In bed* (before sleep, first thing in the morning, waking from a nap)
- *Doing something relaxing* (cooking, showering, gardening)

Very few people—and we're talking professional journalists and writers here—believe they think best in front of a keyboard.

So what's the point (and why should you care)?

Writing is hard work. If you're anything like us (Jerry and Mark), sometimes when you try *too* hard, you lock up. Your brain shuts down. Your words turn as tense as the frown lines on your forehead. At such times, we believe, you're more likely to succeed if you put a mental *Gone Fishin'* sign out and give yourself the space to think. Take a walk. Get a cup of coffee. Look at a bulletin board. Chop vegetables. Not all writing problems get solved through conscious work. Give your subconscious some space and time to click in.

Jerry only began to overcome decades of dread of filling blank pages when he learned this about himself: he writes best moving, something his golden retriever begins to resent (and resist) after hours of walking around the neighborhood. Jerry (but not his dog) has learned to carry a pad and pencil on these walks just in case words or ideas pop into his head. That way, he won't forget.

Fast Drafting

You've heard that in the world of love, opposites sometimes attract? So it is with writing. Let's call it the union of two r's, *relax* and *revise*. Relax is the free spirit of these lovebirds. At her best, she's spontaneous and creative. She's a free spirit who doesn't spend much time second-guessing herself. Revise? He can be a bit uptight. But at his best, he's precise and organized. He helps order the life of Relax while she infuses spontaneity and creativity into his orderly ways.

Relax and Revise are the perfect couple of the written world. Once we've outlined and organized a story, we need to seek out Relax to find the flow, the pace, the rhythm of our words. Once we're done drafting, we need the help of Revise. He'll demand that we circle back two and three or five times to pare unneeded words, clarify fuzzy phrases, sharpen images and analogies.

Enough about our couple. Keep in mind that revision demands precision. But a good revision needs something rich and flavorful to start with, preferably the work of someone relaxed enough to infuse his or her writing with color and animation.

Learning to relax when faced with a blank page can be daunting to many writers. Don Fry, formerly with the Poynter Institute, offered his students this advice: "Draft fast to block the internal censor."

Fry knows that it's impossible to get things right the first time. In fact, trying too much can be the kiss of death for a piece of written work. But let's listen to Anne Lamott, author of the best-selling *Bird by Bird*, explain why. She says it colorfully:

> Perfectionism is the voice of the oppressor, the enemy of the people. It will keep you cramped and insane your whole life, and it is the main obstacle between you and a shitty first draft.

So try drafting fast rather than painstakingly. Don't check your notes before writing each paragraph. Don't revise that paragraph multiple times before you move to the next.

Don't, however, mistake drafting fast for free writing. Before you sit down to draft fast, you should have a plan, at least in your mind. Sometimes fast drafts can be used to capture a scene you've just witnessed or a dialogue you've just heard. That's not really a draft, but a vignette you may stick somewhere in a blog post later on. If you're drafting fast from start to finish, it helps to first look through your notes, links, and other research, and to jot down a few key points. Then put these props aside and write fast before the nag of perfectionism slams you to a stop.

Voice

Mark Leccese plays jazz trumpet; Jerry Lanson sings classical and folk. Maybe that's why both tell students to listen to the words they write, to read them out loud. Some words fly past. Others snap, turn, or stop, steered or lassoed by punctuation.

If, as author William Zinsser suggests, writing is a conversation between writer and reader, we'd all better learn to be better conversationalists. That takes practice.

Fancy writers love the word "voice." Young writers often fear it. It's an elusive concept to define but teachers of writing keep trying. Here are a few attempts from some of the masters of nonfiction instruction.

69

Writes Zinsser in his classic, *On Writing Well*:

> Writing that will endure tends to consist of words that are short and strong
> . . .
>
> Develop one voice that readers will recognize when they hear it on the page,
> a voice that's enjoyable not only in its musical line but in its avoidance of sounds
> that would cheapen its tone: breeziness and condescension and clichés.

Donald Murray, a Pulitzer Prize-winning journalist called the father of writing coaches, wrote several marvelous books on writing during his life. Here is an excerpt from his book *The Craft of Revision*:

> When we write, we speak in written words. The magic of writing is that readers
> who may never meet us hear what we have written. Music rises from the page
> when we read. We call the heard quality of writing voice . . .

And lastly, here are the thoughts of Carl Sessions Stepp, professor, editor, and coach, in his lovely book *Writing as Craft and Magic*:

> Most writers' voices will emerge spontaneously if they just clear away some of
> the obstructing professional underbrush: the artificial constraints, expectations,
> and hobgoblins that haunt many newsrooms, writing studios, and writer-editor
> collaborations.

Voice, in other words, is little more than the real you, dressed simply if with a dash of elegance for a night on the town. It's not something that can be conjured. It's not something that's slathered on top of your work, like blush or eyeliner or layers of cheap lacquer on the fine grain of an old table. To the contrary, it emerges once all the artificial layers are removed from your words.

How do you get there? Again, voice can't be willed. But there are things you can do. Read good writing, lots of it. Write, often. Listen to your words. Out loud. Try, in fact, reading into a voice recorder and playing it back so you can hear the cadence. Be a critic, of your work and others. Imitate what you like. Something drew you to that writer. Ask yourself what.

And above all, don't try to force things.

Let's listen to Stepp again:

> Writers who are steeped in good material, relaxed and enthusiastic about their
> assignment, comfortable in their surroundings, and encouraged to be original
> and inventive do not have to find a voice—it rings out instinctively.

One other thing. No two voices are the same. As in gauging someone's taste in clothing or interior design, we—the readers—know when someone has a voice that draws and know when someone lacks it. But none of us share identical tastes in clothing, music, or food. The same holds true of writing, and the writer's voice.

If writing is a conversation, as Zinsser suggests, not everyone will partake. The writer's task is to engage those who do.

TALIA RALPH

"Blogs work best when readers are responding not just to the topic, but to the person writing"

Talia Ralph is a 20-something multimedia journalist working on a master's degree in food systems at NYU. She earned a bachelor's degree in magazine journalism and design at Emerson College in Boston, where she also studied with the authors of this book. Montreal-born and bilingual, Ralph has kept her own blogs and currently blogs for the food blog *The Sporkful* at sporkful.com. She talked with the authors about blogging and the challenges of developing a distinctive voice.

Talia Ralph
(*Credit*: SARAH JACOBS)

In your view, just what is the difference between the blogs you write and other forms of journalistic work?
Blogs put a premium on personal voice and style, whereas traditional journalism leans towards a neutral voice that is focused on highlighting the voices of others. Blogs work best when readers are responding not just to the topic, but to the person writing. I've found that, especially in the realm of food blogs, readers want to feel like they can trust the blogger and that they know them. They're looking for someone they'd want to cook alongside or ask for a restaurant recommendation in a new city. In light of this, my blogging style tends to be a bit looser, jokier, and more approachable. I feel like my voice is more relaxed, and I'm more willing to go out on linguistic limbs.

What first drew you to blogging?
I've been blogging since the good old days of LiveJournal—back then, my "blog" was a slightly edited diary that I assumed (probably accurately) no one wanted to read. As my blogging matured, and I started to get paid to write online, I really came to value the interactivity of blogs and the ability to engage in conversations with readers. Though the

comments section of a piece can sometimes be a dark and scary place, it also offers a great opportunity to see how people respond to your work and even identify things you may have missed or flubbed. The rapid response time, both to discussing your work and to fixing errors when they do inevitably happen, is a huge advantage of blogging. You can also see your content being shared, referenced, and repurposed across the Web.

What kinds of blogging do you like to do?
Right now, I live in the world of food blogging, and it's a great (and delicious) place to be. I was lucky enough to spend a summer as the editorial fellow at Food52, an amazing recipe resource for home cooks and a platform for some of the freshest, smartest, loveliest voices in online food writing. I also blog for The Sporkful, a podcast on WNYC that discusses the finer points of eating, cooking, and food culture. There's just something about food that connects and excites people, so food blogs become these really vibrant online communities.

What does the nebulous concept of voice mean to you?
In its ideal form, voice is the vehicle by which you let readers know who you are and (hopefully!) earn their trust. It's the perfect average of how you actually sound when you speak and how you wish you sounded . . . I was always drawn to writing because I seem to often find myself either freezing up or putting my foot in my mouth during conversations. Though I wouldn't call myself shy by any stretch, writing (and by extension, my writing voice) gives me the chance to slow down, take a deep breath, think carefully and logically, and best of all, EDIT.

Do you notice any difference in your voice or style of writing when you move between audio and text blogs and more conventional journalism?
"Voice" . . . is one of the most elusive and terrifying things to me as a writer. However, if forced to describe my style of writing, I strive for a tone that's natural, approachable, and highly respectful of my subject matter, no matter whether it's a quick, personally driven blog post or a more conventional journalistic story. Though blogging and radio hosting have both allowed me to loosen up stylistically, I still hold the journalistic ideals of neutrality and making it about others.

Have you blogged strictly for yourself or have you placed your blogs at hub sites that take work from multiple bloggers?
I've done both. A lot of my work for *GlobalPost*, an online international news platform, was redistributed by both print and other online sources like *Salon* and *Business Insider*. Though I've had many iterations of personal blogs, from a fashion dictionary to a photo-driven food blog, none have ever taken off or become wildly successful. I think most were read by an audience roughly the size of my mother and a few kind friends.

[Still], the complete creative control you have over a personal blog is intoxicating, especially when you've been writing or shooting for outlets that have their own style, voice, aesthetics, and structure. However, people don't realize how much work goes into a personal blog, and that is why so many of them shrivel up and die on the vine. You have to be as dedicated to your blog as you would be to training for a marathon or saving for a trip: it requires constant thought, sacrifices, and daily effort. It's also incredibly hard to attract and grow your readership or become profitable. Without eyes on your blog, or a paycheck coming in, or even better, a BOOK DEAL, many writers get understandably discouraged.

What advice would you offer student bloggers trying to establish a foothold?
Learn to pitch, and pitch often. There are so many amazing opportunities to write online, and editors are ALWAYS open to new content. The Web is a great space to write because, well, it's got no space constraints. That means you're more likely to get a 1,000-word feature published there as a new writer than you would be in a traditional print magazine.

The Value of Analogy

73

Some concepts are complex or theoretical. They're hard to translate into plain English in a clear, easily accessible way. Other concepts are clear enough, but dry as a sun-baked dishrag. They lack vitality. In describing either, it can help to use analogy, to compare what's not well understood or is difficult to enliven to something that is clear, well understood, and sometimes more colorful.

Good analogy, in other words, gives writing clarity and energy. We tried to do that in the example earlier in this chapter that compared free writing to stretching exercises at the gym, a warm-up that prepares both gym rat and writer for the heavy lifting ahead. The title of this chapter, too, is an analogy that compares writing to a musical form.

If some analogies make things clearer, others merely confuse. Their comparison is flawed or doesn't accurately reflect what the writer is trying to explain. Put another way, using an analogy doesn't always accomplish what the writer wants it to.

One master of analogy was Lewis Thomas, author of *Lives of the Cell* and an essayist in the 1970s for the *New England Journal of Medicine*. He had a knack for bringing nature and biology to life with his ability to compare the unfamiliar to what we know well. Here, he compares the journey of viruses from organism to organism to the action of bees, flitting through the garden fertilizing flowers. It's a strong and familiar visual image.

> We live in a dancing matrix of viruses; they dart, rather like bees, from organism to organism, from plant to insect to mammal to me and back again, and into the sea, tugging along pieces of this genome, strings of genes from that, transplanting grafts of DNA, passing around heredity as though at a great party.

Analogy is a tool open to any writer, bloggers included. When Josh Rothman began a blog on ideas for the *New Yorker* in June 2014, a subject that can be difficult to discuss with specificity, he turned to analogy to make his point more clearly.

> Like people, ideas have social lives. They're one way when they're by themselves, and another when they're surrounded by their peers. Crammed together, they grow more uncertain, more interesting, more surprising; they come out of themselves and grow more appealing, and funnier. You wouldn't want all of intellectual life to be that social—we couldn't make progress that way. But there's a special atmosphere that develops whenever truly different ideas congregate, and, on the whole, it's too rare.

The analogy here—that ideas, like people, have social lives that take somewhat different shapes in different social settings—is grounded in Rothman's memory of an interdisciplinary college class he took. It works well because, unlike the abstraction of ideas, the image of people in a college group setting ("more uncertain, more interesting, more surprising") is concrete. It is easy to visualize and relate to. We've all been in similar situations.

Talk about easy-to-visualize analogies: David Carr, the late media critic for the *New York Times*, composed a beautifully written column following the death of Ben Bradlee, the larger-than-life editor of the *Washington Post* during the Watergate era, in which he offered up these delightful analogies:

Bradlee, he wrote, "had the attention span of a gnat—anecdotes of him walking away from a conversation he ceased to find interesting were common . . ."

And, Carr added, the hip, much-admired *Style* section Bradlee introduced to the *Post* in the late 1960s had an effect on the news business as "profound as if Chuck Berry had walked into a Glenn Miller show and started playing guitar."

OK, students. A little music history might help you here. Berry played hard-edged R&B. Miller? He was the ultimate during his time in offering up happy, colorless elevator music.

Scenes and Images

Small scenes can help make big stories vivid.

The veteran writing coach Don Fry uses the analogy "gold coins" to capture these. They give a story glitter, draw the reader forward toward them, and cast a bright light on content by bringing it to life.

If Fry's gold coins play the role of the morsels of bread dropped by Hansel and Gretel to mark the path they were taking, their meaning extends beyond that. They not only show the way, they illuminate and enhance it, help the reader sense it and see it, infuse it with images that make the story's surroundings more vivid.

A gold coin can be many things. It can be a vignette, a small, sharp internal anecdote that shows what the writer has said. It can be a selective detail—words of a poem scribbled on a wall, the false teeth of an old-timer found in the rubble of a home wrecked by a tornado, a childhood photo of a person wrongly jailed for decades—that draws a sudden and powerful emotional connection. It can be a sensory example that makes things clear.

Be careful, though, in trying to spread the glitter. Not all coins are gold, and not all details or anecdotes or examples available to the blogger telling a story are germane to what the writer wants to say. Young writers have a hard time selecting among them.

Let's try this example. Just because you know that someone is 5 feet, 8 inches and weighs 175 pounds doesn't mean it belongs in a story. If it were to appear in a story about a football team's smallest wide receiver, this detail would matter. If it was a detail in a story about Silicon Valley's latest wonder boy, it wouldn't.

Other available details, on the other hand, wouldn't apply to the wide receiver but might to the business executive. Do I care that the football player, in a blog about his remarkable conditioning, has a penchant for wearing Levi blue jeans and flannel shirts? Probably not. But that detail might be germane in a piece about the casual atmosphere the Silicon Valley wonder boy fosters at his latest start-up.

Other details are absolutes. I'd certainly want to know that the wide receiver does 60 pushups immediately upon opening his eyes every morning. Or that his neck is so thick his most intimate friends call him *turtle*. And I'd want to know that wonder boy never finished high school because he hated taking orders.

Those are details the reader wants to know. They help the reader understand the subject. Because of this, they are "gold coins," details and specific images that make a story more memorable and more likely to stick with a reader.

DISCUSSION

Bring a short piece of writing you like to class or a writers' group you're in. First, think about why you like it. Read it aloud to a breakout group of four or five people. Get the reaction of others. Then talk about what drew you to the piece. After each member of the group reads his or her choice, discuss which piece draws the most interest (no one can vote for their own) and why.

Is voice generational or enduring? The professor should bring two pieces of writing to class, one a classic, one contemporary. He or she should then read both without identifying the writers or era. The class should gauge its reaction before the titles and authors are revealed.

Each student should bring either two vignettes (anecdotes) or analogies to class from blogs or some other form of journalistic writing. One should be an example the student likes, and one the student dislikes.

Use the examples to discuss the qualities of good anecdotes and analogies vs. those that fail.

EXERCISES

1. Free write for 10 minutes each day for a full week. Keep your efforts in a binder, reading each draft fast, and reading each out loud before tucking it away. At the end of the week, write a few

reflective paragraphs on the experience. Was it all gibberish? Did the writing, gibberish or not, help you relax? Why or why not?

2. Write a fast draft of an assignment. The rules are these: Look over your notes. Take a few minutes to block, or jot down, a few main ideas. Then draft the story without referring to your notes and write it from start to finish without revising. This should take no more than 30 minutes. Write one thing that you gained from the experience and one thing that frustrated you.

Striking up a Conversation

In September 2013, the website editor of the venerable and respected American magazine *Popular Science* announced the site would be disabling its comments functions. Readers would no longer be able to comment on the site's articles or blogs.

"It wasn't a decision we made lightly," wrote Suzanne LaBarre, the online content director. "As the news arm of a 141-year-old science and technology magazine, we are as committed to fostering lively, intellectual debate as we are to spreading the word of science far and wide. The problem is when trolls and spambots overwhelm the former, diminishing our ability to do the latter."

New bloggers need to figure out how they want to deal with reader responses to posts in a comments section. It is not an easy decision.

Interactivity is at the heart of blogging culture. Most bloggers don't just hand down their wisdom; they interact with readers. But some readers are more interested in shouting down or trashing an opinion than civilly disagreeing, and they often do so under the shelter of anonymity. Spammers can quickly overwhelm the comments section with ads for sex sites and unsavory products.

While most bloggers allow—and even encourage—comments, they and news organizations disagree, often sharply, about allowing anonymous ones.

A study by University of Houston Communication Professor Arthur Santana found that of the 137 largest newspapers in the United States, half have banned anonymous comments, 42 percent allow them, and the remaining news organizations do not allow comments at all.

When you start a blog, it's your call what comment policy you want to create. We'd suggest that you link to that policy prominently on the home page. You have five options:

1. **Don't allow comments**. All blogging software has an "Allow Comments" option somewhere in the settings. Uncheck the box and no one can talk back.

2. **Allow comments on some posts but not others**. Many news organizations and bloggers use this policy although few say so publicly. Deciding which posts should allow comments and which shouldn't can be uncomfortable. It demands a kind of selective censorship used in an effort to avoid ugly responses. If you decide on this policy, uncheck the comments box for posts about "hot-button" public affairs matters, such as race, immigration, terrorism, religion, gun control, and the like.

3. **Allow comments only from people who use their real names**. There are two ways to implement this policy. One is to require anyone who wants to comment to send an email to confirm their identity. You'd then add them to a list of your blogging software's approved commenters. The other—and this is a bit more complex—is to allow comments only through a third-party website that uses real names, such as Facebook (huffingtonpost.com uses this policy). In WordPress, for example, you can replace the WordPress comments function with Facebook comments. One advantage is that this option allows you to seamlessly promote your blog on Facebook.

4. **Moderate the comments yourself**. All the most-used blogging software allows you to send comments to a "comments queue" for your review. This allows you to read and approve any before it appears. The problem: This takes time. Be sure upfront that you are willing to take it. A comment submitted and left unposted for days and days is a sure way to alienate a reader. James Fallows, a blogger for theatlantic.com, has never allowed comments. "Unless a comment stream is actively moderated, it inevitably is ruined by bullies, hotheads, and trolls," he writes, adding that he is

unwilling "to commit the ongoing attention necessary to be a real-time moderator of comments."

5. **Allow all comments, even from anonymous commenters**. Just click "allow comments." You'll get comments that are intelligent and thoughtful, and you'll get comments that are insulting and ill-mannered. You'll engage your readers in useful conversation, and you'll get called foul names. Your blog will also be a target for spambots, which we'll discuss later in the chapter.

Unlike Fallows, we believe you should choose option 4, even with the extra work involved. Make yourself the moderator of your own blog comments. At first, anyway, there won't be that many. Blogs at large news organizations may allow all comments from anonymous commenters. But if you're new to blogging, or newly serious about it, you should protect yourself—and your other commenters—from the malevolent demons of the Internet. This attention also allows you to interact with readers in ways that may draw more to your site.

Comments are so important to blogging—and can cause such anxiety and anger—that it is worth talking more about them.

Dan Kennedy, a veteran journalist and journalism professor at Northeastern University, has been writing and blogging about media for years. His blog, Media Nation (dankennedy.net), is widely read, and often the site of active discussion. But he won't let just anyone comment.

"I really believe that if you don't screen comments, you're not serious," Kennedy says. "Allowing unmoderated comments can cause a "toxic environment that drives potential commenters away." For his own blog, Kennedy requires commenters to register with him by email before they can submit comments.

In his book *The Wired City*, Kennedy describes a nonprofit community news website in New Haven, Connecticut, called the *New Haven Independent*. At first, he said, the site "did nothing more than screen all comments ahead of time." But during a contentious mayoral campaign, the comments "grew in quantity and nastiness," he said.

One busy day, the editor of the website quickly scanned the comments queue before heading to cover an event, and accidentally hit "publish" on one that was highly inflammatory. By the time the editor returned, Kennedy said, "the comments had exploded."

81

That incident led the *New Haven Independent* to adopt a policy that limited the right to comment to those who registered under their own name. The commenter, once registered, can use a screen name, but all comments are moderated—and the editor is no longer the sole moderator. The job is shared by several people who work or volunteer at the website.

Why Allow Comments?

Even with the headaches comments can cause, the chance to have a conversation with multiple readers in close to real time makes the Internet different from any other medium. Allowing comments also helps to make your blogging sharper and more accurate (your readers will let you know when you go astray), creates conversation among readers, fosters reader loyalty, and, most importantly, helps build a network of readers and bloggers. Isn't that why you started blogging in the first place?

But be forewarned. It pays to have a thick skin if readers engage honestly. Some of these readers will tell you that you're wrong. Some will disagree vehemently. You'll be called names. Mark and Jerry both engage those posting challenging comments on their blogs as long as the tone is civil. If bloggers want others to listen to and be influenced by their views, presumably based on evidence and context, they have to accept that others can reasonably disagree. At its best, the blogosphere encourages discourse that moves beyond the food fight that too much of the give-and-take, particularly in politics, has turned toward in the United States.

Growing and Nurturing a Community of Commenters

Please excuse our lack of subtlety here, but sometimes you have to state the obvious: you can't build a community unless you *belong* to a community. The community you want to belong to is one of people who research and write about or actively read and comment on topics similar to yours. If you're writing a "locavore" blog—a "locavore" builds his or her diet around food grown locally—then you want to be active in the large community of healthy food bloggers and their followers.

Here are three ways to accomplish this:

1. **Link to other blogs whose topics are similar.** "Link love" is what bloggers call it. When bloggers look at what is known as the "analytics," or readership data, about their sites, they can see who is linking to their blog. That's how they discover who is writing on a similar topic. Other bloggers tend to surf to similar blogs to check them out. The "pingbacks" function in WordPress or Moveable Type helps you encourage such networking. When you link to another blog, your software sends a "pingback" to the blog you linked to, where it will be displayed as a comment.

2. **Comment on blogs whose topics are similar.** Make it a point not just to write comments on other blogs but to write comments that are intelligent and useful to that blog's readers (and to the blogger). If you leave a comment on a blog post about a particular cricket bowler, add an observation that supplements the blogger's. Always use the name under which you blog—if you blog as Charles Smith, then sign into the comment system as "Charles Smith." And sign each comment.

3. **Keep and update a blog roll on your blog.** This is a list of links to related blogs that appears in a column either to the right or left of your blog posts. We recommend listing and linking to 5 to 10 of the best blogs you read.

The best way to draw comments, of course, is to write a well-researched, thoughtful, and eloquent post. Nothing beats quality. A few simple strategies, however, can help entice more comments.

1. **End your post with a question for your readers.** If you've just written a blog post reviewing the new Pharrell Williams album, you might ask: "Do you think this is Pharrell's best album? Let us know in the comments section below." If you prefer a different "kicker", or ending, to your piece, you can ask the question in italics below the post. Don't use a vague question of the "so whaddaya think?" sort, and don't ask a question that can be answered with a simple yes or no.

2. **Include interactive features, such as polls and quizzes.** Invite your readers to participate in your blog. Polls and quizzes have long been standard features of major websites for the very good reason

83

that they attract readers—and keep them coming back. If you've followed our advice, your blog will be more tightly focused than those on major websites so your readers will be more knowledgeable about your topic. That should improve participation. Several WordPress plug-ins allow users to create polls and quizzes, embed them, and keep track of and display the answers. Blogger and Tumblr, on the other hand, have few available plug-ins. You can, however, create a poll or a quiz on a free website and link to it. Surveymonkey.com is the most popular free website for creating polls. Quizzes are easy to build at the free website qzzr.com. Or you can just create a numbered list of questions in your blog post for readers to answer in the comments sections. The quiz plug-ins and quiz-making services referenced above provide easy-to-follow instructions.

3. **Study your analytics to discover who reads and links to your blog**. Publish an article in a magazine, and you'll never know how many people read or thumbed through the lapidary prose on which you labored so long. All you can know for sure is how many copies of the magazine were printed and distributed. On the web, you can discover how many people visited your blog, in what part of the country (or world) they live, how long they stayed to read your blog posts, and a heck of a lot more. The term for these data is "analytics." It is essential to add an analytics package to your blog and check these analytics frequently. The most basic (but still useful) is SiteMeter. Google Analytics is more sophisticated and gathers more information. Any analytics package will require you to add a few lines of HTML code to your blog's coding. But don't worry: You'll get a step-by-step tutorial on how to do so.

4. **Ask friends to help get the comments section going**. We're going to tell you a journalism secret. (Don't spread it around, OK?) In the old days of print journalism, when a newspaper had just started up or an established newspaper approached deadline with a dearth of letters to the editor, friends and family were sometimes asked to write a letter or two. The idea was that those letters would get others to add their voices. When you start your blog, you can ask friends to do the same—as long as their comments are honest and respond to your blog post. A friend leaving a comment that reads, "Great blog post, Tom! See you Saturday night at Claire's!" doesn't help gain new commenters for your blog. This practice is ethical

as long as you don't tell those friends what to write or ghostwrite for them. That would be unethical.

When to Engage Those Who Comment—and How

1. **Ignore trolls and spammers.** On the Internet, a troll is someone who wants to start an argument or upset people by posting offensive or mean-spirited comments. If, as we recommend, you moderate the comments, don't waste your time sending angry emails to trolls. That's what they want. Simply delete their comments from your queue. The same goes for spam: just delete it. Don't try to track down the spammer. Spammers know how to use the Internet to hide their identities. If anti-spam plug-ins are available for your blogging software package, consider using them to lessen your spam-spurred headaches.

2. **If a commenter finds a mistake, correct it and thank the person.** It happens to all bloggers: We make mistakes. Perhaps we spell a name wrong, or, relying on memory (or inaccurate information we found on the Internet), list the wrong bass player in the personnel of a recording session for a famous pop tune. After you have confirmed a mistake, go back into your blog post and correct the error. Put an asterisk next to what you fixed, and, at the bottom of the post, tell your reader about the correction you made: "*This post originally stated the bass player on The Roots' *Undun* album was Owen Biddle. Mark Kelley played bass on the album." Keep this in mind: By pointing out your mistake, your reader is *helping* you maintain a more accurate and reliable blog. So when someone helps you, say thank you with a few words in the comments section beneath the original comment: "Thanks! I appreciate it. I've fixed the mistake."

3. **Respond to comments with interest and respect.** Continue the conversation the commenter started. Don't just respond with a "thanks for reading" or "I agree." You can ask the commenter a question based on what he or she wrote. That's a good way to get a conversation going. If commenters elaborate on a point you make, follow the thread of the conversation and expand on your blog post *and* the readers' comments. Turning the comments section into a respectful and engaged conversation encourages readers to return frequently to see what new comments have been added.

Once again, the key word and concept is respect. The comments on your blog may anger you, sting you, or make you feel dumb, but if you're going to be writing on the Internet for all the world to read, you need to be a grown-up and have a thick skin. Nothing drives readers away faster than insulting their comments.

4. **Email your commenters**. If you decide to require readers to register before they can comment, you'll have their email addresses. An effective way to establish a relationship with a commenter—and to help make that person a loyal reader—is to respond not only in the comments section, but also with a short, personal email. You could write something like this: "Thanks for reading the blog and taking the time to comment. I really appreciate it. If you have any ideas for blog posts or any other suggestions for making my blog better, let me know."

Dealing with Spammers, Bots, and Other Headaches

Spam defines unsolicited and unwanted messages sent in bulk to email accounts, websites, blogs, and other online social media sites. It is usually advertising.

Spamming is good business for those who do it because it costs almost nothing: All spammers need is a list of web or email addresses, which can either be bought cheaply or "harvested" from the Web by special software. Spammers can send 10,000 emails for less than $100.

The increasing sophistication of spam filters has made spammers' jobs harder, but spammers are a determined and knowledgeable lot. Computer security experts estimate about 110 trillion spam emails are sent every year. Make sure your blogging software's spam filter is turned on. Most blogging software now includes a built-in spam filter, which can usually be found on the "Settings" page. These, however, are far from invulnerable. Your email account probably has a spam filter, too, but you still get spam in your inbox every day.

An Internet bot is a piece of automated software that uses what is known as "spidering" to continually search the Web at extraordinarily high speeds and gather data. A bot can be programmed to repetitively search the Internet for the URLs of comment sections of websites and blogs and gather all the URLs into a database. Then a spammer can easily post spam messages to all the comments sections in the database.

Don't be quick to casually dismiss the harm comment spam can do to your blog. You may think readers will recognize it for what it is and ignore it. But spam almost always includes links, and those links are the source of the harm to your blog. Google's search algorithm, for example, takes a dim view of spam links, wherever they appear on a website or a blog, and your blog will appear much farther down the list in a Google search.

What's more, spam comments send the same bad message to your readers as sporadic posting does. They'll likely conclude you're not much interested in maintaining a good blog. They also might conclude that the comments section doesn't matter to you. Once you lose readers, they don't come back.

Moderating your comment section is the best (although most laborious) way to keep spam off your blog. But there are a few other things you can do if you decide not to moderate.

Akismet is widely considered one of the best plug-ins to fight spam on WordPress. Other blogging platforms, such as Blogger and Tumblr, are much less effective in blocking spam.

87

Add-On Software for Managing Comments

Many websites and bloggers either use special software to manage comments, or route comments through a comment management website.

The best comment management website is disqus.com, which calls itself "the web's community of communities." Disqus is free, and it provides a clean, powerful comment system that can be added to Blogger, WordPress, Tumblr, or any other website. It allows you to authorize multiple comment moderators, and easily allows a blogger to share all comments on social media sites, including Facebook and Twitter.

The comment management website web.livefyre.com is new and has many of the same features. Both have spam filters. The comments management website intensedebate.com gives you the option to be notified by email when someone else comments. It also has the strongest spam filter of the three.

Conversations beyond the Comments Section

In announcing that popularscience.com was shutting off its comments section, online content director Suzanne LaBarre gave readers alternatives. "There are plenty of other ways to talk back to us, and to each other," she wrote. "Through Twitter, Facebook, Google+, Pinterest, livechats, email, and more."

Northeastern University's Dan Kennedy said he is finding that the most interesting comments on his blog post now come not from the comments sections, but from social media. Kennedy has a Facebook account set to "public," and said, "I post a link back to my blog on Facebook, and I get many more comments and higher-quality comments."

He speculated as to why.

"Facebook does require real names," he notes. "And I think people are in a different mood when they're on Facebook. 'Here's a picture of a cat.' 'My wife and I just had a nice dinner at a new restaurant.' People aren't in sociopathic mode on Facebook."

Relying on Facebook, however, does give him pause, noting that there are "dangers we don't even understand in turning over a big part of our platform to a huge corporation that has its own agenda."

88

DISCUSSION

1. Why do you think people are motivated to comment on a blog post?

2. Discuss which members of the class read comment sections and which don't. Do those who read these sections tend to comment more often?

3. At the beginning of the chapter, we list five options for managing (or not managing) comments. Divide the class into five groups and assign one option to each. Have each group argue why its option is best.

4. Review the blog comments on a widely read news blog in your area. Discuss the nature of the comments. Are most useful? Are they inflammatory, intelligent, crude, thoughtful, or all of these?

EXERCISE

Find five blogs you like about topics in which you are interested. Submit a comment at each, then follow the comments section for several days to see what responses your comment gets.

89

Why Headlines Matter 6

In newspapers and magazines, headlines serve the same purpose as a store's logo on its window, wall, or door: They are meant not only to inform you of what's inside, but to lure you in. A person walking down the street will take no more than a few seconds to read the store sign and glance in the window before deciding whether to go in. So it is with headlines. The main headline, the top line, is the store sign. Any kind of readout—a second line or deck—is its window display.

We could call this The First Rule Of Headlines: You have two seconds to get the readers interested. As we said in Chapter 2, headlines must be clear. They can be clever, too. But clarity must come first.

Headlines on the Internet do the same—inform and draw the reader into the story. But they must do *much* more, and that is why headlines matter more on the net than in any other medium. Headlines need to contain keywords that will turn up in search engine results and in social media searches. On a blog and on many news websites, headlines not only appear at the top of stories. Recent headlines often also appear along the left-hand or right-hand side of the page to keep them instantly accessible to the reader. These headlines continue to tell and sell the story, reminding readers what they might have missed.

How Readers Find Blog Posts

Some readers will check your blog every day to see what's new. They will be your family and friends, at least at the start. Most won't. So to build an audience, you need to know how people find things on the Web and how to draw them to your stories.

You'll get the vast majority of your new readers through social media (see Chapter 12, "Building Your Blogging Brand"), and from Google and other search engines. Readers scan web pages, surf from one site to another, and go to search engines when a topic they want to know more about pops into their heads. From various studies of Web use, here's what we know:

- About three-quarters of readers use search engines to find news and commentary. They already know the topic they are interested in, and they are looking for information and perspective.
- Two out of three readers come to a news website without ever going to the front page. They get to the page that interests them either through a search or by clicking on a link they've found on social media.
- The average time an Internet user spends on a page is less than a minute; the average time an Internet user spends on a website is about three minutes.

See why headlines matter? To get readers to click their way through to your blog posts, your headlines—your store signs—need clarity and pizzazz.

Writing Headlines for the Reader

- **Build off the main point**. This isn't always in the lede. Blog posts sometimes begin with introductory, scene-setting, or contextual material. The headline should cut to the chase. Give the news or purpose.
- **Don't repeat the wording of the lede**. If the first paragraph of your blog post reads, "The European Union has gone too far in regulating perfumes," don't write a headline that says "New EU Perfume Regulations Go Too Far." Try something like: "New EU Perfume Regs Smell Too Strong."

- **Use the present tense**. The present tense gives headlines immediacy and freshness. Your headline the day after the presidential election would be "Obama wins second term," not "Obama won second term." In English grammar, as well as the grammar of many other languages, this is known as the "historical present." You use it frequently in conversation: "So I'm sitting in my office the other day . . ."

- **Cut to the bones**. Headlines omit any form of the verb "to be" and any form of article. Note that the example of a bad headline above did not read "The Problem Is The New EU Perfume Regulations Go Too Far" (that would have made it even worse). Omitting forms of "to be" and articles such as *the*, *a*, and *an* save valuable headline space.

- **Use commas instead of "and."** Another way to save space: "Festival to Feature The National, Lorde, Bruno Mars."

- **Use punctuation sparingly**. Never end a headline with an exclamation point. A headline, by virtue of being in a larger font size, is already a typographical exclamation. Using an exclamation point at the end of a headline is like shouting at your reader.

- **Choose a consistent style**. Decide whether you want the headlines on your site to be "upstyle," capitalizing each word except prepositions, or "downstyle," in which only the first word and proper nouns are capitalized. Consistency is key.

  - *Upstyle*:
    U.S. Warns Afghans Not to Form "Parallel Government"
  - *Downstyle*:
    U.S. warns Afghans not to form "parallel government"

  Whichever style you choose is a matter of taste. One is not considered more readable than the other, in print or on the Web. nytimes.com uses upstyle, while theguardian.com uses downstyle.

- **Start with the subject.** Headlines typically follow a noun-verb-object construction. This is the active voice—the construction of the famous news lesson: "Man bites dog." "Dog is bitten" wouldn't make much of a story. Dogs bite each other every day. "Dog is bitten by man" eats up a lot of space and backs into the point. Man bites dog? Well, that doesn't happen every day—which is why this story makes news.

Writing Headlines for Search Engines and Social Media

- **Include keywords in every headline**. If you have written a blog post about a recipe that uses cilantro as a spice in crab cakes, your most obvious keywords would be "cilantro," "recipe," and "crab cakes." By including those keywords in a headline ("Chef François Uses Cilantro in His Famous Crab Cakes Recipe"), your blog post will have a much better chance of appearing at the top of the results when a web user searches "recipe crab cakes cilantro." The use of keywords in blog headlines is essential. It is how search engines find them. Search engines work, in part, by constantly combing the web for text and building indexes of the words they find. The better you can match up the keywords of your headline and text to the words Web users submit to search engines, the better chance your post will have of appearing near the top of the results.

94

- **Write headlines that can stand on their own**. In a newspaper, the headline sits atop the story. The web is different. Often, on a web page or a blog, the headline stands by itself—the reader needs to click through to read the story. This, obviously, places more importance on headlines. If they aren't good—and enticing— you won't get readers to click through to your article. We've already mentioned another reason to write headlines that can stand on their own: In most blogging software, the headlines and only the headlines from your previous half dozen or so posts will appear in a column on the left-hand or right-hand side of the page. Good headlines entice your readers to catch up with older posts.

- **Place the most emphasis on nouns**. Yes, active voice demands strong verbs. But online, the "who" or "where" can be the most important elements of the headline because, once again, of those search engines. In the crab cake headline above, the emphasis is on the nouns (cilantro, Chef François, and crab cakes), not the verb (uses). On the web, think of the headline as a label for the blog post. Remember those storefronts?

- **If space is an issue, skip the verb**. Verbless headlines sometimes can be more effective. In print (magazines, alternative newspapers, daily newspapers), such headlines often appear over feature stories, editorials, op-ed columns, advice columns—anything that isn't straight news. Below are headlines taken from nytimes.com on a Monday morning in mid-summer 2014. Note the difference between the news story headlines and the blog post headlines.

News story headlines

- Ukraine Military Finds Its Footing Against Pro-Russian Rebels
- Top Iraqi General Killed in Mortar Attack
- Britain to Investigate Allegations of Sexual Abuse Cover-Up Decades Ago
- Eduard Shevardnadze, Soviet Foreign Minister Under Gorbachev, Is Dead at 86
- Still-Divided Washington Readies for Start of Recreational Marijuana Sales
- Severe Storm Damages Homes, Hurts 6 in W. Michigan
- Obama Weighs Steps to Cover Contraception

Blog post headlines

- 50 Ways to Love Your Quinoa
- Learning "Lear": A King's Gotta Eat
- "The Leftovers" Recap: Laws of Human Nature, Interrupted—or, The Case of the Disappearing Bagel
- Book Review Podcast: Hillary Rodham Clinton's "Hard Choices"
- They Have Seen the Future of the Internet, and It Is Dark
- Rescuing an iPod With a Fishing Knife
- What's News in Washington: Immigration Fireworks

Which headlines are you most likely to click on? Our guess is that you would click on the news story headlines only if the news is of interest to you. The blog post headlines, on the other hand, are written to tantalize you into clicking. *I wonder what it means that "a king's gotta eat" in learning the play* King Lear? (Click.) *Hey, I watched the last episode of* The Leftovers. *What does this writer have to say about it?* (Click.) *How can a fishing knife rescue an iPod?* (Click.) Note, however, the importance of the noun in all three

95

cases. You'd be less likely to click on "A King's Gotta Eat," without Lear. You've got to have iPod and The Leftovers for either head to work.

- **Use question headlines sparingly**. Headlines that ask a question don't work on news stories—after all, the job of a news story is to answer questions. But for a more reflective blog post, the question mark can draw readers. Take this example from a post about the clinical trials for a medication to fight breast cancer. The headline "How Effective is Tamoxifen in Pre-Menopausal Women?" works well because it identifies a drug widely used in treating breast cancer and discusses the results of the latest medical research. Questions can also work atop posts directed at the reader. A financial advice blog post about the advantages and disadvantages of different types of student loans might be topped with the headline "What is The Best Student Loan Package for You?" It limits audience, but it also targets audience.

96

- **Limit headlines to 10 words or less**. Google, the king of the search engines, displays only the first 60 characters (letters, spaces, punctuation) of a headline in its search results. You want the headline to appear in full in search engine results—you wrote it to entice readers. So why sabotage yourself? Here is a headline, 59 characters long, as it would appear in a Google search result: "The Most Important Thing You Need to Know Before You Go to University is." You may think that is a clever way to get the reader to click. It isn't. Without the most important piece of information, the reader will ignore your partial headline, and find one that gives the answer.

- **Keywords alone do not make a headline**. Don't turn yourself inside out to game the system of web algorithms. In the end, humans decide whether and what to click on. Search engines use far more than headlines to rank results. The people who write the algorithms that run search engines became wise to the piling-up-keywords ploy a long time ago. In the end, a headline still must impart information and intrigue a reader. Keywords can help you do that; they can't replace news judgment and intelligence.

BOB TROTT

"Mom was right: You don't get a second chance to make a first impression"

Bob Trott, a former Associated Press reporter, works as an editor and web producer of the "Money" channel at Microsoft's msn.com, ranked by the news analytics company Alexa as one the 50 most popular websites worldwide.

Bob Trott

What makes a good online headline, and how is it different from a print headline?
Online and print headlines are similar in that they've got to grab the reader's attention and sum up the story in just a few words. Obviously it's still the first impression you're making on the reader. The headlines are different because once you're holding a newspaper, the article is right there under the story. Online, it's behind the link, so you've got to make readers want to go beyond the link. Nowadays, the headline has to be more of an enticement that "you need to know what this article says" instead of "here is what this article is about." That has always been important, I think, but it's more so now.

What are the worst sins a headline writer can commit?
A flat headline that says absolutely nothing. I have punched up many a headline along the lines of, "New bank regulations proposed." I also am not a huge fan of question headlines, they're cheap and easy, but sometimes (particularly in personal finance, I find) they can't be avoided. And readers respond to them, so perhaps I shouldn't complain. Also, it's key with online headlines to not give away the punch line. If you read a headline that says "George Springer named AL MVP," you know all you need to about that story. Why click? But a "Surprise pick for AL MVP" headline . . . well, you're going to click on that.

Do you have a mental process for writing a headline? Do you start with a keyword and build from there? Do you start with a subject and verb? Do you consider nouns (who, where, what) more important than verbs?
With the importance on headlines, particularly if we have articles linked on the msn.com portal, we use keywords and phrases that were tied to our Bing search goals as much as possible. "Retirement planning" is one phrase I've worked into more than one headline. Optimizing for search is obviously a concern in any online shop. Same with social media. They're pretty much audiences you have to write to.

I start off by summarizing the story to myself, then trying to narrow down the information to something that: (1) is interesting; (2) makes sense and is coherent as a headline; and (3) could (I hope) be unusual.

How long is too long for an online headline? What's the maximum number of words or characters?

We used to have a strict 35-character count, spaces included, to keep headlines on one line and to make it easier for the home page to run them, to fit easily within our real estate on msn.com. Lately, though, we have let go of that and occasionally we run headlines that spill over onto line two. That said, I still think shorter is better. If it reads like a complete sentence, you've probably written too much.

What guidelines and tips would you give young journalists about writing headlines for the Web?

Mom was right: You don't get a second chance to make a first impression. There are figures out there somewhere along the lines of 8 of 10 people read a headline, and only two of those click through to read the article. And since online headlines often stand alone, with no image or video or other content, those few words are usually all you've got to entice the reader to the entire piece.

Writing Decks

Sometimes two headlines complement one another. The main head (also called the first deck) gives the basics and pulls the reader in. The secondary head or deck expands on the first deck but without repeating words or ideas.

Such multiple deck headlines were the norm until well into the twentieth century. Some papers, magazines, and websites—such as the *New York Times*—still regularly use them.

On the net, decks are less common. They're not summaries, which we'll talk about below. But they do give more information.

When the Titanic sank, 102 years ago, the front page of the *New York Times* on April 16, 1912 offered up no fewer than *18 decks* below the main headline to give the news. These included: "Biggest Liner Plunges to Bottom at 2:20 a.m.," "Rescuers There Too Late," "Except to Pick Up the Few Hundred Who Took to the Lifeboats," and "Women and Children First."

Headline writers today are lucky to get a second deck to tell the story. It's important, though, to know how second decks work with the main headline. A few examples should help.

These are from *Time* magazine and its website, time.com. The site makes excellent use of decks, which, in the case of secondary decks, today sometimes are also called *readouts*.

Two examples from time.com:

HEAD: El Niño Likely to Hit This Summer
DECK: That could mean fewer destructive hurricanes on the East Coast

HEAD: Obama's New Drug Policy Looks Like the Old One
DECK: A new emphasis on treatment and addiction, but no change on marijuana

A few guidelines for writing decks:

- **Don't repeat the headline**. A deck is a supplement to the headline. It should *add* information.
- **Keep the deck short**. Don't write decks any longer than 200 characters. Less is better.
- **Never repeat the same words in the main headline and deck**. The two examples above follow this rule.
- **Dig deep into the article for material**. You don't have to write a deck based on the first paragraph or two of the article. Go deeper and find an interesting fact or angle that draws readers.
- **Decks are always downstyle**. Even if the main headline is upstyle.

Writing Meta Descriptions (WARNING: HTML Ahead)

Even if you use blogging software that allows you to make changes to your blog's and blog posts' HTML tags, learning the basics of HTML will allow you to control what Web surfers see when your blog or one of your blog posts comes up as a search engine result.

If you don't use metadata tags, most search engines will instead display the first 160 or so characters of the article. This can be problematic. Here are some examples:

99

COLUMBIA JOURNALISM REVIEW

The Industry   Politics & Policy   Business   Science   Culture   Magazine   Resources

The Kicker

bits and pieces

04:55 PM - June 25, 2014

Michael Jackson's death is a questionable news peg

The King of Pop died five years ago, and outlets are scraping to say something about the anniversary

By Kira Goldenberg

f ⊻ ✉ ⊠ More sharing ⊕⊕ Single Page

Coverage was...interesting...on Wednesday, the fifth anniversary of Michael Jackson's death. Since there's nothing to cover, so to speak—no new news about the pop star's demise—outlets used the anniversary as a peg to run a strange variety of archival stories and random cultural ephemera.

Compare the first paragraph of this story to the Google search result below.

Here is a blog post from *The Kicker* blog on the website of the *Columbia Journalism Review.*

Michael Jackson's death is a questionable news peg ...
www.cjr.org/.../michael_jacksons_death_is_... ▼ Columbia Journalism Review ▼
7 days ago - Coverage was...interesting...on Wednesday, the fifth anniversary of
Michael Jackson's death. Since there's nothing to cover, so to speak—no ...

Note the second sentence is cut off. Google search results have a maximum of 160 characters.

Here is the Google search result for the CJR blog post. Notice that it cuts off the second sentence of the article when the maximum of 160 characters is reached.

Home | Blogs | Just Now Ago

WHAT'S THE NEXT MOON LANDING IN THE NEW, UNDERDOG AMERICA?

America's reaction to its greatest sporting loss ever recorded proved it: We need a new Moon Landing. We'll let Tim Howard drive the ship.

By Ben Collins on July 2, 2014   ⊻ Follow @bencollins   1,000 followers

f 16 ⊻ 1 ⊞ 0 ⊠   ⊞ ⊞   View All Comments (1)

Jamie McDonald/Getty Images Sport

There were those five minutes at the end when America was beating down the door, where it felt like we were about to do something impossible in the jungle. We were set to, finally, fix the score for our hero on the other end. Tim Howard played the game of anybody's life, and a couple of our own needed to be dragged off the field in the hot Brazilian sun trying to do right by him.

The deck above this story and the first paragraph are different.

Here's a post from the website of *Esquire* magazine, from a news blog called *Just Now Ago.*

Here are the first two Google search results for the esquire.com blog post.

Notice that the first result, in the text under the headline, includes the headline (again!) and the first dozen words of the deck. The second result, from a website that picked up and used the esquire.com post, includes the exact text deck below the headline and the URL.

The second Google result includes the deck because the Web editors added HTML metadata.

(GOOGLE IS A REGISTERED TRADEMARK OF GOOGLE INC., USED WITH PERMISSION)

That's because the producers at the second website used HTML metadata so that the deck would appear in the Google search result—and the producers at esquire.com didn't. Metadata means "data about data," and there are simple HTML tags you can use to have search engines display what you want them to display in the search results.

If you go into the HTML of your blog software, you can add, usually beneath the <title> tag, a meta tag. It will look like this:

<meta name="description" content="whatever content you want to appear in the search result">

w3schools.com, a website that offers free HTML tutorials, has a useful meta tag tutorial at www.w3schools.com/tags/tag_meta.asp.

In WordPress, you don't even need to use HTML to add metadata. All you need to do is add a metadata plug-in, activate it, and type your metadata into the text box provided. It's a bit more complicated in Google's Blogger software, but if you do a search for "Google Blogger meta tags," you'll find some excellent tutorials that will show you how to add metadata.

101

Writing Chapter Breaks

Chapter breaks—also known as subheds—are small headlines placed at intervals through the text of an article. They can be used in any long post, but they are particularly useful in instructional blog posts. If you're writing a post on how to build a birdhouse, each step could have its own subhed.

You should also use subheds, or chapter breaks, in a post that covers more than one topic. If you're writing a blog that offers advice in response to questions from readers, each new topic should start with a subhed.

These small headlines in the body of text serve several purposes: they help the reader move more efficiently through the text by providing signposts; they add "white space"—empty space above, below, and to the sides of the subhed—that breaks up blocks of text to make them easier to read; and they help you organize your writing. Try writing your subheds *before* you write your post and you'll see.

A few quick guidelines for writing chapter breaks:

- **Subheds should summarize what's to come.** So for that birdhouse guide, the first subhed might read "Choose a birdhouse plan."
- **Make the font size 18 point.** You don't want your chapter breaks to be close to the same size as the main headline at the top of the page, but you do want them to be slightly larger than the body text. Put chapter breaks in downstyle.
- **Use parallel construction.** For example, you could start each subhed with an active verb. If the first subhed for the birdhouse is "Choose a birdhouse plan," the next two, to be parallel, might be "Gather your materials" and "Measure the wood and mark where you will cut." Or the first three subheds could be: "Plan," "Materials Needed," and "Measure." Either way, all the chapter breaks should have the same grammatical format.
- **Avoid cute—be clear and complete.** Resist the temptation to use "For the birds" or "A wing and a prayer" or any other ghastly avian puns as subheds in your how-to-build-a-birdhouse post. Not only are they useless to the reader; they confuse.

102

DISCUSSION

1. What type of headline makes you more likely to read the article—a headline that provides factual information ("Government Announces New Low-Interest Student Loan Program") or a headline without a verb that tries to tease you into reading the article ("The Cats of Des Moines")? Explain why.

2. When you use a search engine to find articles on a topic, how many pages of search results are you likely to scan?

3. What do you find most difficult about writing headlines?

4. Are posts on Twitter more like headlines or decks? What about posts on Facebook? How are they different from each other?

EXERCISE

The blog post below was published by one of this book's authors, Mark Leccese, in his media criticism blog on boston.com in early 2013.

Write a headline, a deck, and a meta description for this blog post. Make sure to include at least one search engine keyword (a word that you believe potential readers will use in their search engine query) in the headline, which should be no longer than 8–10 words. Keep the deck to no longer than 200 characters and the meta description to fewer characters than that.

Reminder: a meta description is the words you want to appear in search results beneath the main headline. For example, for a story about the world's largest pumpkin, the headline could be "One ton pumpkin sets world record" and the meta description could be "A Northern California man grew a pumpkin that weighed in at 2,058 pounds at yesterday's Safeway World Championship Pumpkin Weigh-off."

MAIN HED: _____

DECK: _____

META DESCRIPTION: _____

In a little-noticed action just after Thanksgiving, the Federal Communications Commission opened the door for hundreds and hundreds of community groups and nonprofit organizations to start hyperlocal radio stations.

Until its November decision, the FCC had prohibited low-power FM stations in urban areas. That's why there aren't any in the Boston area. But let's imagine a low-power FM station in Waltham, a city of 61,000.

103

Think of the potential for community journalism.

Waltham had a daily newspaper, the News Tribune, until 2010, when GateHouse Media cut the paper to a twice-a-week publication. A year later, GateHouse turned the paper into a weekly. Two years ago patch.com launched a news and features website in Waltham with a full-time staff of one: the editor.

GateHouse, headquartered in Fairport, New York, owns hundreds of newspapers in 21 different states. Patch, a division of AOL Inc., is headquartered in New York, New York and owns and runs more than 850 hyperlocal websites across the U.S.

A hyperlocal radio station in Waltham with a 100-watt transmitter in could reach every corner of the city. The station could use volunteers to cover School Committee and City Council meetings, the Mayor's office, and all the other community events that used to be covered by the local newspapers.

In addition to news, the station could program call-in talk shows about local issues, shows featuring local music and musicians, shows about books or computers or food—all community-based. The station could even step into the space abandoned by public radio in Boston and air a daily jazz show, like WCRX in Columbus, Ohio.

Best of all, a low-power FM station in Waltham would be owned and operated by a organization or group from the community.

I'm just using Waltham as an example here—it could be any city or town.

There are already 12 low-power FM stations in Massachusetts, each with a broadcast range of about 3.5 miles—just enough to create a local community of listeners. Seven of the existing LPFM stations in the state are owned by churches, Nichols College in Dudley owns one, and the other four are community stations.

The community stations are a pleasure to listen to—quirky, opinionated, eclectic. They all have web streams. Check them out: WBCR in Great Barrington, WVVY in Tisbury on Martha's Vineyard, WXOJ in Northampton, and WMCB in Greenfield.

The Prometheus Radio Project, a Philadelphia-based nonprofit founded in 1998 to advocate for community radio stations, helps groups across the country looking to start community radio stations. When the FCC approved the new LPFM regulations, Pete Tridish of Prometheus waxed inspirational:

A town without a community radio station is like a town without a library. Many a small town dreamer—starting with a few friends and bake sale cash—has successfully launched a low power station, and built these tiny channels into vibrant town institutions that spotlight school board elections, breathe life into the local music scene, allow people to communicate in their native languages, and give youth an outlet to speak.

What would it take to be one of those small town dreamers who launches a low-power station—besides a heck of a lot of work and some devoted collaborators? Prometheus estimates "a fairly minimal" start-up investment in the necessary equipment would be about $10,000. The blog Engineering Radio has done a breakdown of the cost of starting a hyperlocal radio station and sets the cost of a full set-up somewhat higher. You can check out prices for equipment at The LPFM Store.

Some existing low-power stations are getting serious about doing community journalism. KSOW in Cottage Grove, Oregon ("Real Rural Radio") just published a guide to radio journalism resources for its volunteers.

I'm dreaming, you say. No one listens to the radio anymore. (Actually, more than 90 percent of adults listen to the radio.)

At a time when so many community media outlets have become skeleton-staffed cells on a corporate spreadsheet in some distant finance department, we need to think creatively about community media.

The federal government, after a decade of stalling, is offering communities an opportunity to create new hyperlocal media. Who's going to step forward and start creating community radio?

Beyond Words 7

Text, pictures, and graphics comprise newspapers. Radio delivers sound and the imagination it elicits. Television merges that sound with video. But only one medium can use all these tools—text, pictures, graphics, audio, video—to tell one story: the Internet.

From picture books to podcasts, TV reality to the tumblelogs that bring you a little of this and a little of that, weblogs have evolved into a new kind of journal.

Words often aren't the best way to tell a story in this digital age. If "a picture is worth a thousand words," as the cliché has long held, what is a slide show worth? And what if it is accompanied by audio?

Even when words are best, they aren't always enough. That's why a blogger with something to say needs to consider the right medium for saying it.

This chapter will consider the world of blogging beyond words— or at least the elements that enhance the story those words tell. We'll start with the challenge of choosing good pictures to accompany word blogs, move to slide shows, and then evolve to the magic of multimedia.

Choosing the Right Photos

Every blog should have a photo. But not *any* photo. The first and most important rule of using photos in blogs is to choose those that reinforce the message of your text. If you're writing a basketball blog and you write a post about the importance of keeping your head up and your eyes forward while dribbling, don't use some random photo of a basketball court or a group of players in the midst of a game. That's generic, and generic photos don't work. Find a photo—or take one yourself—that shows a player doing exactly what you have described in your post.

Or, better still, choose an image that in some way adds to that message. On the blog *Cognoscenti*, featured on the website for the National Public Radio affiliate in Boston, WBUR-FM, blogger John Sivolella wrote in June 2014 about the wider political meaning of the primary defeat of Republican U.S. House Majority Leader Eric Cantor. The editors at *Cognoscenti* illustrated his post with a photo of a dejected Cantor giving his concession speech the night he lost the election.

The photo of a dejected Eric Cantor after his election loss complements the main point of the blog post.

The Art of Writing Captions

The American photographer Elliott Erwitt took a photograph of a black man drinking from a water fountain in North Carolina. Almost 50 years later, the *Telegraph* of London named it one of the 10 photographs that changed the world.

The man's head, slightly out of focus, appears in the right third of the photo as he either is bending down for a sip of water or straightening up after he has taken his drink. Much of his body is outside the frame. Above the hat on his head, a small sign reads "colored." In the left third of the photo, a much larger (and unoccupied) drinking fountain has a sign above

The 1950 photo by Elliott Erwitt tells the story of segregation in the American South in an image.

(CREDIT: ELLIOT ERWITT, MAGNUM PHOTOS)

it that reads "white." The photo's center third is largely a blank wall, but for a pipe that connects the two fountains.

The *Telegraph* editors felt the picture told the story of racial segregation in the United States.

Even a single picture can tell an entire story—or be an entire blog post. Often, it is the words that accompany the picture—the caption (called a cutline in newspapers)—that increases impact and provides context. These words generally appear directly below the photo.

Next time you look at a photo in a newspaper or on a good website, notice *how* you look at it. The photo (if it's good) will arrest your attention. Then your eyes will look for words that explain the photo, and then you'll look back at the photo with the knowledge you didn't have before you read the words. Now the photo carries more meaning.

Here are two possible captions for the Elliot Erwitt photo:

1. *Segregated water fountains, North Carolina, 1950.*

2. *An African-American man takes a drink from a "coloreds only" water fountain in North Carolina.*

Which caption packs more punch?

The first one gives readers the basics: what is happening, where, and when. Readers look at the photo, read the caption, and learn these are segregated fountains in the American Deep South before the civil rights movement, and look back up at the photo with new eyes—and a new understanding of how in 1950, something as common as getting a few sips of water was strictly segregated by race.

The second caption provides much more information than a reader needs to grasp the impact of the image. It states what the reader can see: that the man is African-American and that he is drinking from a water fountain. It tells more than the reader needs to know to perceive the impact of the image: Does the man's name and age matter, or that he was in a bus station? Or is it more important to say when this happened?

Here are some guidelines for writing captions:

- **Explain the image, don't repeat what the reader sees**. Tell your readers the situation they are looking at. A dramatic photo of ominous storm clouds approaching could be anywhere. The simple caption "Dark skies outside Lewisham before yesterday's hail storm" adds information to the photo. It says where the photo was taken and what happened afterwards.

- **Explain details an image adds to the story.** If you write a yoga blog and you post a photo of a man doing yoga in a studio while his dog sits beside him, the reader is going to be a bit befuddled. What's the dog doing there? Tell the reader "West Side Yoga Studio offers a 'doga' class every Saturday. Participants can bring their dogs."

- **Add information the photo does not give.** If you have posted a photo of the exterior and interior of a magnificent Gothic cathedral, tell your readers the location of the cathedral, its name, and other details that add to the readers' appreciation. If, for example, you have taken photos of the Cathedral-Basilica of Notre-Dame de Québec, and choose one of a tomb inside the cathedral, tell readers what they are looking at: "The tomb of Saint François de Laval, appointed the first Roman Catholic bishop of Québec in 1674." This is known as "writing to the corners of the picture."

- **Use present tense.** A photograph captures a moment and suspends it in an eternal present. Whatever is happening in a photograph is happening when the viewer looks at it. Use present-tense verbs in captions: "A bowl of clam chowder steams as Bill Bishop ladles it from the pot for guests at St. Stephen's Soup Kitchen."

- **Avoid the obvious.** No need to write "Seen here . . ." or "Shown above . . ." or any of the other empty words one sees in the photo captions of small-town newspapers or amateur blogs.

- **Be brief.** Captions needn't always be complete sentences. If you're writing a family history blog, a caption reading "Uncle Steve and Aunt Nancy, Brighton Beach, 1956" works just fine.

Telling a Story with a Photo Blog

Speaking of family photos, consider this analogy as we move to the next step, photo galleries.

Perhaps someone in your family keeps a scrapbook of photographs from pre-digital times (which, hard as it may be for you to believe, weren't all that long ago). Turning the pages of that old scrapbook is not only fascinating, but evocative—the facial expressions of the people in the photos, their style of clothing, the cars and scenery in the background, the posture of the subjects.

As you turn the pages and learn a little about each photo, perhaps by reading, perhaps by listening to a family member, a family narrative takes shape in your mind, often built around the passage of time. The photo blogger provides a similar narrative for his or her audience, using images that tell a story. Often these images use the passage of time, chronology, to tell a story with beginning, middle, and end. The story, as a writer might say, has an arc. The pictures are organized in an orderly manner, not at random.

Photo Galleries: Creating Narrative from Images

You'll find many poor examples of galleries online. Photo galleries blanket the Web like weeds. Most are "clickbait"—if you make your way through a 20-page gallery, that counts as 20 page views for the website, and page views is one of the metrics that determines popularity and advertising sales. Open up your browser and you'll find gallery clickbait without trying. "No Snack for You: 20 Vending Machine Failures." "13 Amazingly Ridiculous Hairdos." "14 Reasons Your Cat Actually Owns You."

Serious news organizations love photo galleries, too. As the 2014 U.S. Open was being played on a golf course in North Carolina, the *Kansas City Star*'s website posted a photo gallery of 37 images from the second day of the tournament. The editors could have made this gallery an interesting narrative. The first photo could have shown an establishing shot of the golf course with a sign of the tournament. (An establishing shot typically is a wider view that sets—or establishes —the scene and place of the gallery.) The next few might have shown spectators arriving at the golf course, golfers warming up, perhaps caddies lining up the golf carts. Then the photos could have shown the top golfers playing the first holes. The middle might have shown the favorites in triumph and tragedy—the leader with a birdie putt and perhaps the leader from the previous day blasting out of a sand trap. The slide show might have closed with shots of the best golfers and the leader doffing his cap after the final hole. Perhaps the final photo could have shown the scoreboard at the end of the day.

These photos, working together chronologically, would have told a story. Instead, the viewer gets 37 photos in random order, probably

111

the order in which they arrived at the computer of the Web producer (or intern) who created the photo gallery. It was a boring gallery and, more importantly, one that did not tell a story.

When you've gathered together images for a gallery, think about two things: (1) What is the story I want to tell? (2) What is the best order for me to sequence the photos to tell it?

"First and foremost, the gallery needs some kind of logical order," says Craig Nickels, online production editor at the *Milwaukee Journal Sentinel*. "In most situations, photos can go in either chronological or reverse-chronological order. That helps create a narrative structure to the gallery: first this thing happened, then this other thing happened, and so on."

"If we have photos from multiple days or geographic locations, I often try to group those together," Nickels says. "I may also do the same if I have several photos of the same person. That allows me to avoid duplicate explanations in the captions. If my gallery is 'Democrats celebrate Obama's victory' and I have six photos from a bar in Philadelphia, I can say, 'Crowds gathered at Johnny's Pub, a small dive bar in South Philly, to celebrate . . .' in the first caption. Then in subsequent Philly photos, I can say, '. . . at Johnny's Pub . . .' without re-explaining what or where Johnny's is."

If the photo gallery is of an ongoing event—a game, a festival, a protest—Nickels puts the newest photos first, so that readers can come back to the page and get new content. "This means that these galleries will be in reverse-chronological order. While this is slightly less intuitive for the reader, it's still easy enough to digest if the structure is predictable and consistent."

Almost any piece of photo storage software can create a gallery. If you choose Google's Blogger software, Picasa (a free Google product) has numerous options for making and embedding a gallery in your blog. There are a number of WordPress plug-ins and widgets that can create and embed a gallery, too, but perhaps the easiest is Cincopa (www.cincopa.com). Heavy users can pay for Cincopa's premium service.

Nickels uses a plug-in called NextGen to organize photos and create galleries on his personal WordPress website. He uses Photoshop for photo editing, but there are other, free, choices.

Nickels offers this final piece of advice: "Photo galleries are pageview gold mines. With that in mind, I might suggest that if there's a question about whether to do the gallery, do the gallery. If there's a question about whether to include a photo, include it. Be reasonable, obviously, but lean toward the side of 'more.'"

Taking It to the Next Level: Audio Slide Shows

If you master simple audio editing (and it's easier than you think), you can create a narrative with images *and* sound. That's a powerful combination.

First, a few definitions. With photo galleries, the user has to click to move from one image to the next. They are static and have no audio. A slide show moves from image to image automatically and usually has the potential for audio.

One great slide show example is "One in 8 Million," an nytimes.com project that can be found at www.nytimes.com/packages/html/nyregion/1-in-8-million/). Each slide show tells the story of a New Yorker going about his or her life. The stories last two or three minutes and feature an audio track of the subject talking and interacting with others. But the key here is how well the images and the audio complement one another.

The slide show titled "Jessie Villanueva: The Sneaker Connoisseur" begins with audio of Villanueva speaking: "I keep them in closets, I keep them in containers, I keep them at the store so my wife doesn't know I have them, I keep them wherever I can keep them so I can keep them. Now I have probably 150 pairs of my own shoes." The photos that appear as he speaks are of three tall stacks of clear plastic shoe storage containers, a photo of a closet jammed with shoe boxes with Villanueva in the background, and a photo of a dozen pairs of shoes lined up next to a bedside table.

You can find more excellent examples of audio slide shows—these from around the world—at the website of the *Guardian* (www.theguardian.com/audioslideshows), based in London.

The audio slide shows on the websites of the *Times* and the *Guardian* were made with the same software, Soundslides, which is available for Mac and Windows operating systems. Soundslides is powerful, flexible, and intuitive. A stripped-down version costs $39.99; the better version, Soundslides Plus, $69.95.

Keep this in mind: not everything lends itself to audio. Sometimes simplicity is your best option.

113

For example, Nickels, of the *Milwaukee Journal Sentinel*, has found readers prefer galleries.

"Generally, more reader control is a good thing and galleries allow [the reader] to consume the photos and captions at [his or her] own pace."

Still, if you've got really good audio, go with a slide show.

Building the Slide Show

Once you've got the images and audio for a slide show, review all your assets. Do you have what you need to tell the story? Do you have good images and enough images to complement the audio package?

Next, edit your audio down to two or three minutes. Anything longer is likely to lose the audience. (You may already have a basic audio editing program in your computer, but, if you don't, we recommend Audacity, which is free, easy to use, and can export MP3 files. We'll talk more about audio later in this chapter.)

In Soundslides, the length of your audio determines the length of the slide show—your slide show can only be exactly as long as your audio clip. You'll probably want human voices of some kind: narration or sound bites from an interview. Natural sound helps transport the audience to the scene. You also can use music that is copyright-free, or your own music. If you are going to use narration, write a script and rehearse it before recording.

Next, choose the images you want to use. Don't choose too many, or they'll fly by the viewers' eyes too quickly, and don't choose too few, or they will remain on the screen too long. A two-minute slide show should be between 16 and 24 images. Process and prepare the images before you load them into your slide show program.

Once you've got your audio and your images loaded, arrange the images in the order you want. Now you can start to use the power of the program to make something more than just a photo gallery with sound. Soundslides Plus, for example, allows you to:

- Choose different "skins" (outer borders and overall design look) for your slide show.
- Make the transition between slides a quick cut, a cross-fade, a fade out/fade in, and more.

114

- Adjust the time each slide remains on the screen. One slide could be on the screen for eight seconds (that's a really long time for a single visual) while another could appear for only, say, four seconds.
- Add effects to an image or to the slide show such as "The Ken Burns effect," named for the producer of serialized documentaries on the American Civil War, baseball, and jazz. For the *Civil War* documentary, Burns (obviously) only had still images from the period. So he would have the camera slowly pan and zoom on the still image to create motion. You can do the same in your slide show.
- Offer the reader captions for each image.
- Export the completed slide show in a format that will easily embed in your blog. This is a bit complex with Soundslides. If you are not sophisticated with HTML code, you'll need to create a video version of your slide show, which you can do by going to the Soundslides video conversion website (http://tools.soundslides. com/converter/). Once you create the video, just upload it to YouTube, copy the YouTube web address of your video, and paste the web address into your blog. The video of your slide show (with the audio) will be embedded. All the reader needs to do is click "Play."

There are plenty more audio slide show tools out there, such as ProShow Gold. When you look for audio slide show software, aside from price (which is always a factor), look for three things: ease of use, editing and formatting tools, and range of formats. That last one is important—you want to be able to add an audio slide show to your blog with as little hassle (and coding) as possible.

Some of This, Some of That: Tumblelogs

When we think of blogs, we tend to think of a text-heavy website.

But as early as the mid-2000s, some bloggers were experimenting with what were known as "tumblelogs." Instead of being text-heavy, these featured posts that relied more on images and videos. When a Web developer named David Karp couldn't find software to create one, he teamed up with another developer, Marco Arment, and the two created their own tumblelog platform. They called it Tumblr.

That caught the eye of Jason Oberholzer and Cody Westphal. In 2008, they started personal Tumblrs to keep in touch with their college buddies.

"We were drawn to the platform as a place to do what we and our friends would naturally do if we were all still in the same dorm together—share media," Oberholzer says. "Check out this picture! This video! This cool quote!"

A year later, they were swapping charts they'd found on the Internet demonstrating how bad the economy was.

"This took on a certain gallows humor, and we decided we should spin off a blog," Oberholzer recalls. "We quickly moved off that as the content idea, and into our general love for charts and how many of them we were able to find online. There are so many."

Their new Tumblr, called *i love charts*, soon caught the eye of Tumblr's head of content, who gave it a promotional shout-out on "Tumblr Tuesday."

"We woke up the next day with 1,000 followers and have been improvising ever since, trying to figure out the most fun we can have with the people who show up and care," says Oberholzer.

They blog funny hand-drawn charts, including a bar chart titled "Tops to wear to appear slimmer" and ratings of the tops on a scale of "uncool" to "very cool." Right beneath it is a chart from 1894 showing the working parts of a Remington typewriter. There are serious charts, too, such as one that displays the percentage of people in the United States who did not have health insurance from 2009 to 2014.

At first, the two men combed the Internet for interesting charts. As the blog's visibility grew, Obberholzer says, "people started creating more of their own charts and sending them in. When we got noticed by the world outside Tumblr, . . . organizations, blogs, newsrooms, etc. began sending their charts to us in hopes we would share them. Now, it's a mix of all these approaches."

The reach of Tumblr is broad and deep. When Yahoo! bought Tumblr in September 2013 for $1.1 billion, Yahoo! CEO Marissa Mayer revealed that Tumblr hosted 105 million different blogs, had 900 new posts each second, and drew more than 300 million unique monthly visitors. An average of 120,000 people were signing up for Tumblr every day.

Like Twitter, Tumblr is considered a "microblogging" platform for short-form posts of mixed media. It couldn't be easier to use.

When you log in, there is a dashboard atop the main page with icons for the seven things you can post on Tumblr. These are: text, a photo or other image, a quote with the source underneath, a link, a bit of conversation from a chat, an audio MP3 file, or a video (which can be either uploaded or imported from another website).

In the upper right of the Tumblr page is a search box. Check it out. A search for the 1970s rock band Little Feat turns up audio and video files of the band, and it also leads to Tumblr "tags." These are the same as Twitter hashtags except a space can be placed between words. The search for Little Feat turns up the tags #Little Feat, #Lowell George (the band's leader), #Classic Rock, #70s, and so on. Click on any one of the tags and you'll be taken to Tumblr posts with that tag.

The beauty of Tumblr is that as easy as it is to use, it is built for mixed-media posts.

Many of the most fun, interesting, and popular Tumblr blogs are primarily images.

Magazines and major news organizations maintain Tumblr blogs. Al Jazeera America has one of the best news Tumblrs, with an emphasis on photos and people. National Geographic digs into its archive of 125 years of extraordinary photographs for its Tumblr called *Found*, which features wonderful images from around the world and across more than a century.

Brandon Stanton, a University of Georgia graduate now in his early thirties, lost his job trading bonds on the Chicago Board of Trade when the economy went sour in 2010. He decided, he writes, "to move to New York City and take portraits of strangers on the street." After some trial and error, he started the Tumblr blog *Humans of New York*, in which he photographs New Yorkers on the street and collects quotes from them. Occasionally, he writes a story. He has taken more than 5,000 portrait photos, written more than 50 stories, and, as he says, "met some amazing people along the way."

A publishing house spotted Stanton's Tumblr and signed him up to create a book from *Humans of New York*. It was released in late 2013 and almost instantly became a No. 1 *New York Times* bestseller.

117

ALVIN CHANG

"When creating a data visualization, the first question I ask myself is: 'Why am I visualizing this?'"

Alvin Chang is a journalist, a coder, and an artist. He combines those skills to make a pile of numbers clear and interesting to readers.

Today, the power of computers and the variety of tools available on the Web have made visualizing data—turning complex data sets into easy-to-understand infographics—a powerful journalistic tool.

Chang is data editor at the *Connecticut Mirror*, a nonprofit news outlet founded in 2009 and staffed by veteran journalists. He holds a master's degree from New York University's Interactive Telecommunications Program and has also written for a variety of newspapers.

Alvin Chang

For Chang, data visualization means telling a story.

"For those starting out, it's important to understand that these storytelling tools are just that: tools," he says. "It's easy to become enamored with flashy visualizations. But the goal for storytellers isn't to use the tool. Rather, it's to tell the story in the best possible way."

Asking the right questions, he said, helps keep the focus on story.

"When creating a data visualization, the first question I ask myself is: 'Why am I visualizing this?' Sometimes, a single sentence works better than a visualization. But other times, a visualization helps a user understand a concept in a more nuanced or dramatic way. Once I can articulate 'why a visualization?' then it's all about conceptualizing different ways I can tell that story."

Using a database that listed the locations of all the Starbucks and Dunkin' Donuts stores in the United States, Chang made a map of the U.S. showing every Starbucks location as a green dot and every Dunkin' Donuts location as an orange dot. The reader can look at the entire United States or zoom in on a particular region or city. (If you're curious, the Northeast and Florida are very orange; the West Coast is very green.)

Chang offers these guidelines—he calls them "workflow"—for data visualization in the service of storytelling:

1. Articulate the story you want to tell.
2. Plan the story with a tool that encourages you to think more than to create. Something, for example, as simple as paper and pencil works well.

3. Take out everything in the plan that doesn't contribute to the story.

4. Gather the tools needed to create this story.

Learn just enough of the tool to create the story (mastery takes time). Among the open-source software Chang uses:

- **Leaflet:** for online mapping (http://leafletjs.com)
- **Highcharts:** for charts (www.highcharts.com)
- **Data-Driven Documents:** when he wants something beyond a bar/line/pie chart (http://d3js.org)
- **Open Refine:** when he needs to "clean," or fix, incorrect or incomplete data (http://openrefine.org)

Chang said he also uses the commercial product Microsoft Excel for quick "data parsing," or taking a block of data and sorting it in a useable form such as rows and columns.

Keep in mind, however, that tools can change with lightning speed. Don't discard those that have weathered the assault of newcomers. Do look around for those that might improve on them.

I Am a Radio Station: Podcasts

Human beings have no older tradition than the oral narrative. Never underestimate the power of the human voice to draw others into a story.

That's the power of today's podcasts, nothing more than radio shows that you can listen to whenever the spirit moves you. If you're willing to spend about $200 and put in the time, you can be your own radio station, producing programs and making them instantly available to anyone with an Internet connection.

Producing a podcast requires more technical sophistication—and more equipment—than writing a blog post and inserting an image. If you want to get deeper into the technical side, there are hundreds of articles and dozens of books that will take you there.

But to start, you'll need three important pieces of equipment: a portable recording device, a microphone, and audio editing equipment. Don't drop a bundle on the highest-end equipment; the editing system Audacity, for example, is a free program that will meet your editing needs (http://audacity.sourceforge.net). But some expense is inevitable. Gathering sound on your cellphone won't cut it without a microphone. Do your homework.

Getting Started

What kind of podcast do you want to build? What is it you have to say? Just as with text blogging, keep your topic narrow but rich enough to sustain the show. So, if you want to do a podcast on beer, you could feature only local beers and focus on a different local microbrewery each week.

Decide whether you want to do the podcast alone, or have a co-host. We've listed some podcasts below with one host and co-hosts. Listen to them. There is something about co-hosts that keeps the listener engaged. The pace seems quicker, differences of opinion or approach create a spark, and listeners enjoy the variety of more than one voice.

Building Your Podcast

- **Keep it short**. You'd be surprised how much effort it takes to produce just five minutes. That's one good reason why a solo podcast should be under 15 minutes. The audience's attention is the other. Divide even this length into segments, changing your subject or approach for each. Three five-minute segments offer enough depth and variety. The University of Texas at Austin, for example, has created a series of (so far) more than 60 podcasts called "15-Minute History." These often are among the five most listened-to podcasts on iTunesU. Frequency matters. Most successful podcasts upload a new episode once a week. But too much ambition can turn podcasting into a full-time job.

- **Use natural sound**. Sound evokes imagination. The more varied the sounds you can include, the more the listeners' imaginations will be roused. In the field, look to record "natural sound," the background sound that's all around us. It can be the clinking of silverware and clatter of plates in a restaurant, the chirping of birds and the rustling of leaves in the forest, the starter's gun and the slapping of running shoes during a marathon. The nature of "nat sound" depends on the topic.

- **Write a script**. No matter how articulate you think you are, you're not articulate enough to sit in front of a microphone, press "Record," and create a seamless 15-minute podcast. Not a chance. So write a script, and practice reading it before you record. And time yourself to get a sense of how much you devote to narration, natural sound, music, and interviews. If you want your podcast to sound more like a conversation between two or more people, you needn't script everything. But still jot down extensive notes—complete with key phrases or sentences. When you're ready to record, do so in a quiet place away from traffic or people.

- **Make your podcast sound professional**. Listen to and model successful podcasts. They'll likely start with theme music. As the music fades, the host or hosts will introduce themselves. Do the same. Then state the name of the podcast and preview that you'll be featuring. Eliminate the "ums" and "ahs" and "y'knows" from your speech (this takes practice). Pace your delivery—not too fast, not too slow. Speaking a little bit faster than normal gives your delivery extra energy. And *modulate* your voice. Don't read in a monotone. Oh, and one more thing: *no dead air*. On live radio, three seconds of silence seems an eternity.

- **Find a hosting site**. Once your podcast is done, export it as an MP3 file. Now you need to find a place to store it so listeners can access it. The major podcasts—the ones with financial backing and advertising—often rent space on Web servers. There are two simple and free alternatives, though neither offers all you want.

  The website *Soundcloud* (https://soundcloud.com) will host mp3 files for free.

  Then you can add the Soundcloud URL to your blog, where visitors can listen to it. But they cannot download your podcast to play on their own devices.

  It is possible to upload your podcast to the Apple iTunes Store, from which anyone can download your work easily. But that demands storing the podcast on a Web server with a URL address. You also have to create an RSS feed for the file to be hosted at the iTunes Store.

  Want to build a library of podcasts? You'll need to find server space. As a start, ask around at your college or workplace. Many provide the space for free.

121

Here are a half-dozen podcasts we consider good models. Check them out:

- **News:** *Today's Takeaways* (WNYC and Public Radio International)
- **Politics:** *Slate Political Gabfest* (www.slate.com)
- **Arts and Entertainment:** *WTF with Marc Maron* (Independent)
- **Music and Movies:** *Who Charted?* (Independent)
- **A bit of everything:** *TED Talks* (TED Conferences LLC)

TV Reality: Video Blogs

We're going to keep this section brief. There are lots of books about video production. Our aim is to give you some tips on getting started with your "vlog," or video blog. Or you can link to someone else's video to accompany your writing.

Whatever your topic—music, food, fashion, cars, pets, politics, fitness—there are hundreds (maybe thousands) of videos on YouTube or Vimeo. If you're reviewing a band's new release, why not include a video of the song in your post so listeners can hear it and see the band?

This is called "embedding" a video. YouTube and Vimeo make it easy. In fact, with WordPress, all you need is to copy the URL and paste it into your blog. The video will automatically embed. With other blogging software, just go to the video you want to add on YouTube or Vimeo, click on the "Share" icon, copy the HTML embedding code, and paste it. Be sure you are in HTML mode when you paste.

If you fancy yourself a budding TV personality (and who doesn't?), start a video blog with your own material. It's the visual equivalent of a podcast.

The same guidelines for a good podcast apply here (flip a few pages back and you'll find them). Once again, figure out a niche topic, keep your posts short, post regularly, gather material, write a script, and work on your voice and presentation.

Here are a few tips specific to creating vlogs.

If you don't have a video camera, use your phone. The quality of video recording on smartphones continues to improve. But there are two major problems with shooting smart phone video: The camera is not stable and secured, and the built-in microphone is terrible. When you're shooting for your blog, attach a microphone. And get a tabletop or full-size tripod on which to mount your phone. *Always* do an audio levels check through headphones before you start shooting.

Frame and light your shots. In the field, be aware of light levels and of shadows. If you are in your "studio"—which should be a quiet place with uncluttered, neutral-colored background—make sure your shots are well lit. In both your shots from the field and in the studio, *stay tight* on your subject, whether it be a fountain in a plaza or you talking to the camera. When shooting in the field, always be aware of the shot's background (is it distracting?) and any unwanted audio (a jet flying overhead).

123

Edit with care and precision. Editing always takes longer than anticipated. But it's also what will make your video look and sound professional. The industry editing standard is Final Cut Pro. After a few tutorials, you'll be surprised how easy and intuitive it is to use. But even a package as basic and inexpensive as Apple's iMovie is powerful. You won't need 95 percent of what the software can do, but you will need to learn to edit, trim, and paste clips; to add text to your video; and to use basic transition effects, such as fades and dissolves.

Most essential: Make the first 15 seconds of your video as engaging and interesting as you can, because that's about all the time you'll have to hook your viewers. It's not much different from writing a lede. On the Web, "time to boredom" is measured in seconds.

It helps to have a good name for your video blog. And you'll need to host it at YouTube, Vimeo, or elsewhere. Once you've created what the video hosting services call a "channel," you're ready to post.

DISCUSSION

1. Twenty-five years from now, as you and your family look back, would you rather be looking at a scrapbook of printed photographs or a photo gallery of digital images? Why?

2. What is the most evocative photo you have in your phone's photo gallery? What makes it good?

3. Are still photos more emotionally powerful than video, or is it the other way around? To put it another way: Can an audio slide show pack more emotional punch than a video? Why or why not?

4. Which classmates do you believe have the best voices for podcasting? Why?

EXERCISE

Create a podcast and several other blog posts that are primarily image-based. Make sure to write captions for your photos.

Stories of Everyday Life

8

One of the gifts of being a writer . . . is that writing motivates you to look closely at life, at life as it lurches by and tramps around.
—Anne Lamott, *Bird by Bird*

Whether your blog is about living a green lifestyle or maintaining a rooftop garden, raising kids as a lesbian mom or rescuing dogs and stray cats as a good Samaritan, there's a good chance a huge slice of your work will be generated from your everyday experiences.

The key is to spot the experiences that matter, to train yourself to recognize a good story and give it shape.

That takes practice, but it's also fun. Life's a lot richer when you pay close attention to what's unfolding around you. Or, to quote Lamott again, "We are a species that knows and wants to understand who we are."

Find Universal Connections

Look around more. Or let your imagination roam. If you do, you'll find that daily life is neither mundane nor routine. It's filled with surprises.

Your past can teach you that. Remember the time you got nabbed as a kid for stealing candy? The time your mother tried to teach you the facts of life? The first time you beat your dad in a race? These aren't just passages; they are stories. By sharing them and more contemporary personal tales—some no bigger than a conversation— you, the writer, can strike a *universal chord*. This is not summoned through incantation. It's just a fancy phrase for a sense of connection, a way that readers can engage in your life and experiences by filtering them through the prism of their own. Think of it as blogging's version of swapping stories at the bar or coffee shop. Most of us got nabbed as kids with our hand in someone else's candy jar. We all had to learn the facts of life from someone, as embarrassing as it seemed at the time.

Author Jerry Lanson came to understand the power of universal connections in the 1990s when he wrote a column called *Muddling Through Midlife* for the Syracuse, New York, *Post-Standard*. In it, he recounted tales about daily life as a dad, husband, and 40-something guy losing hair, teeth, and memory.

Jerry still has a passion for writing such little stories, but today he writes blog posts. He, his family members, and his dog Murphy often serve as the characters in his pieces for *The Huffington Post*.

One day, for example, his granddaughter Devon, then 6, announced her plans to seek higher office, which Jerry turned into a short post titled "A 6-Year-Old Launches Her Political Career." It went like this:

> As I was driving my granddaughter Devon home from first grade on Friday, the subject turned to politics.
>
> "Ada," she said, using the name she invented for me about as early as she could speak. "I would like to be president."
>
> "You're not old enough," I replied.
>
> "Do I have to be 10?" she asked.
>
> "No, a little bit older."
>
> I refrained from telling her that given the current political climate, she had to either be crazy or a closet member of the Tea Party to even consider running for president. I had to know which.
>
> "Why do you want to be president?" I asked.
>
> "So that I could tell people what to do," Devon replied.
>
> I didn't want to crush her dream.
>
> "I'm not sure it actually works that way," I told her. "What would you tell them?"

"The first thing I'd do is give everyone recess for the entire day," Devon said.

"Congress has already done that," I muttered under my breath. "Maybe you should run for the House of Representatives."

But this was Devon's show.

"What else would you do?" I asked.

"I would take naps."

"But who would run the country?"

"I would tell my assistants to do that," she said.

Clearly she's a George W. Bush Republican in the inner circle of a family of liberal Democrats. Still, I'll vote for her. She's too delicious to turn down.

If five-minute conversations can be fodder for a story about everyday life, just about anything can. But it takes practice—and an understanding of the difference between self-indulgent rambling and story.

As the humorist, novelist, and one-time journalist Mark Twain said, "You can't depend on your eyes when your imagination is out of focus."

Every story has a point, even the smallest vignette. Every story needs a beginning, a middle, and an end. Sympathetic (and funny) characters help a lot, too. In this case, the point—the universal connector—was nothing more than a play off the funny things that kids say (who hasn't known a kid who at some point announced plans to run for president?). Just as it can be amusing to eavesdrop on a conversation between kids and their parents at the beach, it can be amusing to read about similar conversations in a blog.

But the writer first has to register them. Writers should always be on high alert to what's going on around them. Writing about everyday life first requires watching, listening, recognizing what makes you curious, and recreating on the page what makes you smile—or squirm. It's a reason writers "gather string," jot notes on their phones, tablets, or pads about what catches their eye or ear.

Writing about everyday life does *not* mean looking in the mirror and telling the world why you look so good in red or what you think is cool today. It's an exercise in sharing honest experience, not ego or narcissism.

Bridgette White understands this. She tapped a deep vein with *Huffington Post* readers when she wrote about a family outing at the beach and a conversation with her kids that changed her self-perception about the way she looked. Titled "Exposed by My Children for What I Really Look Like," her post went viral. It was shared more than 25,000 times, drew 200,000 likes, and attracted hundreds of comments. She had struck that *universal chord*, as was obvious from the words that many wrote.

"Thank you so much for this article," wrote one mom. ". . . Yes, I know I'm overweight. But if it bothers someone else, then it isn't necessarily my problem but rather theirs."

ROSHNI CHINTALAPATI

"You have to find your own writing style or else your words don't ring true"

Roshni Chintalapati writes about everyday life: her own as an *Indian American Mom*, the blog's name. Chintalapati, who lives with her family in San Diego, California, started the blog in mid-2012. She writes this to the site's visitors: "If you have ever wanted to know how an Indian American household functions; how Indian Americans bring up their kids; what festivals Indian Americans celebrate; what Indian Americans eat; why Indian Americans move about so weirdly every time a Bollywood number starts playing; this site may be able to answer these questions (regarding the last one though; it's just genetics!)"

Roshni Chintalapati

The blog's subtitle is "Juggling two rich cultures through life and parenthood."

Chintalapati's blog caught the authors' interest because her words and their cadence carry her personality and sense of humor. The blog, in short, is a good read. Chintalapati answered a series of questions by email.

Why do you blog?
I enjoy writing and interacting with the blogging community. I used to read blogs on a daily basis and once the urge to contribute hit me, I set up my site. It's nice to be a reader and commenter, but of course, most of us also want to voice our own ideas and pretend that other people care about our opinion.

What are the challenges of balancing a job, two kids, a husband, and a blog?
Obviously in that list a blog is and should be the last priority. So, the challenge of maintaining a blog that you are serious about is to keep to a regular posting schedule. Of course, nowadays, social media presence and interaction [are] key to blog promotion; no one just posts articles

and sits back any more. So, the challenge of being always present and ready to chat on social media is there. Frankly, I can't and don't have the luxury of time for that; I do the minimal and leave it at that!

Is it at all difficult to keep your blog fresh? How often do you post?

Because I've worked out the topics of my blog very clearly, I don't have too much trouble in figuring out what to post. My theme is the Indian American lifestyle, perspective of a mom, a parent, an Indian American parent, and, finally, posts about my childhood and my extended Indian family. It's specific enough to keep my readers interested, yet broad enough to give me a wide range of subjects to blog about. I try to post once a week, though there have been times where I haven't been able to hammer out a post because life gets in the way.

Has the nature of your blog changed at all over time?

Yes indeed! It started out as a mommy blog, but I expanded my topics a lot shortly after.

When you began blogging, had you done much writing before?

I always loved to write. I used to keep journals, I loved writing essays in school, and I wrote for my college magazine. I didn't really take writing very seriously, though, since I was pursuing a science degree.

Clearly, you are a reader. You mention that in your biography. Do you believe that has helped you as a writer? Why?

Yes and no. By that I mean, I definitely am enriched by the wide variety of thoughts and writing styles to which I have been exposed as a reader. But, ultimately, you have to find your own writing style or else your words don't ring true. For instance, I love P.G. Wodehouse and I used to write articles in his style; but I quickly understood that only Wodehouse can and should write like Wodehouse.

How did you find your voice as a blogger? Do you think of your blog as a letter to yourself? To friends? Do you have any audience in mind or simply enjoy telling stories?

If I wrote with someone in mind, it would definitely hinder me from expressing myself freely. Some of my articles, like my post on bedwetting (www.indianamericanmom.com/2013/08/bed-wetting-older-kids.html), were quite unnerving to write, but I thought of someone whom I didn't know but who would derive some comfort on reading that article, and so I wrote and posted it! For other posts, like about my family, my grandmother, I wanted to have a written record of the so many endearing and amazing things that they had done, and so I posted those for myself to read over and over again. Finally, there are subjects that I am passionate about, like my post on rape (www.indianamericanmom.com/2013/01/she-was-asking-for-

131

it.html), and I posted my frank views on it without any regard to how others might view it. So, ultimately, you should write for yourself; that's when you can be your most authentic.

What advice would you offer a young blogger who wants to get started?
I learned that it is true that content is king. Sometimes, it feels like many blogs become big over a post that went viral or because these bloggers have thousands of Facebook followers. I agree that there are many wonderful blogs that deserve such recognition. But the blogs that endure are the ones that have a loyal band of readers because it is the writing that draws them back again and again.

Start Small and Specific

Bridgette White's story, like Jerry's, grew out of an interaction with children. But hers was anything but light-hearted. Instead, her conversations with her son and then daughter gave her a new lens and new courage through which to look at the issues of weight and body image, issues with which nearly everyone grapples. The story grew out of a single photo of her lying on her back at the beach.

132

My first reaction is shock. Who took this hideous picture of me?
Self-loathing and disgust [well] up and threaten to bring me to tears.
Just as I am about to hit "delete," my boy walks in the room.
"Do you know anything about this picture?" I ask him.
I turn the screen so he can see it. He smiles huge.
"I took that of you in [Lake] Tahoe," he says. "You looked so beautiful lying there. I couldn't help it Mom."
"You need to ask me before using my phone to take pictures," I say.
"I know," he says. "But Mom, seriously, look how pretty you look."
. . .
I still see my dimply fat thighs.
I also see a mom collapsed on the shore who just explored the lake for hours with her children.
I see chubby arms.
I also see the arms of a mom who just helped her kids across the rocks and hot sand so their feet wouldn't hurt.
I see a fat woman wearing a black dress bathing suit to try to hide her weight issue.
I also see an adventurous mom who loves her children something fierce.

White has established a tension here: this mom is at best ambivalent about her body. But as the post continues, her conversations with her children help her resolve her self-doubt and make peace with the picture and herself. She ends her piece like this:

> I don't hate my body anymore.
>   That's huge for me to admit, and hard to even wrap my mind around.
>   I'm not giving up on exercising and getting healthy . . . Right now, though, I just want to love my body where it is. I want to be OK to see myself the way my kids do.
>   Thank you, kids.

The simplicity and honesty of White's story are why it works so well. Built off one picture and an exchange with her kids, it says much more. Blog posts can be like that. They can examine big issues of day-to-day life—in this case, weight, body image, and the impact of both in a culture that venerates youth and shapeliness. But to take on those big issues effectively, to touch readers, they need to approach those issues in small, specific, and human terms.

It's essential to establish a story's point and place before expanding its purpose. Save preachy for the Sunday pews.

133

Inventory Your Own Life

Those who blog about everyday life can find stories with impact by simply paying attention to what they're doing, thinking, and saying.

As we noted in Chapter 3, "Getting Started," story ideas come from lots of places. Blogs on politics, economics, the media, and public affairs often come from monitoring the Web, social media, public records, and other written sources used to find angles that others haven't tapped. Writing about everyday life is different. It demands living in the present and tuning into it with heightened alertness. It means noticing what's around you, what's changed. It means thinking about who is affected by actions and how. And it means changing routines, going places at different times of day, walking places you haven't walked, taking public transportation if you usually drive.

"Inventorying the obvious" is how Jerry describes it in his book, *Writing and Reporting the News*. It works in newsrooms, too. Once, when he lived in California and worked as a newspaper editor, Jerry found his home overrun by ants. Rather than writing a personal blog about it—this was the 1990s—he asked a reporter at the *San Jose Mercury News* to make a call. Was this a widespread problem in the region? It was. The story made Page 1.

On your own blog, you are Page 1. You call the shots. The story needn't be big and widespread. Interesting and personal will do.

Serendipity often plays a part. So again, be alert. Just yesterday, for example, Jerry drove to his daughter's house in Woburn, Massachusetts. On the way back—once again with Devon—there was a traffic jam and commotion on Route 38, in front of Stop & Shop right before a rotary at the entrance to Route 128. People were standing on the median, leaning forward, their cellphones out to take pictures. Cars waited patiently. As in the famous children's story, *Make Way for Ducklings*, a parade of winged animals was crossing the road. Only these were geese—nine of them—who, oh-so-slowly, marched across the six lanes in single file. It was a cute moment that surely had the makings of a blog, with photo, had Jerry not been intent on writing this chapter.

Perhaps he'd have started with something like: "Forget those cute ducklings in Boston's Public Garden. In my neighborhood, geese rule the roads."

The lede, after all, doesn't have to tell the whole story. It only has to get the reader to the next paragraph.

Enlist Example as the Seed of Stories

Here's a way to find stories: ask yourself when you get home each day what the day's biggest "holy mackerel" moment was. How would you finish this beginning: "Hey, you'll never guess what happened to me this afternoon." Those kind of personal "headlines," small, specific moments in the day, often point the way to a blog post.

Jerry's wife Kathy, for example, was sitting on their patio in their busy Boston suburb a few summers back when a red fox trotted by just a few feet away. It was the kind of moment that would be the "talker" with anyone Kathy met that day. It certainly surprised Jerry.

In this case, after a few phone calls, he wrote a *Huffington Post* blog titled "When Life in the Suburbs Gets Wild." It began like this:

Perhaps she hunts by bankers' hours, the red fox who lives in our neighborhood. Or maybe her kids are growing up fast, demanding more to eat.

The first time we saw her close up, several weeks ago, we were eating breakfast on the patio between our garage and house at about 9:30 a.m. She loped down the street, perhaps 30 feet away, straight toward Massachusetts Avenue, the main road of our historic, Revolutionary War village. Not a care in the world.

Then, on Father's Day, Kathy was sitting on the same patio, talking on the phone to her mother at 5:25 p.m., when the fox emerged from the shadows behind the garage, not 5 feet away. It walked another 10 feet to the lilac bush, stopped, turned and stared, not hurried, apparently not the least bit afraid. Kathy sort of was. She raced into the house, slammed the screen and blurted out the news.

Instead of cat and mouse, we've been playing fox and man of late in our neighborhood. Or, occasionally, coyote and golden retriever.

Unlike the fox, the coyote doesn't dally. He raced by at 10:30 a.m. sometime last week while I was walking our dog Murphy on a dirt connecting road on the hill behind our house . . . Our most haunting neighborhood addition has yet to show its face. That's the fisher, sometimes erroneously called the fisher cat. Late at night, three times last week alone, we've been awakened by its screech, something akin to the sound of two cats fighting in an alley or a ghoul cornered by the Ghostbusters. It's enough to make me pull the covers just a bit closer.

135

Unlike Devon's run for the White House, this story needed some explanation. Why all the wild animals? So Jerry called Lexington's animal control officer, Stephanie Doucett, for her thoughts.

"We've had wildlife in the neighborhoods for a long time," said Doucette, who has been on the job more than seven years. "They just do their own thing."

She told him one fox family with five babies lived two blocks from his house.

So what should he and other residents do about it? A state wildlife education official offered tips on how to scare off wildlife and discourage them from prowling; useful information for readers elsewhere, too.

"Their first response is flight, not fight," said Marion Larson, chief of information and education for the Massachusetts Division of Fisheries & Wildlife. But she added, it doesn't hurt to show them who's boss. ("My mother is over 70 and she yells at bears," she said.) That might mean "whooping it up" to scare the animals away, turning on bright lights or throwing something at them. Preferably—and this is my suggestion—from behind a very large fence.

Jerry's piece linked to the website of Larson's agency, which had a list of further advice for dealing with wild animals. There are two more lessons here: small stories about everyday life still can involve reporting and still can allow readers to learn something new.

A Little Humor Goes a Long Way

Make me smile and you'll make me your reader for a long while. Most funny things take but seconds to deliver. Don't prolong them needlessly.

Kelcey Kintner, a former journalist, author, and mother, keeps an active blog called *The Mama Bird Diaries*. She's from Florida and, as she explains, "drives a used gold minivan because you can't fit five kids on a Vespa."

Her blog, filled with advice, is casual, colloquial, and often funny. Here's an excerpt from a blog on breastfeeding titled "how to breastfeed (alternate title: this is not a wet T-shirt contest although you could totally win if it was)."

136

> It takes a village to breastfeed. You need experts. Probably not your well-meaning noisy neighbor whose dog just had puppies so now she's sure she knows all about nursing. You need people in your life that know stuff.
>
> I had no natural instinct when it came to breastfeeding. I didn't magically know how to properly get my baby to latch on. I didn't know what to do when my breasts became the size of two gigantic honeydew melons. And you probably won't either.
>
> So utilize the lactation nurse at the hospital who can help you position yourself and your baby correctly.

Kintner sometimes tweets short-and-sweet posts, niblets really, on Twitter. Here's one:

> 4-year-old: I need Band-Aid.
> Me: Don't have one.
> 4-year-old: I need a Band-Aid. NEED A BAND-AID NOW!
> Me: Oh, wait. I found one.
> 4-year-old: Not that one.

KELCEY KINTNER

"Life is so tragic and so serious. Humor is the escape."

Kelcey Kintner began writing her humorous blog on marriage and motherhood, *The Mama Bird Diaries*, seven years ago. She's written funny posts about changing her daughter's name when she realized she didn't like it, visiting Naples (Florida, not Italy), and something she called "emails in a marriage," a way of showing how different the lives and minds of working dads and stay-at-home moms are.

Kelcey Kintner

We caught up with Kelcey, whose work is excerpted in this chapter, at her Florida home. She answered our questions by email.

How did you go about approaching your blog when you began? Was it a hobby? Or did you see it all along as a potential business?

I always viewed blogging as a part-time job (not a hobby), I guess because I went to journalism school and consider writing and journalism my profession. So I always viewed it as a way to potentially make money. I don't remember exactly when it became profitable. But as my traffic grew, I was able to charge for ads, and it led to paid freelance writing opportunities.

Why did you start in the first place?

I had kids, didn't want to work full-time and the freelance schedule is very unpredictable. I thought blogging was a great creative outlet and I just hoped I could make some money doing it.

To what extent do you write for yourself and to what extent for others?

I write for my readers. This is not a diary. I write hopefully funny posts that parents and others can relate to.

What do you see as your blog's mission or focus, and how has that changed over time?

It's always been a humor blog on parenting, marriage and pop culture. The focus hasn't really changed. I just think I've become a better, sharper writer over time. At least I hope so!

How have you gone about building traffic to your blog?

Slow and steady. Through other blogs, freelance writing, social media like Twitter and Facebook and writing consistently.

We first saw your name on a compilation of short dialogues—tweet blogs for lack of another name—on *Huffington Post*. Do you periodically try your hand at these as well?
My goal is to tweet funny, relatable things that will be shared on Twitter and other outlets like *The Huffington Post* and Nick Mom.

Do you write your tweet blogs in part to draw traffic to your bigger blog or are they just quick and fun, or both?
I enjoy tweeting and it's definitely fun. But my goal is to build my audience, which helps to attract sponsors and other money-making opportunities.

What in your mind makes a great blog on everyday life?
Something that is easy to relate to. Like I wrote a post about wearing the wrong thing to a shiva call [a visit to pay respect and give comfort during a mourning period in the Jewish religion]. Everyone can relate to wearing the wrong thing to an event. I also strive to make my writing concise. I hate longwinded blogs.

What advice would you offer a young blogger starting out with this kind of blog?
Be true to yourself. You have to find your own voice. And find some writers that you really admire that can take you under their wing.

How important in your mind is humor in connecting with your readers?
Life is so tragic and so serious. Humor is the escape. If you can make someone laugh, you have really given [that person] a gift. Readers have written to me that my blog got them through some horrible thing in their life and that is just amazing.

Use Dialogue

Conversations are a big part of everyday life. Yet reporters look for "quotes," sentence- to paragraph-long comments meant to accentuate a point, give expert opinion, or add another voice.

Real people speak in dialogue, the give and take of conversation. Dialogue conveys action and interaction, and is a much more effective way of engaging readers in a scene. Here once more is where gathering string comes in—carrying a small audio recorder, your phone, a tablet, a pad—to record or get down the best such exchanges.

Dialogue needn't merely anchor a story. It can be the story, as was the case with Kelcey Kintner's tweet. Or it can be most of the story, as was the case in Jerry's piece above about his granddaughter's quest for the presidency.

To work, dialogue needs to be short, punchy, fast-paced, and, whenever possible, funny. Remember: Think of those stories you'd share with a friend that begin, "Hey, you wouldn't believe what I overheard today."

Here is an example from the *New York Times* blog, "Metropolitan Diary," which captures snippets of New York in essays, dialogue exchanges, and poems. The pieces are not bylined.

> At my West Village Pilates class last week.
>
> Instructor: "What do you want to work on today?"
> Me: "Abs."
> The woman on the mat to my left: "Stretching. My back is soooo sore."
> The woman on the mat to my right: "My butt."
> The woman to her right: "World peace."
> A pause.
> The woman to my left: "O.K. Brunch."

Everyone Has a Family

Just as we all can be characters in our own stories, so, too, can those who know us best—the members of our family. The influence of family goes a long way toward defining who we are. Like it or not, no one knows us better, and vice versa. And since just about everyone has a family, few topics provide a more natural bridge to readers than those that tie into family.

As always in writing, ground your story in specifics. Don't just write stuff. Think small.

Let's say, for example, that you wanted to write an essay for Father's Day. You wouldn't get far by launching into a bunch of generalities about "why I love my dad."

> My dad is the biggest, kindest and strongest man I know. He's always there for me, and he's the only person who can always make me smile in the worst of times. We share an interest in a variety of sports and both like to cook sometimes. We also both like animals. But what I like best about him is that we share a love for baseball. We go to games together, compare our favorite players, even keep batting averages.

So what's the problem? The sentences are short enough. The individual sentences are clear. But they lack focus, example, and specificity. As the writing coaches at the journalism center, The Poynter Institute in St. Petersburg, Florida like to ask: "What's the point? Why should readers care?"

Start plotting your post by answering these two questions for yourself. Writing a good headline can help (see Chapter 6, "Why Headlines Matter"). Maybe the headline "Dad, Baseball and the Lessons of Life" would work. Or "Memories of Bonding at the Ballpark." Whatever the answer, writing a headline will help you figure out where you are heading.

Next, when you write that first sentence, interest readers in something that *shows* your character or main point rather than merely tells about him or it. Let's start over.

> My Dad taught me the art of sneaking into the best empty box seats at Fenway Park when I was 5. He was born for the part. Dad was a distinguished-looking fellow, with a round, bald head and a rim of prematurely white hair around its fringe. Shortly after a game's first inning ended, he'd scout the most expensive empty seats below, and, with newly purchased popcorn in hand, lead the way toward them with the air that they were his.
>
> It was such adventures at the ballpark that forged our relationship, the reason, as Father's Day approaches, that my memories always turn toward Fenway.

See the difference? The first paragraph establishes the theme. The second anchors it, gives what journalists call the *nut graf*, or *so what graf*—in this case, that baseball forged a relationship you still think of every Father's Day.

The specifics here take no more space—and they say something much clearer, better grounded, and more universal. The story may move beyond baseball at some point, but if it's a good story, it will come back to this original theme at the end. That's what staying on topic or theme means.

As is the case with this Father's Day piece, family stories often can be planned by keeping track of the calendar. Anniversaries give stories something of a *news peg*, a reason for being written when they are. Thanksgiving, Christmas, Mother's Day, Valentine's Day, the start of baseball season, graduation season, camp season, anniversaries, and birthdays are but some of the dates that might prompt a particular family story.

Family stories needn't all be nice either. David Sedaris has built much of his career as a humorist writing about his largely dysfunctional family. And while most of what we read about moms on Mother's Day keys on special memories of a special person, this story was distinctive because it took a decidedly different tack. It was written by blogger Lucy Ball.

> The last time [my mom] hit me was when I was about 11 or 12. She swung at me. I had planned it in my mind over and over and I finally got the courage this time. I grabbed her wrist and stopped her arm mid-air. And I told her, "Don't you ever lay a hand on me again. Ever."
>
> But there were many times when her words and behavior hurt people worse than her hand ever could. Like the day of my wedding.
>
> So, sadly, this Mother's Day I will not be filled with joy and admiration for my mother like a good daughter should be. I will not reminisce about the times when we played dress-up or she let me put on her makeup. If any of those things did happen, they were overshadowed by the traumatic memories and long since forgotten.
>
> What I can do though is forgive her. She has changed. And the death of her own mother has awakened the sleeping elephants no one would talk about until now.
>
> I can also tell others my shameful embarrassing story.
>
> Not because I am ashamed of my mother, but to show others that the cycle can be broken.
>
> But only when you stop ignoring the elephants. Find someone to talk to. Get help.
>
> There is no shame. Let your elephants go.

141

Ball ends her *BlogHer* post not by thanking her mother, but by forgiving her.

Tighten the Focus of Your Everyday Life Blog

Too many blogs about everyday life try to cover just about everything and end up covering next to nothing. Don't make that mistake.

When a family in Wiltshire, England, decided to start a blog together, it titled its effort *Everyday Life on a Shoestring*. It shared the family's efforts to live frugally and green. That's focus.

In contrast, a blog titled *The Kitchen Sync, Thoughts on Work, Life, the Cloud and Other Topics*—and this is real—needs to decide what it is about. The play on "sink" is nice, but the whirlwind of topics needs some boundaries.

Pick an aspect of your everyday life—the place in which you live, parenting, preparing for a marathon—and make it the topic of your blog.

Tracy Kaler, for example, writes a readable, multimedia blog about all things New York titled *Tracy's New York Life*. It's personal, conversational, and filled with pictures and graphics. She posts regularly, keeping her spotlight on her life in the city, from one entry about noisy neighbors to another about a graffiti tagger some consider an artist and others a vandal. Along the way, she passes on tips and advice.

The best blogs about daily life sometimes inspire book ideas, or, better yet, calls from publishers. Colin Beavan published his book, *No Impact Man*, in 2009, after spending a year blogging about his efforts to reduce his environmental impact on the planet to as close to zero as possible. He later ran as a Congressional candidate for the Green Party and has converted his blog into a voice for energy conservation.

Mason Currey's story is the kind that should give bloggers encouragement as they begin posting in what is often a wilderness inhabited by only a few friends. In 2007, he began a blog called *Daily Routines* on the work habits of "artists, writers and other interesting people." The blog is no more; it has become a book, titled *Daily Rituals*. Here is how Currey tells the story.

I launched Daily Routines on a Sunday afternoon in July 2007, while procrastinating on a writing assignment due the following day. It was intended as a hobby, and for the first year and a half I had a readership of about a dozen friends, coworkers, and family members.

Then, in December 2008, Slate wrote a story about the quest for the perfect morning routine that quoted liberally from my blog. Suddenly I went from having a record of five visitors in one day to almost 18,000, and more than 80,000 visitors for the month.

Along with all of these visitors came a steady stream of comments and e-mails—including a few e-mails from editors and literary agents suggesting that I turn the blog into a book. Two weeks after the Slate article came out, I signed on with one of those agents; over Christmas vacation, I wrote a book proposal. By April 2009, after lots of back-and-forth with several editors, I signed a contract with my dream publisher, Knopf.

Now, four years later, the *Daily Routines* book—officially titled *Daily Rituals: How Artists Work*—is finally coming out. It presents the routines and working habits of 161 creative minds.

We can all dream of such an opportunity. But first, sharpen your focus.

DISCUSSION

1. In small groups, discuss the difference between simply keeping a personal journal and telling stories about everyday life. How is it different to write only for ourselves and to write about everyday life for an audience? Within your groups, discuss whether any of you have either kept journals or blogged about everyday life before. What did you write about? How might your approach change after reading this chapter?

2. Discuss the challenges of using dialogue in writing. Do you consider it more effective, less effective, or simply different from using quotations? Why? What skills do you believe you need to develop to introduce dialogue into your work?

EXERCISES

1. Gather string for a week about your own life. At the end of each day, answer the question: "Would you believe what happened to me today?" Analyze these answers in small groups and decide whether and why some of the answers could be the basis of a story. What would that story need?

2. Think of the quirkiest person in your extended family (every family has at least one). Write about that person, but not in general terms. Instead, write about a day, a visit, a memory. Try to convey the person's character and personality by recreating a scene—an interaction, a conversation, a shared experience.

On the Road Again

The Travel Blog

Travel bloggers have a choice. They can submit their work to places that publish paid or unpaid freelance work—from Lonely Planet (paid) to *Huffington Post* (unpaid). Or they can set out to write their own blog and scramble to build an audience.

They can try to line up a paycheck in advance or send pitches to editors, known as query letters, after they return from a trip. Or they can find a distinct niche, post a lot, market their posts through social media, and hope to capture attention.

In the latter case, warns Tim Leffel in *Travel Writing 2.0*, "Remember that the root word of freedom is 'free' . . . That's what you'll be working for day after day, week after week, for six months to a year until your shiny new blog gets some traction—if it ever does."

Author Jerry Lanson had read Leffel's admonition before he headed to France for six months in January 2014. Still, he chose to take the risk. He didn't expect to strike it rich, which is a good thing. He did expect to learn. He had contributed freelance travel blogging for pay of sorts at trueslant.com. He'd blogged about travel for free at *Huffington Post*. But he'd never built and sustained his own travel blog. If the experience was humbling—and it was—it was even more gratifying.

Jerry's www.slowlanetravel.com survives as a practical yet reflective guide to all things Provençal and back-road travel in Provence and other parts of France. He posted almost every day for six months, a pace that taught him the pressures and the pleasures of starting and maintaining a personal travel blog. He chronicled cultural differences, profiled people he met, and shared his experiences living in the city of Aix-en-Provence. He built slide shows and galleries, always making sure that they—like all good stories—anchored the audience in place and then moved logically, and often chronologically, from beginning to end. He offered tips on travel off the beaten path, whether writing about how to decipher the French road system or how to find hikes away from the tourist hordes.

Blogging helped Jerry reflect on his time overseas while he was there. It also gave him a way to meet locals and make new acquaintances among those readers who would comment regularly.

But Jerry missed opportunities to build the foundation of a bigger potential audience before he arrived, and he realized too late that his blog was too broad in scope.

It took four full months to reach an average daily readership of 100 page views. And when he returned to the United States six months later, no Hollywood contracts awaited. No one had recruited him to write a travel book. No one, in fact, had offered him a dime.

Still, he'd gained a new cadre of Twitter followers in France and England, including the travel publisher Rough Guide. Several active blogs in France republished his posts, some after asking (frenchnews online.com) and others by simply copying (gradegood.com). He'd been interviewed by expats.com, a blog that serves expatriates worldwide, and his college's website. And, the greatest pleasure to him, he'd gained a following among his French teachers.

All blogging requires planning, something you've already read in Chapter 2, "Two Models: The Reporter Blogger vs. The Op-Ed Blogger." But barriers of culture, language, custom, and technology make that planning much more imperative before you head out on the road. Prepare with care.

Getting Ready

We've touched on some of these tips elsewhere. But the travel blogger needs a checklist.

Narrow Your Blog's Focus

You'll recall from Chapter 3 that one of Mark's favorite student bloggers wrote solely about where to find the best chicken wings in Boston. That may be meaty stuff (sorry), but it's also so tightly focused that it doesn't even take in the whole bird. One of Jerry's travel writing students built a strong blog titled "10 from the T" that gave tips on the most interesting walks within 10 minutes of the Massachusetts Bay Transportation Authority's subway stops in the Boston metropolitan area. Boston is a city of neighborhoods so the topic offered lots of opportunities worth exploring. Its point, however, couldn't have been more clear.

Focus was something Jerry struggled with in France because of what he came to realize was a flaw in his blog's conceptual design. On the one hand, he wrote a series of "Letters from Provence," posts about life in one of France's prettiest and most easygoing regions. On the other, he wrote about "Slow Lane Travel," places to go and things to see off the beaten path. He'd designed this duality because of twin sabbatical projects. But in hindsight, it was a mistake. He needed a single, fully integrated focus.

To help you establish a title and topic for your travel blog, we propose an exercise. Once you've chosen a blog topic, ask five people you trust whether they'd read it, why, and what they consider its biggest weakness. Then, research what other blogs have written on the topic using *Technorati* and other directories of blogs. Finally, force yourself to break your topic into three potential sub-topics. Ask yourself whether one of these alone might be rich enough for a blog. The tighter your focus, the better your odds of success.

Practice Close to Home

Writing a travel blog doesn't mean you have to go anywhere. It means you need to interest others in something about a place you know well. And that's likely to be close to home.

Just as reporters can learn the skills to cover Washington, D.C. by covering local government, travel writers can prep for that big journey

147

by writing about things they know better than others. Like chicken wings. Like walks near the stops on Boston's subway system.

So if you live in Rome, New York, instead of Rome, Italy, build your first travel blog there.

Take Wendell Jamieson. He published a piece titled "My Borough, Your Destination" about Brooklyn, the New York borough in which he'd lived for more than four decades. Jamieson didn't write his piece for a personal blog. He wrote it for the *New York Times* travel section cover.

Travel blogging close to home costs a fraction of what you'll pay to see the world. It gives you a built-in core audience of friends, neighbors, and relatives. It lets you think about something you know best.

That might be underground music stores or cool sites for hang gliding. It might be the best farm-to-table restaurants or food trucks with panache. Whatever your passion, turn it into a travel blog in your own backyard.

Choose Your Technology with Care

Jerry cut his journalistic teeth decades before the world turned mobile. He prefers to write on keyboards, not smartphones or iPads. But he neither wanted to haul around the 4.5 pounds of his MacBook Pro nor consume all his computer's memory mid-journey. His solution was to buy a new MacBook Air (3 pounds for a 13-inch screen) and to pay extra for twice the memory. He carried it in a foam sleeve he could slip into a backpack.

Jerry had neither the money nor space to buy a big professional camera with multiple lenses. But he wanted to take pictures that captured culture and knew this would require a decent zoom. After talking to friends and looking over product reviews, he settled on a Canon SX50HS, which he bought with case, batteries, and two memory cards for a little over $500. Its best feature: an optical zoom lens with 50x magnification.

Think carefully before you hit the road about what equipment fits you best. Carry back-up batteries and memory cards. Be sure you have enough memory and the right electric current converters. Verify, too, that you've bought space on a reliable server and that you have enough space reserved to meet all your blog's demands. It was here that Jerry ran into trouble. During his first few months in France, he battled problems with server space, blog speed, and spam, in part because his grad assistant also was new to the business of building and operating a personal blog. The lesson: It's not good enough in today's world to say, "I'm a writer, not a techie."

Give Your Readers a Home Page Search Function

As a blog grows, the ability to search its archives becomes crucial. Be certain to install a home page blog search function that allows visitors to type in keywords to find past stories. In fact, explore whether this function can readily appear on every page. It helps hold readers.

Scout for Potential Allies and Audience on Social Media

Chapter 12 is devoted to "Building Your Blogging Brand." For now, let's just say scout early when entering new territory. Twitter, Facebook, and other social media outlets are natural allies in a digital world in which every blog has hundreds of direct competitors and millions of people competing for attention. Be sure to "friend" and "follow" influential or active users in the place or topic about which you will be blogging before you get there.

149

If you're traveling abroad, seek out international online communities. Some bloggers specialize in making sites that index other blogs. Such hub sites can serve as a good source to see what's written about an area, who is writing it, and whether you'd like to link to them. For example, *Expats Blog* (www.expatsblog.com/blogs) lists 2,492 blogs around the world by country and region within country.

A few other travel sites worth visiting:

- *The Travel Blog Exchange* (www.travelblogexchange.com). Among other things, this site offers a 30-minute video on how to build a travel blog.
- *The Travel Writers Exchange* (www.travel-writers-exchange.com). Offers travel writing tips, book reviews, and forums. You can also submit an article to the site.

Create an Email Newsletter

So you think email is old hat? Not so fast. Here's what David Carr wrote in a June 2014 *New York Times* column on newsletters:

> Email newsletters, an old-school artifact of the web that was supposed to die along with dial-up connections, are not only still around, but very much on the march.

Travel bloggers can use newsletters to help identify loyal readers and converse directly with them, either as a group or individually.

Design a Blog That's Both Attractive and Dynamic

Entire books are devoted to Web design. We'd recommend *Beautiful Web Design*, by Jason Beaird, since design isn't the primary purpose of this book. But design bears mention. In planning your travel blog—or any other for that matter—find a balance between creating an attractive home page and one that's easy to navigate. Ideally, you want your home page to be both.

Busy blogs that lack a clear, compelling title and cram too much on the home page can scare visitors off. They offer too many choices, provide no clear sense of purpose, and lack a dominant "entry point"—think of a sort of welcome sign in the form of a dominant photo or graphic element. They look cluttered.

On the other hand, pretty blogs that don't give readers the chance to click through to enough different features, to access archives, and to interact run the risk of being too static, or just plain dull.

Prefab templates at places such as WordPress or Blogger work just fine to create your first blog. But if you're in this for the long haul, either read a good design book before you launch or find a design-savvy friend who will help you build the right look.

Whether or not you're the designer, you should make the final call. The blog's look, its usability, and its content should complement one another.

CAZ AND CRAIG MAKEPEACE

"Have a very clear vision for your blog and how you want to help your readers"

Caz and Craig Makepeace write that "we like to call the world our home." They travel it for a living. Or, more precisely, they make enough money writing about it to support themselves and two young daughters, who go on the road with them. The Australian couple are the authors of *y Travel Blog* (www.ytravel blog.com), ranked third among the top 50 travel blogs by *The Expeditioner* in the third quarter of 2014. It's a blog devoted to inspiring others and showing them that they, too, "can travel the world on little dime." We caught up with the Makepeaces in Western Australia, which, their blog says, they've been traveling around for 15 months "with no end in sight."

Caz and Craig Makepeace with their daughters, Kalyra and Savannah

What gave you the idea for your blog?
We had spent eight years living and traveling around the world and so knew we had a lot of experience, stories, and tips to share with people who wanted to do the same. A travel blog seemed like an easy and fun way to connect with other travelers and help them travel more and create better memories.

Why do you think your blog took off?
We started blogging already with authority as we'd had so many years of experience traveling around the world. We also understood our readers very well because of this, which meant we could easily provide them with what they needed to create similar travel experiences. We worked hard to provide useful, relevant information for them. We also worked hard to create a community around our blog, similar to the hostel couch. We've created a place that is fun, engaging, friendly, and welcoming, that shares stories and tips about travel.

Our story is very inspiring to many people. They can relate to us and we help them to feel they can live their travel dreams too. I think that is very powerful.

How long did it take you to make your first dollar?
I think it was about three months and it was $75 for advertising. We thought that was amazing! To make money doing something that filled me with such joy AND helped people as well. That money was like hitting the jackpot as it showed me what was possible.

Now we are full-time with our blog earning more money than we did in our jobs that we hated.

How often did you post when you started? How often do you post now?
We posted almost every day when we first started. We now consistently post at least three times a week. Our current road trip with our children slows us down so we can't publish as much as we'd like.

What advice would you give students who set out to write their first travel blog?
Have a very clear vision for your blog and how you want to help your readers. This will guide every decision you make and when you think about your readers' needs, then you create content that nourishes them. That is how you build long-term success.

Types of Travel Blog Posts

152

A blog post can be a 50-word snippet or a series of "odds and ends"—short, unrelated bits, separated by dashes or boxes that each stand on their own. Or a post can be a 1,000-word essay or full-blown profile. It can be a single photo and cutline. Or it can be a sequence of photographs—15, 20, or more—with extended captions or a slide show with narrative, words, and music.

Variety builds reader interest. Good bloggers have their own style, their own voice. But they don't deliver stories that always take the same form or are set in several prefab forms. Allow yourself to experiment. If something interests you, it'll interest someone else.

Two tips will help here:

- Don't write a single word more than your post needs.
- Write clear headlines that work with your lede and ground your reader in place or topic, as we explain in Chapter 6, "Why Headlines Matter."

We won't try to give you an exhaustive list of travel story types here. We bet you can invent something new yourself. But here are some standard posts worth knowing about.

Tips for Travelers

Big websites like *Huffington Post* love lists.

These can be trite at times—"12 Tips on Using the Language of Love." But readers do appreciate concrete information. Don't be shy about providing it. Among the posts Jerry put on his blog were "15 Tips for the Best of Aix," "12 Tips on Getting from Here to There in Provence," and "Aix: What's Hot, What's Not." His most successful blog, which he also put on the *Huffington Post*—where it drew 721 likes—was "12 Tips on How to Spend 6 Months in France Without Going Broke."

Jerry wouldn't call it among his best. But it gave specific advice about something travelers care a lot about: good value. And the headline identified a country, France, to which a lot of people travel. Such things count in getting readers to the page (see Chapter 6, "Why Headlines Matter").

The post began like this:

From the start, the math didn't add up.

Kathy and I were headed to France for a half year. I'd be on paid sabbatical, but Kathy was retiring, and we weren't ready to tap her Social Security. Even with our house rented at a discount, complete with our lovable if wacky golden retriever, the basic math looked daunting:

Overall income: Down 40 percent

Basic Expenses: Up at least $1,000 a month

Outlook: A bit scary

From there, the story launched into Jerry's 12 tips. Here's an excerpt:

- Cancel everything you can before you leave home. We shut down our phones, parked our cars, canceled Netflix, a French language TV station, my school parking space and newspapers. It adds up.
- Get credit and debit cards that don't charge a fee. Most cards tack on a 3 percent overseas transaction fee. Not Capital One.
- Keep track of daily expenditures. This allows us to monitor ourselves and reward ourselves. It takes little effort. I keep a running tally in a notebook in my back pocket.

Such advice blogs can take many forms. In Paris, Jerry wrote about three restaurants worth eating in and two scams to steer clear of. He told his readers that "In Chamonix, Choosing a Trail's Direction Is No Small Matter," explaining that the far less-traveled and slightly

153

steeper direction on the North Balcony trail kept the view of the Alps directly in front of the hiker while the more downhill direction that hikers chose more often was crowded and left the view at their backs. He took readers on a photographic boat tour of Lake Annecy. And he explained, in "Medieval Fortresses of Provence: 1 for the Masses, 1 in the Wild," why he considered it much more interesting—and much less expensive—to head to medieval ruins of Fort du Buoux in the wild than to go to the wildly popular and crowded Les-Baux-de-Provence.

All these blogs included specific information, delivered directly:

> If [Les Baux] is for you, gird yourself for the crowds and carry a bit of extra cash. Admission from spring through summer costs $14 a person and that doesn't include parking.
>
> Fort du Buoux? It has no audio guide, no demonstrations of weaponry, no snack bar, no bathroom, only modestly restored ruins—and no people. Yet it's only an hour's drive . . . from Aix-en-Provence.

He gave this advice on "Getting from Here to There":

> If you're renting a car, book as far ahead as possible.
>
> We've found that Orbitz gives us the most flexibility and the best prices. But that's only when we book early. The cost differences between renting a week ahead and a day or two ahead are sometimes staggering. And since Orbitz demands no deposit at the time of booking, there's no disincentive for booking early.

Sound practical advice builds readership.

Stories about People

As wanderers, we don't just travel to see Roman ruins, the paintings of the masters, or the landscapes that drew them to places like Provence. We go to meet people, learn about their culture, and try, sometimes using multiple languages (and gestures), to communicate with them. We may rush to show our friends pictures of the Acropolis in Athens, Big Ben in London, and Machu Picchu in Peru. But the stories we tell often have more to do with the people we encounter or the predicaments we find ourselves in. (Jerry calls the latter "adventure stories." You'll read more about them in the next section.) The key point: people, not things, are at the heart of most interesting travel memories, and your audience will want to meet them.

When Jerry found a great lunch spot in Aix-en-Provence, he wrote about it through his own experience in interviewing the lively and lovely owner, Fanny Jehanno. He titled the piece, one of his best read, "When You Eat at Fanny's, Don't Forget to Order the Fondant au Chocolat." It began like this:

> Some French chefs study at schools like Le Cordon Bleu in Paris. For others, cooking is a family affair.
>
> Fanny Jehanno falls into this second group. She's the owner, chef, welcoming committee and, quite possibly, chief bottle washer at Fanny's Bistro Gourmand, a hole-in-the-wall-sized lunch place in this Provence city that serves up fresh, farm-grown food, warm blends of tea on cold, damp days, and some of the best chocolate fondant—Jehanno's specialty—that you'll find anywhere.
>
> I interviewed Jehanno a few weeks ago, in French, on a slow afternoon. Given the sad state of my language development, this means I understood about half of what she said during 90 minutes of conversation. But I do trust my taste buds, and I can tell you that Fanny's is a place to go with an appetite and time to spare.

As the piece continues, it talks about the food, but also shares the backstory of Jehanno:

> A fit and outdoorsy-looking former tennis teacher, with the hint of smile lines at the corners of her clear blue eyes, Jehanno grew up near Paris, cooking with her parents and grandmother. From her father, she learned to cook fresh vegetables from the garden and mushrooms that she and he would pick in the forest. From her mother, the "queen of potato salad," she says, she learned "simple but very tasty cooking." And from her grandmother, she learned how to make fondant au chocolat, a chocolate dessert that melts in your mouth. It remains her specialty to this day ("tout ma vie le fondant chocolat," she says).

Travel stories come to life when they have characters. Sometimes the main character can be the writer himself: As we've said, there's no prohibition against using the first person in blogging. Sometimes it can be a companion. Jerry often used his interactions with his wife Kathy to incorporate humor and humanity in his posts. But when possible, push yourself to interact with and learn about the people who live in the places you visit. It'll make your travels—and your blogs—that much more interesting.

Adventure Stories

The cliché has it that "misery loves company." But it also might be said that "company loves misery," at least, that is, when the "company" is your audience. Too many travel writers forget that the best stories can grow out of what goes wrong.

Life isn't a fairy tale. Neither is travel. When we, as writers and people, struggle and sometimes fail, people see something of their own lives in our hardships. This isn't voyeuristic. We've all had hardships. That's why Friedrich Nietzsche wrote, "What does not kill me makes me stronger."

Jerry's journey to France got off to an inauspicious start. A blizzard blanketed Boston with more than a foot of snow the night before he left. And though he made it to the airport in bitter-cold conditions, his jubilation soon turned to frustration as his flight was delayed three times and then canceled for mechanical difficulties.

Jerry and Kathy spent 25 hours waiting at and near Logan Airport before they finally boarded. They missed another connecting flight in London. By the time they reached their Aix-en-Provence apartment, 46 hours had passed since they'd left home.

Jerry was too exhausted to ever post to his blog about this experience (his French class started the morning after his arrival). But he did post four times to Facebook, where a growing group of friends starting commenting on his mini-drama.

By his final post, 18 people weighed in with comments after he wrote:

> Time spent sitting at Logan Airport in the last two days: 16 hours. Time spent getting from Marblehead, Mass., to London following the big snowstorm: 36 hours. Number of engineering problems on British Airways Flight 212: 3. Number of times British Airways communicated clearly with passengers: 1, when people nearly levitated after the second significant delay in two days. Number of times Massachusetts State Police were called down to the gate to make sure things stayed calm: 2.

In hindsight, Jerry is sorry he didn't post the whole thread on the blog. That's because company, it seems, truly does love misery.

Some of the best adventure travel writing can be found in the books published by *Lonely Planet*. They tell of travelers lost near war zones, turned desperately sick in strange lands, determined to test their stamina in the teeth of winter on the South American coast. They allow the reader to imagine, to worry, and to come along for the ride. So remember: bad experiences can make the best stories.

Essays on Culture and Place

At its best, writing can help us figure out what we think and why.

Yes. We know that sounds awfully self-indulgent in a book about blogging for others. But the worst mistake a blogger can make in writing about experiences in a distant or strange place is to hide emotion or reaction behind the Big Voice, to try to make sweeping and often uninformed generalizations.

Such essays read like hot air, expansive and empty. At the opposite extreme are blogs, essays, and articles so intent on being reportorial that they abandon the author's personality, an important aspect of sharing experiences others haven't had. Travel essays that find a balance between the know-it-all and the report-it-all show the humanity of the writer by sharing the surprises, discoveries, and sometimes frustrations that are part of understanding life in an unfamiliar place. They balance observation, specific example, and reflection.

To help you find this balance, we'll offer this piece of advice about writing, one easier to give than to receive: "Be yourself. Don't try to be the expert you're not."

Jerry tried his hand soon after arriving in Aix-en-Provence in an essay titled "Slow Lane Travel Starts as a State of Mind." Looking back, he realizes he was guilty of the dreaded "wind-up"—the writer, not quite in his comfort zone yet, covering up for his insecurities by saying too much. Here's how that essay began:

> In our first two weeks in France, we have never sat in a car, never taken a train, only once boarded a bus.
>
> So what gives with the name "France in the Slow Lane?"
>
> As we walk to language school each morning—dodging la crotte (dog crap); watching the high school students walk past, puffing on cigarettes and acting cool like kids everywhere; passing workers who sip espresso at stand-up, open-air bars; squeezing past umbrellas and their owners on sidewalks but a foot or two wide—I concentrate on the moment.

It was all wind-up. In retrospect, Jerry believes he should have started with his fourth and fifth paragraphs when he settles into being himself:

> I'm starting to realize that "slow lane travel" is more a state of mind than a particular mode of getting somewhere.

157

In Provence, Kathy and I are learning again how to absorb the sounds, scenes and scents of daily life, how to live as nearly as possible in the present. To me, it is as extraordinary a change in daily routine as was the moment this week when I realized I was taking notes in French for the first time.

Two points here:

- Small daily events can be the fodder of interesting travel essays.
- When we strain to convey meaning, we often unnecessarily expand space.

Redrafting helps. So does the simple act of putting your work aside before doing so. But start with this mindset: Blogging in many ways is the art of the small point. As mentioned in Chapter 4, be a miniaturist, not a muralist. When we try to make too much of a single post, it starts to crumple from all that weightiness.

Four months later, Jerry returned to the notion of the slow lane of daily life. By this time, he'd relaxed. He titled his essay "Life on the Set of Aix-en-Provence." The piece built on the metaphor of Aix-en-Provence as a movie set. Several things prompted the idea: the markets that grow and recede like some kind of organism in the squares each day, the penchant of Aixois to dress elaborately in what seem like costumes on market day, and the extraordinary experience of living someplace where most of the surroundings are hundreds of years old. With this metaphor in mind, Jerry decided to take his readers on a ground-level tour, addressing them as if they were there accompanying him. He read the piece out loud, something he always advises, to listen to how the sentences sounded.

It began like this:

For nearly five months now, we've lived on a most remarkable movie set, a place of music and laughter, outdoor life and ancient buildings, cobblestone streets and old-fashioned street lights, suspended from metal stanchions. In a dozen days, the time will come for us to move to a new set, meet a new cast . . .

First, though, walk with me one more time, and I'll show you what we've liked best about life in this city of Provence, a place first settled in 123 BC.

It's a walk we take daily, usually twice—a walk that never fails to lighten my mood, peel away worries, ease the pressures of goals unrealized and time passing too quickly. The more we walk, the more time slows down.

Come with me first to the park, a misnomer really for this 17th century mansion, Pavillon de Vendôme, built, says Aix's official city site, so that the Duke of Vendôme had a country home in which to pursue "his passionate love affair with Lucrezia de Forbin Solliès called 'Belle of Canet.'" Today, a new generation of lovers—along with guitarists, painters and dreamers—sprawls on the wooden and stone benches across the well-trimmed lawns, looking at the twin figures of Atlas, one on either side of the massive doors, watching as the facade warms from yellow to orange in the late afternoon sun.

Through another gate, past a second garden of hundreds of roses, we enter a narrow residential street.

Now the set takes on more energy as we head toward the Place de l'Hotel-de-Ville, slightly uphill, past fruit stands and wine bars, stylish women's shoe shops and dress stores, narrow iron balconies and buildings boasting faded block letters with names from another era. There's an African clothing store, its colorful costumes spilling onto the street; a children's book store where the kids come for Saturday readings; an oddly out-of-place funeral supply store on the left. We dodge cars and *crottes*—every set has its pack of dogs and Aix's leaves its fair share of droppings behind—and weave between the actors, sauntering in their seasonal best, issuing heartfelt French sighs, tugging carts for the market behind them . . .

As you travel, do write essays about what's on your mind and what you observe. But don't try to make these reflections monumental.

159

Picture Stories

People love to see a place. Chapter 7, "Beyond Words," is all about multimedia blog posts. Here, we would simply like to reiterate the centrality of images in a robust travel blog. Jerry typically posted one or two galleries of slide shows each week.

These are never merely random collections of photos. He'd often shoot 100 photos a day and use 10 percent or less of what he'd taken. These he'd arrange as a story, sometimes chronologically, sometimes geographically, but always with purpose. (His galleries included "The Signs of Provence," "Cassis: 'The Poor Man's St. Tropez'," and "Touring Lake Annecy.")

Whether told with words or photos, stories need a clear shape that the audience can follow.

The Outtakes of Daily Life

The best newsroom stories get told at the water fountain, not on the air or in the newspaper. If this is a newsroom cliché, it's a true one, and that's a shame.

The same needn't be true of travel blogging. Some exchanges aren't worth a full story. They are worth a quick post. Jerry is partial to building "bits and pieces" using several of these.

Some of his, like this one, center on miscommunication:

> I shudder to think what comes out of my mouth when I get stuck in French and revert to the lost cause of literal translation. Because as I read efforts to translate French directly into English in various pamphlets and publications, I often can't help but chuckle.
>
> These, shall we say, highly descriptive phrases about the ambiance of Provence appear in the press kit of the Tourist Office in Aix-en-Provence:
>
> "In fact pleasure is an integral part of everyday life here. Be it thru its fragrant cuisine, its regional wines which accompany it, the taste for 'good things' and wellbeing is a way of life: 'the Art of Living.' Spoiled by nature and climate, the capital of Provence could have well fallen into leniency, being not for its engrained sense of balance."
>
> Before I, too, risk "falling into leniency" as I return to my French studies, let me bring you one more excerpt from "Aix-en-Provence and the Aix Region," the Tourist Office Press kit:
>
> "The power of initiative at the service of eclectic artistic vitality has given rise to a buoyant culture life."

Little blog posts can keep readers interested. Certainly, anything that draws a smile counts.

Telling the Story

Pick the Right Medium

As we discussed in Chapter 7, "Beyond Words," picking the right blog form makes for a more interesting site. A visit to Wrigley Field in Chicago or Central Park in New York on a warm summer day would lend itself well to an audio slide show. Why? Because of the natural sounds: the crack of the bat and hot dog vendors in Wrigley, the sounds of laughter and notes of musicians in the park. These soundtracks comfortably accompany still photos.

When Jerry soared 9,000 feet from the Chamonix Valley to the foot of Mont Blanc, Europe's highest mountain, he chose a photo gallery with captions to capture the cable car's ascent, the icicles hanging in mid-summer off the mountaintop restaurant, and the panoramic view of the Alps. Video might have been even better because of the sweep of the view; Jerry took some for himself but didn't post it.

Not all posts, however, need extensive multimedia.

A blog post about a special art exhibit in the Metropolitan Museum of Art would best be accomplished with words and a few pictures. For one thing, it would need context. For another, it would demand specific information (price, times, background on how it came to be). And for a third, it seems a waste of photography to try to replicate the artwork of masters.

Block That Empty Cliché

One of our favorite books on writing is William Zinsser's *On Writing Well*. In it, he rightly pokes fun at the empty frothiness of too much travel writing. He writes:

> Nowhere else in nonfiction do writers use such syrupy words and groaning platitudes . . . Half the sights seen in a day's sightseeing are quaint, especially windmills and covered bridges; they are certified for quaintness. Towns situated in hills (or foothills) are nestled—I hardly ever read about an unnestled town in the hills . . . In Europe you awake to the clip-clop of horse-drawn wagons along a history-haunted river . . .

161

Zinsser urges writers to ban "travelese" from their vocabulary before they sit down to write. He warns:

> Travelese is . . . a style of soft words that under hard examination mean nothing, or that mean different things to different people: "attractive," "charming," "romantic" . . . One man's romantic sunrise is another man's hangover.

Pause when the words come too easily. Look for something fresher.

Say Something Specific, but Be Selective

Verbs drive sentences. Facts and selective details steer stories.

So if you want to block that cliché, replace it with something that grounds the reader in a place and gives valuable information.

Here's what Jerry had to say about France's odd mix of Bayou-like marshlands and cowboy country:

> Let's face it: The Camargue is just different from other parts of Provence, different I would guess from anyplace else in France.

This is a region, south of Arles, where one cafe we entered had a saddle mounted on a sawhorse across from the bar. It's a place where *taureau* (bull meat) is a staple on any self-respecting restaurant menu, where bullfights are advertised at the town's Tourist Office, and where honest-to-goodness cowboys, the *gardians*, ride white horses. And even all this is but one sliver of a region with exotic birds, flooded rice paddies, miles of beaches, and an annual multinational gypsy pilgrimage, culminating each May 24 with ceremonies honoring "the black Madonna."

Given that the piece was written in mid-May, it contained links to information about the gypsy pilgrimage, a good place to eat, and a modestly priced hotel. Mixing story and specific advice usually makes sense.

Be Human

On the road, the main character of a blog often becomes the writer himself. Since travel involves surprises—some pleasant, some funny, some embarrassing or uncomfortable—it helps for that traveler, that main character, to show some humility. Few readers find pleasure reading the exploits of a blowhard. Put another way, most of us like to engage in the stories of someone we might someday like to meet.

One way to be human is to poke fun at yourself when warranted. Another is to share those moments in a strange place that confound or simply make us feel uncomfortable. Jerry shared his own insecurity the first time he attempted to interview someone in French:

> As a professor, I've often witnessed the discomfort that comes with that first assigned interview. Each semester, someone from an introductory-level skills class knocks on my door and either slinks or saunters into my office to ask me questions . . .
>
> At times these first-ever interviews tickle me. They're reminders that the ability to draw information from another person is far from an innate talent.
>
> This Thursday, I'll be keenly aware of my past amusement and sometimes poorly veiled impatience. That's because I will find myself in something akin to the shoes of these first-semester journalism students. I'll be interviewing— or trying to interview—Juliette, my unusually patient young French teacher at IS-Aix, about what motivated her to become a teacher and what challenges she faces as a professor of adult learners.
>
> And, *bien sur*, I'll be doing this in French.

Travel Blogging and Ethics

Only you can decide what kind of blogger you want to be. Do you want to sell stories or products?

Journalism demands a high standard of ethics. Most large news organizations prohibit staff from accepting any gifts of significant value, any food that they can't consume at a sitting, or anything that will compromise their ability to write what they discover, without fear or favor.

Travel is expensive. The temptation to accept the free trip, free lodging, a free travel adventure is always there. If you do so, however, the not-so-subtle expectation is always there that you'll write something uncritical in return. Ask yourself: Are you willing to disclose to your readers that you've accepted that five-star hotel room for free? If not, don't accept it.

The authors of this book were print journalists for many years before we became bloggers. So we strongly recommend that you follow the story and decline the freebies, known as swag. A good blogger—one who files useful information—can't be any more beholden to his subject than a good journalist. That said, too much purity, particularly in a culture in which it might be considered insulting to turn down someone's offer of a glass of wine, can create its own poison. Jerry grappled with this several times in his travels. His rule of thumb was a bit more fluid than it is in the States, where, as a matter of practice, he never accepts anything.

When the owner of an Ardeche wool mill took him for lunch at the firm's new restaurant, Jerry offered to pay, graciously said thanks when the owner declined, and then bought several books at the firm's new bookstore. When the owner of a small bistro in France gave him a taste of her chocolate dessert after an interview, he tried to pay but didn't turn it down when she said no. (He might in either case have sent a check after the fact, but chose not to because it would have been considered rude.)

Jerry teaches journalism ethics at his college, and he's a believer that the reporter always has to work through the individual situation. It's always possible to say "no," but if the gift is small, genuine, and consumable, it sometimes can be a cultural mistake. Just remember: If you feel bought, you are.

Don't ever ask for a free meal or gift. But keep an eye out for cultural cues in deciding how to respond to a modest act of kindness.

163

DISCUSSION

Travel is expensive. Debate with your classmates whether and, if so, when travel bloggers should be allowed to write about things without paying for them. In considering your arguments, put yourself in your audience's shoes. Would you trust someone who wrote about a resort, for example, where the writer was staying for free? Why or why not?

EXERCISES

1. Find a blog topic that in some way builds off the neighborhood in which you live. First, research whom else blogs in the neighborhood and find out what the niche of these bloggers is. Then put yourself in the place of a visitor arriving there for the first time. What would you want to know? What's missing from the ground covered by other bloggers? Draw up a list of three possible blog topics and pitch them to your classmates, providing an initial list of blog topics and a rationale for writing the blog.

2. Travel writers must be keen observers of scene and selective in the details they choose to describe it. This assignment is designed to sharpen your skills of passive observation. Go to an active place in your community, choose an unobtrusive place to sit or stand, and watch for awhile. It might be a bus station or food court, a schoolyard playground or neighborhood basketball court, a Saturday market or a street concert. Your task is to be on the lookout for a small scene or exchange that you can describe in 150–200 words.

   The rules are strict:

   1. You may not identify yourself or ask any questions.
   2. You should use all your senses: what you see, hear, smell, even touch.
   3. Write not what you assume, but what you observe. A man with a child on his shoulders might be a father, but it also might be an uncle or friend. So don't assume the relationship between child and adult.

4. Look for a passage of time—it might be no more than a minute or two—in which something happens that has a beginning, middle, and end. An international customer trying to order the right coffee at Starbucks is a scene. So is an argument between biker and driver at a stoplight. Scenes are all around us.

5. Listen for dialogue, exchanges that take the reader to the scene.

6. Look for telling details. Does that Starbucks customer have a tat with a word in another language?

7. In writing your passive observation, be sure to tell where the scene is unfolding. Location matters.

8. Try to give your little "story," or blog, a beginning, middle, and end.

Blogging about Politics and Journalism

Everyone has an opinion about government and journalism. But that doesn't mean anyone can write an intelligent and effective blog on these topics. The blogger might start by asking: What can I add to the conversation? How can I be a voice and not an echo?

167

It's a question more easily asked than answered. This is a crowded blogging environment; there's lots of competition. So, in truth, most blogs on these topics echo rather than reverberate with insight. Bloggers who live in the ring of politics and journalism—and these are raucous worlds—can build their audience by reading a wide variety of news sources and blogs that span the political spectrum. They can gain credibility by making clear to readers where they got their facts. And they can carve out a niche for themselves by finding a place to stand, developing a fresh take or under-covered angle in these much-covered realms of news and opinion, making strong, logical arguments supported by facts.

Blogging about Politics

Read a Lot and Mix up Your Reading

You can't comment on politics if you don't know what's going on. Start by building a list of news websites you'll visit at least once a day. That list will depend upon where you live, of course, but we recommend that it include some of the largest and most visited sites around the world: *BBC News*, *CNN*, the *New York Times*, *Reuters*, *Bloomberg*, the *Guardian*, the *Washington Post*, and perhaps *China Daily* for a start. It should include some less widely followed but well-respected sites such as *Vox*, *Slate*, *Vice*, the *Christian Science Monitor*, and *Politico*. You should also monitor online video sites watched by news junkies on the right and left. These range from the TV websites of foxnews.com (right) to democracynow.org (left), and the magazine websites of *The National Review* (right) to *The Nation* (left).

If you're monitoring the news media themselves, follow specialized media criticism such as NPR's *On the Media*, the Poynter Institute's website poynter.org, and mediagazer.com.

Finally, you can also check in regularly with what are known as "news aggregators." These sites don't produce news stories, but instead gather the most popular articles from thousands of newspapers around the world and present the top stories on one page. The two best are *Google News* and *Yahoo! News*.

There are ways to organize these reading habits to make them easier. If you're working on a desktop computer, for example, create a folder full of bookmarks for your go-to websites. When you sit down to read the day's news, you can open all of them at once by using browser tabs. (In Chrome, go to the "Bookmarks" menu, scroll down to the folder, and choose "Open All Bookmarks" from the drop-down menu; do the same in Safari, except choose "Open in Tabs" from the drop-down menu.) Or, as we discussed in Chapter 3, "Getting Started," you can use an RSS reader.

If you have a tablet or a smartphone, there are several useful free apps with simple customization features you can use to follow news websites, including Flipboard, Pulse, Zite, Feedly, and News360.

Choose a Place to Stand on the Political Spectrum

When Skip Murphy and a friend decided to start a blog in 2006, they already knew where they stood on the political spectrum: they were conservatives who supported the New Hampshire Republican platform. These core political beliefs still guide their blog posts.

The two named their blog *GraniteGrok*—New Hampshire's nickname is "The Granite State," and the slang word "grok" means to understand something so well that you are a part of it. "Our concentration is New Hampshire, a small state where one person *can* make a difference and retail politics still holds sway," Murphy says. "I literally can walk down the street to yell at my state representative, and my state senator (a Democrat) is just a town over."

Writing from their political "core foundation," he says, "has earned us the trust and confidence of our target audience." The readers who know where they stand on the New Hampshire political spectrum seek out *GraniteGrok* because they stand in the same place. Political bloggers attract an audience by staking out and maintaining a clear political perspective.

DAVID GOLDSTEIN

"Write fearlessly"

David "Goldy" Goldstein of Seattle, Washington, is the founder and chief blogger at the *Horse's Ass* political blog. Goldstein has worked as a staff writer at *The Stranger*, an alternative weekly newspaper in Seattle, and hosted "The David Goldstein Show" on Seattle's news/talk station 710-KIRO from 2006 through 2008.

David "Goldy" Goldstein

Why did you start your blog? When did you start it? How long did it take to build an audience?
I transformed *Horse's Ass* into a blog in May of 2004. Readership took off in November 2004, during the recount and legal battles over Washington state's incredibly close 2004 gubernatorial election. It gradually built over the next few years, peaking at about 5,000 visitors a day during the 2008 election.

How do you come up with ideas for blog post topics? What news sources, blogs, and other sources of information do you regularly read?
I mostly focus on Washington state and local politics, with an emphasis on media criticism, so my primary muse is our local media. Additionally, I tend to follow national news media and national blogs. That said, because I have proven to be such an effective muckraker over the years, some of my best stories come to me in the form of tips. Blogging at its best comes from seeing the real story in the same news that everybody else is reporting. It is a form of conceptual journalism.

How frequently do you post to your blog (in an average week) and how many hours each week do you spend working on your blog?

When I was blogging full time, I posted three to five times every week day, depending on the length of the pieces I was working on, at least once a day on weekends. And it was a full-time job. I probably spent 50 to 60 hours a week writing. Frequency is absolutely crucial to building and maintaining an audience. If you don't have a fresh content, readers do not come back.

With so many political blogs out there, how have you made yours different and unique?

You need to build a personal relationship with your readers. This is a first-person medium—I read the news, pick out the important stories, focus on the best (or worst) reporting, blockquote out the significant sections, and then attempt to put it all in context. Readers come to me because they trust me to do all this work for them. Lacking a newspaper banner to automatically grant us credibility, successful bloggers must build and maintain that trust.

As for *Horse's Ass*, part of our success is just damn good writing. I'm a writer first. I care about words. And that comes through. Also, I provide an aggressive style and attitude that readers quietly crave out here in passive-aggressive Seattle. I say the things a lot of respectable people wish they could say. And so that makes me fun to read whether you love me or hate me.

What advice would you offer young people who are just thinking about starting their own political blogs?

1. Above all, write for yourself. Write the kind of blog that you want to read. Chances are you'll never find much of an audience; most blogs don't. So if you write for yourself, at least you'll be happy with the result. But if you try to write what you think people may want to read, chances are it will suck, and then you still won't find an audience, but now even you won't be happy with your work.
2. To heck with objectivity. Wear your bias on your sleeve and trust people to be smart enough to read you in that context. It's more honest. And it is incredibly freeing. If you don't have an opinion, you've got nothing to say, and if you do have an opinion but don't share it, that is a lie of omission.
3. Never lie and always correct your errors.
4. Choose your enemies. The best way to build your readership and credibility is to get into a pissing match with somebody who has much more readership and/or credibility. And never go after the weak and the powerless—that includes the underage children of the powerful. Children are off limits.

5. Don't bother blogging unless you are willing to devote the time and energy necessary to blog successfully.

6. Write fearlessly. I've always been enamored of Gustave Flaubert's advice to a young writer: "Be regular and orderly in your life like a bourgeois, so that you may be violent and original in your work."

The best-informed political blog readers, of course, will seek out competing perspectives. Though most readers in today's politically polarized world seek confirmation of their own views, here's an example of what can be learned by looking a little further.

When the U.S. company Burger King bought the Canadian company Tim Hortons, Burger King executives announced plans to move the company's headquarters to Canada, thus paying the lower Canadian corporate tax rate. *The Federalist*, a right-wing blog, and *Daily Kos*, a left-wing blog, offered two very different takes on the news.

Conservative blogger David Harsanyi at *The Federalist* wrote:

171

> Burger King plans to merge with Canuck coffee-and-doughnut chain Tim Hortons and base the company's headquarters in Canada, where it will enjoy the kind of reasonable corporate tax structure that Democrats continue to obstruct here in the United States. And the move has provoked a fresh round of moral panic, faux patriotism and confusion.
>
> It's doubtful there will be much of a real backlash despite much wishful thinking. Most obviously, the majority of fast food customers are probably less inclined than the editors of the New Republic or the petitioners of MoveOn.org to mistake high tax rates with patriotism. This kind of distorted understanding of national loyalty may work in populist politics, but not so much in markets. Few reasonable humans will meditate on Burger King's corporate tax "inversion" or its fiduciary duty to stockholders—or even its Brazilian owners—as they wait for the frozen French Fries to be dropped into the deep fryer.
>
> Nor should they. The four best-selling cars in America so far in 2014 are the Toyota Camry, Nissan Altima, Honda Accord and Toyota Corolla. One of the best-selling cell phone brands is South Korean. And so on. Does a Whopper taste like a Whopper? That's all that matters. And it's all that should. Nothing really changes for the consumer.

The next day, partly in response to Harsanyi, liberal blogger Jon Perr of *Daily Kos* made it no less clear where *he* stood:

> The merger of Miami-based Burger King and Tim Horton's of Canada is adding fuel to the raging debate about the so-called "tax inversion." While Jordan Weissman questions Burger King's denial that the decision to base the new fast food giant in Canada was motivated by a desire to lower its corporate tax bill, Megan McArdle and David Harsanyi argue BK's royal decree is just common sense.
>
> But lost in the debate about the degree to which Burger King will screw American taxpayers is the inescapable fact that it already has. Thanks to a different gaming of the tax code that can rightly be called the "Romney perversion," Burger King's private equity owners already redirected millions of dollars from the U.S. Treasury to line their own pockets. And among those who padded their own bank accounts at taxpayer expense was Mitt Romney himself.

Harsanyi and Perr's references may be obscure to the casual reader—such is the world of political blogging. But their positions on the issue couldn't be more clear. They've taken a stand.

Show Your Readers Where Your Facts Came From

172

In Michigan, one of the 10 most populous states in the United States, the website michiganliberal.com, serves as a blog "hub"—a place to which many bloggers contribute—to present "commentary and information from a vaguely leftish point of view."

A post about the City of Detroit's controversial plan to shut off the water to thousands of homeowners who had not paid their water bills talked about two mainstream media reactions to the news. The post attacked a *Detroit News* columnist and praised a columnist for the *Detroit Free Press*. (Just so you know before you read the example below: michiganliberal.com refers to *Detroit News* columnist Frank Beckmann as "Fried Chicken Frank" because of a column Beckmann once wrote, seen by many as offensive, that used the stereotype of African Americans' supposed love of fried chicken.)

> Fried Chicken Frank's column this morning on the Detroit water shutoffs was the awfulest thing written about it yet. It's about how the real victim in the shutoffs are suburbanites and if you had any lingering doubts that Fried Chicken Frank is something of a racist this should erase them. We can debate the merits of whether the water department should just be up and shutting off people's water, especially since there are apparently two different policies regarding residential water and water for businesses, but attacking a bankruptcy judge because he didn't take the time to listen to suburbanite whining is the very essence of white privilege.

The underlined words in that paragraph link to the "Fried Chicken Frank" (Frank Beckmann) column the blogger finds not just awful, but "awfulest." The blogger continues:

> I would advise skipping the column. It adds nothing of value to this issue and will only make you think about those two minutes you'll never get back, plus the one minute thinking about those two minutes.
>
> Go instead and read <u>Nancy Kaffer's column</u> [in the Detroit Free Press], which unlike both the columns written by Nolan Finley and Fried Chicken Frank, appears to have involved research and thought.

The underlined words in this paragraph link to the Kaffer column the blogger admires. (There is no link to Nolan Finley column.)

Just as reporters use attribution (". . . according to Police Chief John Smith") to tell readers the source of a piece of information, bloggers identify the source of information by linking to that source, so readers can examine it for themselves.

Linking to a source becomes even more important when you are blogging about *facts* rather than opinions. Murphy of GraniteGrok wrote an outraged blog post about a New Hampshire school committee that limited public comment at its meeting. He wrote a second blog post on the topic when he read that another town's school committee had taken a similar action.

173

> I wrote about the Gilford School Board's brazen decision to limit the First Amendment Right of Gilford parents <u>(here)</u> . . . I also told them, face to face, they were holding themselves unaccountable by NOT answering questions posed to them during public hearings.
>
> I thought it was an isolated event with one school board, but <u>then I saw this</u> on the Cornish School Board.

Murphy links in his first paragraph to a previous post on the GraniteGrok blog to help the reader understand the background. Then he links to the news story in a local paper that served as the basis for this second blog post.

Later in the second post, he links to a *primary* source: the website of the New Hampshire School Boards Association. When a political blogger links to a primary source, it allows readers to see for themselves what a document contains rather than just a report by a media outlet (which may or may not be reliable). It also demonstrates to the reader that the blogger has done independent reporting.

Political bloggers can find mountains of primary source material available on the Internet—texts of politicians' speeches, pieces of legislation, court decisions, and almost unlimited data gathered by government agencies. This serves readers by allowing them to see firsthand the actions and decisions of political leaders and politicians whose actions are the fodder of bloggers. It also allows bloggers to contribute as reporters by giving context that the secondary sources to which they link, such as news stories, have not included.

Take, for example, a blogger writing a post about unemployment rate data released by the government. The blogger could link readers to a short news story or a blog post about the unemployment data. But it would be more useful to the reader to link to the full report of the data that the government will have posted on the Internet.

The lesson, then, is not only to link, but to link to primary sources whenever possible. Most bloggers don't do that.

Build a Single, Strong Argument

If you are going to write a blog post blaming the government for the high unemployment rate, don't wander off halfway through to talk about war in the Middle East or how someone stole the last election. Save those topics for other posts.

Here is the roadmap for building a powerful, focused political argument:

- **Research your topic and take notes**. Facts always build arguments, especially when you're writing about politics. Open up a blank word processing document on your computer when you start your research and name it "Notes." When you find a fact to support your argument, copy and paste it into your "Notes" document—copy the Web address, too, so you can link to the page in your post. You may also want to copy a few direct quotes from your sources. Make sure you put these in quotation marks and attribute them. Using the exact words of others without quotation marks is plagiarism. So is stealing their information without attribution.
- **State the main point of your argument at the start of the post**. Most inexperienced writers start a piece of writing with platitudes and generalities—throat-clearing, basically—before they get to what they really have to say. The reader isn't interested in all that phlegm. Go straight to the point.

A post on the conservative blog *PowerLine* begins with a forceful perspective:

> Doran Ben-Atar, a professor of history at Fordham University, is an outspoken opponent of calls by the American Studies Association for a boycott of Israel's academic institutions. And wisely so. The boycott is an affront to the free exchange of ideas that should be at the heart of the academic mission.

That last sentence makes it quite clear where the author stands. But another post on the same blog, headlined "Alex Mooney's opponent makes desperate Holocaust reference," begins with the writer rambling:

> My friend Alex Mooney is running for Congress in West Virginia's second congressional district. He is one of our PowerLine Picks. I wrote about Alex here and here, among other places.
>
> Alex's opponent is Nick Casey, a lawyer/lobbyist. Alex has consistently led Casey in the polls. However, the race has tightened. In fact, Real Clear Politics has moved it from "leans GOP" to "toss up."
>
> Casey is a liberal Democrat and, as such, well out-of-step with West Virginia. For example, in responding to the National Right to Life Committee questionnaire earlier this year, Casey replied that he would not vote to protect pain-capable unborn children.

175

The reader has to plow through the writer's talk about his friend and how he has written about him before, and who his friend's opponent is, and what the polls are saying, and how Casey is "out-of-step," until, *in the eighth paragraph*, the writer finally gets to the point: Casey calls his opponent's characterization of his position on abortion "a lie," and adds, "It's like they said I was at Auschwitz. It isn't true." The writer of the blog, it turns out, finds this reference offensive. His offense is not noted until two-thirds of the way through the post.

- **Use the facts you gathered to back up your point**. Go through your notes and make a quick outline—nothing too elaborate—of the facts that you want to use in the order that you want to use them. This will help you think about how to build your argument most effectively.
- **Anticipate the arguments against your position**. All political positions have at least two sides. Often, they have more. Thinking about what other bloggers may write, or reading what they already

have written, will allow you to make a stronger case for your own position.

- **End with a suggestion of how to fix the problem.** You don't have to come up with a solution yourself. Odds are, a politician with whom you agree already has done so. By all means use it. Readers want to leave a blog post with not only a new understanding of the problem, but with some ideas about how it can be solved. Ending a post with a call for action helps readers engage. For example, a September 2014 post by the *Economic Intelligence* blogger Chad Stone on the website of usnews.com ended by recommending actions the U.S. government should take to decrease the number of people living in poverty. "Policymakers should have expanded the Earned Income Tax Credit for childless adults long ago," he writes, referring to a tax break for low-income workers. "States that have not yet adopted the Medicaid expansions should take a hard look at the costs of their decision."

Be a Voice, Not an Echo

176

Since the advent of political blogs more than a decade ago, the political blogosphere has been criticized by some scholars and commentators as relentlessly partisan. Conservative bloggers only read and link to other conservative bloggers, they say, and liberal bloggers do the same with liberals. Cass Sunstein, in his book *Republic 2.0*, called this "the echo chamber effect."

With hundreds of thousands of political blogs out there, one way to be distinctive today is to serve as a marketplace of conflicting ideas, to take a clear, intelligent position while at the same time linking to and taking on the opinions of those with contrary views.

Blogging about Media

In democracies, a free press serves as a watchdog of those in power. But, as the Roman poet Juvenal wrote, *Quis custodiet ipsos custodes?* Who will watch the watchers? Thoughtful (and sometimes contentious) media criticism has exploded since the creation of the World Wide Web, with bloggers leading the way.

Before the Web, only a few magazine and alternative weekly newspaper writers regularly published criticism that evaluated, judged, and put into context the day's journalism. Now, anyone with Internet access can read and watch an almost limitless number of news sources from around the world and write a media criticism blog.

A few bloggers for traditional news outlets, such as Jack Shafer at Reuters and Erik Wemple at washingtonpost.com, cover media from coast to coast. So do a few outside the mainstream media, most notably Jim Romenesko at jimromenesko.com. But there are hundreds of good media critics who take a narrower focus. Most center their work on the journalism of one city or region. When Mark wrote a media criticism blog for the website of *The Boston Globe*, for example, at the top of every post appeared this line: "Mark Leccese watches Boston and the people who report on it."

Once again, it starts with a little homework.

Closely Follow the Media Outlets in Your Niche

This should go without saying. If you're going to present yourself to the world as a media critic, you need to keep up with the news and opinions being produced in your geographic or topical niche. When the editors of *The Boston Globe* asked Mark to write a media criticism blog for the *Globe*'s website, he already subscribed to four print newspapers (the two Boston dailies—the *Globe* and the *Herald*—along with the *New York Times* and the *Wall Street Journal*). He also listened to all-news radio on AM in the morning and NPR on FM in the afternoon, watched at least two nightly newscasts (local and national), and checked in on various news websites and blogs over the course of the day.

If that sounds like a big time commitment, it is. It's not that Mark did nothing but follow the news all day. He didn't, because he had classes to teach and meetings to attend and deadlines to meet. Most of Mark's news consumption came first thing in the morning, before going to the office, and in the evenings, when he had some time to catch up on the day's events. But Mark always had opportunities throughout his work day to keep tabs on the news: listening to news stations on the car radio, checking the Web in free moments, and reading news and blogs on the mobile phone while eating lunch.

Mark's news consumption habit solidified into routine during his 30 years in the news business, but anyone can pick up the habit. It takes a little work, but following the local news will not only keep you informed enough to write about media intelligently. It's where you'll get most of your ideas.

As you read and watch, think critically—and by critically, we don't mean disapprovingly, we mean analytically. Study how the stories were put together: who was interviewed, what documents were cited, what gets emphasized in the story (and what doesn't). Look, too, for gaps in coverage and errors in coverage. Think about what kinds of stories are overemphasized and which are barely covered or simply missed.

Reading the two Boston daily newspapers over breakfast one morning, Mark noticed the papers emphasized very different aspects of a story about the Provincetown, Massachusetts school committee voting to make condoms available to students in its elementary schools and high schools. He knew he had the makings of a blog post.

Rather than describe the two stories to his readers, Mark showed them, quoting the first two paragraphs of each story so the readers could see for themselves the difference in emphasis.

The *Herald* story began like this:

> A new policy in Provincetown to make condoms available even to first-graders is being called "absurd" and a frantic overreaction to sex education.
>
> "What next? Birth control pills?" asked Kris Mineau, head of the conservative group Massachusetts Family Institute.

But the *Globe* story began like this:

> Students in Provincetown—from elementary schools to high school—will be able to get free condoms at school under a recently approved policy that takes effect this fall. The rules also require school officials to keep kids' requests secret, and ignore parents' objections.
>
> "The intent is to protect kids," said School Superintendent Beth Singer, who wrote the policy that the Cape Cid town's School Committee unanimously passed two weeks ago. "We know that sexual experimentation is not limited to an age, so how does one put an age on it?"

Mark then told his readers that the 12-paragraph *Herald* story devoted six paragraphs to sources in favor of the policy, three paragraphs to sources against, and three paragraphs of neutral information. The *Globe* story had three sources who spoke in favor of the policy and three against.

To Mark, the *Herald* story was clearly biased. He noted while the *Herald* had only three paragraphs "devoted to a hostile opponent, *those are the first three paragraphs of the story*, and that makes the emphasis of the story clearly hostile to the Provincetown policy."

Analytical thinking needn't always lead to earnest writing. During his years as the media criticism blogger for the *Boston Globe*, Mark tried to have a little fun, for himself and his audience, whenever possible.

Boston winters are long, cold, and snowy, and Mark, as a lifelong Bostonian who always pays careful attention to the TV meteorologists' forecasts, decided to take a look at who was the most accurate. For one predicted snowstorm, he set up a contest. Using his DVR to tape all five local newscasts, he recorded each meteorologist's prediction 24 hours before the storm was due to hit. He didn't tell his readers about the contest before the snowstorm, but, after the storm, he described setting up the contest in the present tense to give his writing more immediacy:

> The meteorologist who comes closest to predicting the total snowfall in Boston, as reported by the National Weather Service, will be declared the winner.
>
> I know, I know—New England snow storms are unpredictable and forecasting snowfall totals 24 hours before the first flake is complicated business. "The storm is still 24 hours away," WBZ-TV meteorologist Todd Guttner said at 5:30 Tuesday evening. "Things could shift around."
>
> But, hey, why not judge the weatherman on a tough forecast? We're trying to rate meteorological chops here.

179

Once he had dug out from the storm, Mark checked the National Weather Service's snowfall totals for Boston, switched to the past tense, and ranked the competition:

> The winner: Matt Noyes of New England Cable News. He predicted exactly 12 inches and, by golly, we got 12 inches.
>
> The runners-up: Pete Bouchard of Channel 7 (prediction: 9 to 12 inches) and Harvard Leonard of Channel 5 (prediction: 6 to 12 inches), on the ground of imprecision.
>
> The loser: The Brookline Department of Public Works, which issued this statement Tuesday night: "Brookline DPW expects 2 to 4 inches of snow and does not plan to declare a snow emergency."

It wasn't a tough post to research: as mentioned, watching TV news is part of Mark's daily routine. The writing, too, practically took care of itself. What counted here was the idea. It had a natural audience. We all know everyone talks about the weather. This time around, contrary to a lament oft misattributed to Mark Twain, Mark Leccese did something about it.

Keep Up with Other Media News Bloggers and Critics, on the Web and Twitter

For all those media bloggers out there, only a handful report on the media daily. Following their posts can tell you what issues are drawing attention. It can also help you hone your own skills by dissecting how these sites cover the issues. And if you're really paying attention, you'll see what angles they've missed. Here are some bloggers worth watching each day:

- jimromenesko.com. His was the first—and is still the best—of the media news and gossip blogs. In fact, when Romenesko started the blog in the 1990s, it was called "mediagossip.com." It's still something of the Bible of blogs for those who work in the news industry.
- *Poynter MediaWire*: www.poynter.org/category/latest-news/media wire/. Poynter's website also maintains a blog written by various authors on media news.
- mediagazer.com. This website publishes media news and media criticism from a wide variety of sources and is updated throughout the day.
- *Columbia Journalism Review*'s *The Kicker*: www.cjr.org/the_kicker/. A blog by various authors of media news, commentary, and media "must-reads," compiled by the venerable *Columbia Journalism Review* magazine.

Be Tough but Fair

Call 'em as you see 'em. No one wants to read a tentative, indecisive piece of analysis. A good piece of media criticism states an opinion and backs it up with facts and examples.

Journalism is a high-pressure business with inviolable deadlines; the goal of journalism isn't to produce the best story possible, it is to produce the best story possible *by deadline*. Reporters, copyeditors, and the top editors at any news organization must make hundreds of quick decisions each day, and some of them may be wrong. Or at least open to question.

That's where bloggers come in. A good media critic focuses on the story or stories journalists produce, not on the journalists themselves (with the exception of egregious ethical choices). *Ad hominem* attacks are always unfair. Sharp, reasoned criticism of the decisions made by reporters and editors in putting together a story, or choosing what to emphasize in a story, is not unfair.

Mark had an agreement with the *Globe*'s editor that he could write critically about the *Globe* on its own website as long as he didn't take any "cheap shots." (Mark also declined to be paid for his blog, because he believed accepting money from the *Globe* would create an inherent conflict of interest.)

When the *Globe* published a story about the Archdiocese of Boston reportedly blocking a local blog, critical of the archdiocese, from gaining access on its office computers, Mark found the story unfair and unbalanced—and said so:

181

> This morning's lead story on the Globe's Metro Page, "Archdiocese limits access to critics' blogs," is 25 paragraphs long—and only five of those paragraphs present the archdiocese's perspective.
>
> Fifteen of the paragraphs present the perspective of the bloggers. Three paragraphs provide background information. The final two paragraphs quote a third-party expert in support of the bloggers.
>
> Counting the number of paragraphs in a story that gives the perspective of each side isn't the only way to assess whether a news story is balanced, but when one side gets three times the space the other side gets, the evidence for an unbalanced story seems pretty solid.

The blog avoided "cheap shots" by using a fact-based analysis as the basis of a tough critique.

By being tough but fair, the media blogger establishes his or her credibility with journalists and readers alike. Strong opinions based on facts and factual analysis can provide a formula for success.

Don't Expect to Make Friends

Journalists, like everyone else, don't much like to read what others write about their work or their organizations. They can be thin-skinned. Media bloggers can't afford to be anything but thick-skinned.

Mark wrote a blog post about the "sad, inevitable" decline of alternative weekly newspapers, including his city's local alternative weekly, the *Boston Phoenix*. The post was quoted by a writer at salon.com in a post on the same topic, which in turn provoked the editor of the *Phoenix*, in his own blog, to express his displeasure:

> Another sidenote about Salon's sloppy aggregating: they quote a blog post by someone named Mark Lecese [*yes, he spelled it wrong*] and imply that this person is a media writer for The Globe. By which they mean the opposite: the blog post they quote contains a disclaimer that says, unequivocally, "This blog is not written or edited by Boston.com or *The Boston Globe*." From what I can surmise, then, Lecese is some sort of sad, failed journalist who can't land a paying gig, isn't smart enough to figure out Tumblr, and therefore has to settle for the community blogs on Boston.com. Dear *Salon*: If that's the guy you found to proclaim that the *Phoenix* is "stodgy," please kill yourself.

Not only won't media bloggers make friends, media bloggers—and political bloggers—will almost certainly at some point be personally attacked, called names, and have their intelligence called into question and their motives challenged.

This was not the only time Mark faced a sticky situation in writing about the news media.

In late 2012, Mark wrote a post about *The Boston Globe*'s handling of a case of plagiarism—an editorial writer had substantially plagiarized from an opinion piece at another Boston news website.

In the first half of the blog post, he used blockquotes to quote passages from the original opinion piece. He followed these quotes with passages from the offending editorial so that readers could see the similarities for themselves—and decide for themselves whether this was a case of plagiarism.

Boston is not a large city, and professional and personal connections among people who work in Boston media are frequent. Many people who worked in Boston media, and who knew the plagiarist personally, insisted this was not a case of plagiarism, but of carelessness.

Mark strongly disagreed. He considered it a clear-cut case of plagiarism and began to draft a blog post, a decision a couple of good friends encouraged him to rethink. It was an uncomfortable place to be.

But he wrote the post anyway. Why? It was an important story. And his "beat" was Boston news media.

Nor did he mince words:

> Plagiarism in an editorial is even more damaging to the integrity of a news organization than plagiarism by a reporter or a columnist because the editorials are the voice of the institution. It is as if the institution had committed plagiarism, and that is why I believe *The Globe* should have taken responsibility more clearly for presenting as the opinion of the institution the work of another writer.

The *Globe*, in an Editor's Note, had said the editorial bore "some similarities in phrasing and structure" to an opinion column published by the website of the local NRP affiliate, wbur.org, and called that "inconsistent with Globe policies." The writer who had plagiarized—who is also a columnist for the paper—was suspended for two weeks and then returned to writing a column.

As the controversy brewed, a panel of veteran journalists—including a good friend of Mark's—appeared on the local TV talk show *Greater Boston* and argued the *Globe* writer did not plagiarize, but only used another writer's work "as notes" and made "stupid careless mistakes."

Mark's blog spoke to the editorial, the paper's reaction, and the defense mounted by the offender's friends:

> When a major news organization issues only a trivial sanction against the offender, and when prominent journalists excuse away the act as mere sloppiness or carelessness, accepted standards of journalism suffer where it matters most—in the eyes of the public.

Writing about the news media's actions—and failings—demands exceptionally high ethical standards. Many media critics, like Mark, first spend years working in the media. That's not a prerequisite. But anyone who starts writing a media criticism blog because he or she wants to get even or wants to take on acquaintances and former coworkers shouldn't be writing a media blog—unethical motives lead to unethical writing. On the other hand, media bloggers who are fair and honest and aren't afraid to tick off people they know are widely respected and widely read.

183

DISCUSSION

1. Discuss what websites or blogs you visit regularly with classmates. Be honest: the point of this discussion is to discover the range of reading habits in a class and how these reading habits affect ideas for blog posts.

2. Discuss the pluses and minuses of having news media experience before working as a blogger specializing in media criticism.

3. Discuss whether you are more likely to read a blog about local politics or national politics. Consider why.

EXERCISES

1. Select a news story in the last few weeks that has elicited significant coverage either locally, nationally, or internationally. Review the coverage in multiple outlets and across different media. Write focus statements of two or three sentences (see Chapter 11, "I'll Be Your Guide: Advice and Review Blogs") to pitch at least two blog ideas on the coverage.

2. Watch a political debate or a speech by a major political figure in your city or state. Write a 500-word blog that gives insight into the event you choose by placing what was said in the context of the politician's past comments. This will require significant background work. What insight can you provide about the politician's inconsistency or consistency by reviewing past statements?

I'll Be Your Guide

Advice and Review Blogs

Everyone likes telling other people what to do and what to think.

No, that's too cynical. Let's try again.

Everyone likes to share with other people lessons they've learned, knowledge they've gathered, and their opinions about the music, books, movies, and other arts that have brought pleasure to their lives.

We've all hunted the Internet for advice, whether it is "how to" guidance or general advice on something we want to know more about: paying for a college education, for example, or dressing well on a budget. And we've all gone to our favorite websites and blogs to get a different kind of advice about movies, music, dance, and other arts interests. We seek out reviewers we respect to see what they are saying, and whether they think buying a ticket or paying for a download is worth the money.

Keep in mind that on the World Wide Web, every consumer can also be a producer. You needn't be just a reader of advice and reviews. You can offer your own. Giving advice, whether about what community theater to attend or how to find discount coupons for shopping, is one more way to build a community of readers. You may not think of yourself as an expert or critic, but odds are you know more about something than others—and probably more about several somethings.

If you've spent countless hours going to clubs and bars to listen to live music, and you've thought about what you listen to, then you're an expert on the local music scene. Your experience gives you the knowledge to blog about the latest indie band, particularly if that's your genre. The stronger your passion, the tighter your niche, the more successful your efforts are likely to be.

If you've always had a dog as a pet and you love dogs, you're something of an expert on dogs.

But if your dogs always have been golden retrievers, a breed whose eccentricities range from eating anything in sight to swimming for hours in circles with a log or ball firmly wedged in one cheek, you'll write an even more interesting blog about that breed. Why not write a blog that offers advice to owners and would-be owners of golden retrievers? It can be funny and practical: how to keep your puppy from chewing the kitchen wallboard, for example, is pretty important advice.

188

Writing an Advice Blog

Even though you'll be writing from experience, advice blogs should bring in facts and evidence that builds your expertise. After all, readers will always ask: How do I know your advice will work?

Here are a few guidelines:

Incorporate the Advice of Other Experts and (Once Again) Link Like Crazy

You're not the only expert in your subject area on this big round earth, and you are not the only expert in your subject area on the Internet. It helps to cite—and link to—advice offered by others. This not only helps your readers, but benefits you: It makes other bloggers in your subject area aware of your blog. If other bloggers know you, they may link to you, and, as mentioned earlier in the book, that's an effective way to build an audience. If you *disagree* with other experts you nonetheless respect, link to them as well and then explain why you're challenging their advice. This can lead to a lively discussion.

Don't Be Afraid to Offer an Opinion

This is your show. Don't be wishy-washy or offer two-handed advice ("on the one hand . . . but on the other hand"). Melinda F. Emerson of Pennsylvania is known as the "SmallBizLady" online and writes a useful blog about starting and running a small business at her website succeedasyourownboss.com. Her advice is succinct and confident. "I've been in business more than 15 years," she says, "so I know what the issues are when you are running a small business." That's confidence.

Mix Advice and Demonstration

Don't just tell people what to do; show them. This is an area in which multimedia elements can make your blog so much better. Use photos. Use videos. Use charts or graphics. If you're writing a baking blog, for example, and you've written a post about how to make chocolate chip cookies, don't just write out the recipe. Take your own photos as you make the cookies and include them in your blog. Break out a simplified step-by-step sidebar of measured ingredients. It always helps readers seeking advice to not only be told how to do something, but to *see* how it's done.

Remember the "Three S Rule"

Good advice comes with a caveat we call the "Rule of Three S's." Keep your writing succinct, simple, and sincere. If you find you've written a draft of an article that's long and wordy and incorporates three different pieces of advice, break it into three blog posts (and edit for wordiness). Each post should have a narrow and specific focus.

Consider these excerpts from two posts about looking for a job. The first is by a "career transition coach." Do you think she follows the Three S's Rule?

> Transformation seems to be the word of the year. Everything is transforming, everybody is transforming. It used to be good enough to change, but not anymore. You've got to transform.
>
> The two words are often used interchangeably and they are certainly related; yet they are quite different. In fact, on the outside, depending on what it is, transformation and change may look exactly alike. The real difference between the two lies on the inside.

What do you think? Our guess is that your answer is something like, "huh?" The first paragraph here uses "transform" four times and insists transformation is different from change. It doesn't say how, though. The second paragraph tries to explain that difference—and fails utterly.

You needn't be a virtuoso of words to be clear. This excerpt from a company advice blog gets to the point. Want your resume read? Here's how:

> Think about how your resume looks to the busy hiring manager who's reading it for the first time. Here at Integrity Staffing Solutions, we often receive hundreds of resumes in a week, or even a day, so we must be able to scan them quickly to see which ones meet our requirements. The resumes most likely to get our serious attention are those that:
>
> • Are arranged in a way that makes sense.
> • Don't waste our time with information we don't need.
> • Present us with the case for the applicant's employment.
>
> The standard resume format is to start with a summary, then your job history, and lastly your skills and education. But your primary consideration should be what the hiring department needs to know first. Organize your resume information in order of importance to the job in question:
>
> • Put your experience first when—The job you want is one that is focused on the skills and accomplishments that you've made at previous jobs.
> • Put your education first when—The job you want is based in academia or your education is the only thing that links you to this new job role.
> • Put your skills first when—You don't have job experience or you need to show that your skills outweigh your education or your job history.

Not everyone has to agree with your advice. It does, however, need to be clear.

- **Build your own club.** Succinct, simple, and sincere doesn't mean dull. Have fun when you write. Don't be afraid of being clever; just don't force things (see Chapter 4, "Writing as Rap"). No reader wants to wade through your oh-so-witty prose to find the advice buried somewhere in the eighth paragraph. Your fans do want to be engaged by your voice, however. So be an interesting personality—yourself, not some facsimile of yourself filled with hot air.
- **Make your blog a conversation.** As an advice columnist, you should always answer your readers' questions. Sometimes, though, you don't just want to do this under comments. You also can address readers' questions in subsequent blogs. That's what Melinda Emerson does.

190

She begins one blog post by quoting a query from a reader:

> One of my loyal blog readers asked: I've learned from you and others that personal branding is a must if you want to set yourself up as an expert in your given area. I have a few trusted advisors who are black women. They suggested that I needed to take my face off of my site to create a "colorless" business if I wanted to be known beyond the black construct. They said that I should use a white woman and not myself to be the face of my business. Did you go through any of this? If so, how did you overcome it?

Emerson gives the reader a straight-ahead answer:

> Thank you for asking me this question. First of all, I will answer your first question. No, I've not really faced this. But I also never write or talk about being a successful black woman in business. I only talk about how to become successful in business. I don't think anyone cares that I'm African-American. They only care about whether my information can help them in running their small business better.
>
> Now, your business is very different from mine; I am selling information and my small business expertise. You are selling services. In your case, I would not necessarily brand your name or your face to your business other than on your "about" page. Look at your top competitors. I do not see many who focus on their personal brand. I think you should consider renaming your business and do the same. No one cares that you are black, they just care that you are good.

DAVID WELIVER

"Blogging is neither a sprint nor a marathon—it's a journey that will take years"

David Weliver of Maine is the publisher of moneyunder30.com, a personal finance website that offers advice to young professionals.

Why did you decide to start your blog?
I began my career at a national financial magazine but later moved into a non-editorial position. I began blogging as a way to continue writing, but also because I saw a need for content that fit a specific niche—basic personal finance advice for young professionals that was presented in a clear, non-judgmental way.

David Weliver

I started my blog as a hobby, but I always kept an eye on the possibility of growing it into more than that. After two years of blogging I was able to sell some advertising and make a bit of money from it on the side. In my blog's fifth year, it became my full-time job.

How do you come up with ideas for blog post topics?

In the beginning, coming up with topics was easy because I wanted to cover my subject area—personal finance for young professionals—as comprehensively as possible. So I looked at other publications like *Money* magazine and the *Wall Street Journal* and tried to cover the most popular topics in a way that my audience would enjoy.

As I exhausted some of the more basic topics, I began turning to my readers for ideas. Many post ideas now come from readers who email me with questions and from semi-annual surveys I send to readers asking what their challenges are with money and what they'd like to read more about.

How frequently do you post to your blog (in an average week) and how many hours each week do you spend working on your blog?

Today we publish four or five articles a week. I spend 35 or 40 hours a week on the blog, but I'm only writing 10 to 20 percent of this time. The rest of the time I'm editing other writers' work, developing post ideas and an editorial calendar, selling advertising and managing advertiser relationships, promoting the blog, and handling technical updates.

What are the three most important things a new advice blogger needs to know?

1. Choose a niche. In a sea of millions of websites, it's difficult to stand out. Spend a good amount of time becoming familiar with other bloggers who cover your topic and ask yourself, "How will my blog be different?" Can you bring a colorful voice to the subject or choose a narrow sub-topic that allows you to become a trusted commentator in that niche?

2. Write for your audience, not yourself. The best way to get your blog read is to connect with people who want to hear what you have to say. Your first readers (aside from your mom and best friend) will be the hardest to get. Show them appreciation by responding to comments and writing thank you emails. Most importantly, ask them what they want to read. Not only will it give you good material to blog about, it will encourage them to come back again.

3. Be persistent. This is the most important advice I can give. Blogging is neither a sprint nor a marathon—it's a journey that will take years. Getting started will be frustrating and slow, there will be highs and lows along the way, and you'll make mistakes. Set a writing schedule that you can stick with (more isn't necessarily better), try new things, talk to other bloggers and keep going. Eventually good things will come.

Writing Reviews

We're all reviewers. We offer friends our opinions on music, fashion, movies, food, cars, and more every day.

"Yeah, I saw that movie last week. It starts kinda slow, but when the two guys rob the casino it really gets interesting. The scenery is great, too. You oughta see it."

"No, I wouldn't go to that new restaurant, Tavolo's Kitchen. They cook the pasta until it's like wet newspaper and the sauce tastes like ketchup. You want good Italian food? Go over to Mechanic Street and eat at Amici's. Get the veal osso buco—fantastic. And try the zabaione for dessert. You won't empty your savings account either. The prices are reasonable."

It's true that putting this kind of advice into written words demands a little more craft than the casual comment. But the idea is the same. Write in the tone you'd use giving advice to a friend. We suggest you do the following as well: Be clear and confident in your opinion; describe what you're reviewing with concrete language and examples; know the subject's context well enough to link to other resources; and, again, keep things succinct, simple, and sincere. And don't be dull. If you can make your friends laugh, you can make your readers laugh, too.

Deciding what to review can be tricky. Topics are almost limitless—there will always be a new album or concert, a restaurant you've never visited before, and new fashions about which you've got plenty to say. Unfortunately, so do tens of thousands of other bloggers (and thousands of professional journalists).

That leaves you a choice:

1. Choose a niche that isn't already crowded with bloggers. Instead of reviewing pop music, for example, review one type of pop music or only the pop music produced by bands in your city or your slice of that city. Instead of reviewing fashion, review lipstick colors.
2. Go ahead and review the bands, pop music, and fashions everyone else is reviewing, but work to stand out from the pack. If you don't have a niche, you need both a distinctive voice (see Chapter 4) and substantive knowledge.

193

Remember: Blogging gives you the freedom to break out of the formatted styles you've learned in school or at work. It will take time and a certain amount of trial and error to develop your own voice, but that's part of the fun of blogging.

Blogging gives you the incentive to explore, discover and learn things. You want to write about classic films? Then study the great actors and directors and what's been said about them. It's not good enough to say that the chemistry between Humphrey Bogart and Lauren Bacall made the movie *Key Largo*. You'd better know that the two fell in love on the set of their first film together, *To Have and Have Not*, that they married, that he called her "Baby," and that she was 25 years his junior. Not that you have to flash all that knowledge in every review. It's just part of what journalists call "doing your homework," knowing the broader-based context of your area of expertise.

Liam McCarthy and Corey Plante knew this even before they began their blog Snippet Studios (www.snippetstudios.com), devoted primarily to movie reviews, after they graduated in 2011 from Rhode Island's Providence College. They'd been writers at their college paper and they missed writing for publication. Today, the pair spend 10 or more hours a week each on the blog, writing or editing posts of contributors, and adding to an archive of hundreds of reviews.

McCartney offers this advice: "Watch every movie you can get your hands on. Then look up criticism on those movies. Build a library of knowledge about film that you can draw on."

"Learn about filmmaking," he continues. "Learn about the jobs and their responsibilities. Learn about cameras and cinematography so you can write about the look of a film, the way it might use color, or framing, to tell something. Know the ins and outs of the process of making a movie. This will only help you appreciate films more and enrich your ability to write about them."

Reading film scholars, however, does not mean sounding like them. The voice of the blogger is more conversational than that in other forms of writing. In fact, think of blogging as some mix of talking and writing—*well-edited* talking, we should add. When you do find your blogging voice, your readers will let you know.

If you're not convinced that voice matters, consider these two examples in which bloggers review the same album.

Example 1:

Iggy Azalea is an artist I have been following since her early mix tape days and watching her music and techniques evolve has been incredible. 2014 see's the release of her highly anticipated debut album rightfully titled The New Classic. This album is an impressive collection of material that see's Iggy staying true to her roots with music that reminds me of her mix tapes Ignorant Art and Trapp Gold. Her honesty and sassiness is something I have always loved and lyrically the songs featured on the album are quite personal and has seen her open up to the world. "I Don't Need Y'all" is the most passionate and honest songs on the record and has quickly become a fan favorite. "And if you wasn't here when I was down then you won't be here when I'm up. Now the same one you looked over be the same one that blew up." It's lyrics like this that most artists would be too scared to say but she's not afraid, not even a little.

Example 2:

She's a singer and a rapper, the first white woman to appear on the cover of XXL, and an uninformed expert on Aborigines. She has scored three U.K. Top 20 hits but endured the delayed release of her debut album, the optimistically titled *The New Classic*. Iggy Azelea, in short, understands the vagaries of third tier stardom in the 21st century. "Have you ever wished your life could change?" she asks on "Change Your Life," a collaboration with former label mate T.I. Eleven tracks later the question lingers. Zippy, squeaky, and context-free, *The New Classic* establishes the Australian artist as a competent rapper with a decent ear for hooks, but that's about it.

The fustiest part of the album is helmed by Norway's The Messengers, the duo responsible for the stuttering, whirring, processed beats and manipulated multi-track harmonies for the likes of Justin Bieber, Chris Brown, and Pitbull. What that leaves Iggy with is a state of the art 2011 album, designed to compete with the 2014 versions of Nicki Minaj and Rihanna: good luck.

195

Forget whether or not you care about Azalea. Ask yourself, which review draws your interest? We'll take odds it's the second.

In the first, the writer's voice is tentative and uses the first-person pronoun needlessly (it's a review; we know it's your opinion). A ghastly serial spelling mistake (*see's* instead of *sees*) makes the reader stop and reread a couple of sentences. Straining to describe the music, the writer falls back on empty and general descriptions: "incredible," "impressive," and "passionate."

The second reviewer writes with more style and snark. Both make the review distinctive. The writer varies the sentence length to create pace and chooses evocative, original words like "zippy," "squeaky," and "stuttering" to describe the music. The review's last two words, "good luck," deliver the verdict with snap.

So far, we've focused on two important skills in casting successful reviews: establishing a voice when you write and building expertise before you start.

Here are four more suggestions of how to achieve success.

Study the Stars of Your Field

Everyone has writers whose work they admire. It helps to study their work, to emulate the way they build a review, their choice of detail, their use of language, the way they reference old works or other current works as a means of comparison.

Imitation isn't plagiarism. Imitation is how we learn. The jazz trumpet player and teacher Clark Terry taught students how to play jazz and improvise in three steps: *Imitate. Assimilate. Innovate.* As you read writers and bloggers whose work you admire, you imitate them. As you imitate, you begin (slowly at first) to absorb the style of writers you admire and it becomes part of your own style, your own voice. Over time, as you build the frame and details of your style by assimilating, you begin to innovate, to speak in a voice that is *yours*. Your growth as a writer starts with reading others and, if you work hard enough, your own style flowers.

Miles Davis, another trumpet player and one of the greatest musicians in the history of jazz, told a documentary filmmaker he spent the early part of his career imitating other musicians. "You have to play a long time," Davis said, "before you sound like yourself."

Be Original

"Given that many will write on the same movies, it helps if you can think of an original angle," suggests Roy Flannagan, who started a popular blog, *The Film Doctor: Notes On Cinema*, after he was laid off from a job as a newspaper critic in 2008. "For one review, I compared a blockbuster movie to a plastic cap for a bottle of grape juice."

Put What You Are Reviewing into a Larger Perspective

For a few years, before the days of blogging, author Mark Leccese made a modest living writing about books. For one publication, Mark

196

wrote a 2,500-word profile each month of an author. To prepare, he would read each author's previous books, or at least a significant slice of them. It helped him formulate questions and explain how the author's new book fit into his or her body of work.

When the writer Leslie Epstein, for example, published *Pinto and Sons*, a novel about a Hungarian Jewish immigrant in the American West during the gold rush of the 1840s, Mark read Epstein's previous novels. Eleven years earlier, Epstein had published his most acclaimed (and controversial) novel, *King of the Jews*, a dark comedy set in a Jewish ghetto in Poland during World War II.

When writing about Epstein's new novel, Mark discussed how the writer's new novel differed from his most famous—and perhaps most similar—previous novel:

> As in *King of the Jews*, the battle of hope and charity against the world's blind cruelty dominates Pinto and Sons. But the naïf Pinto, unlike King's vain and clever Trumpleman, is nearly swamped by humanity's brutal passions: greed, fear, anger, force, ignorance and solecism.

197

The more you know about someone's old work—an author's, musician's, film director's, dance choreographer's—the more intelligently you can review what's new.

Every review begins with background work: Where did the artist and the art come from to get to this point?

Be Fair and Thorough in What You Review

Your readers expect you to cover your topic area fully. So don't only cover what you think will appeal to you: "Particularly with something like amateur film criticism, it's easy to slip into the habit of only reviewing the movies you want to," says Corey Plante, a co-founder with McCarthy of Snippet Studios. "This is really, really dangerous. If you want to exercise your critical eye then you're going to need to see the movies you don't want to. You're going to develop your critical eye and be able to articulate why a terrible movie is so terrible. [And] be critical of the movies you love, because even those have their faults."

The same advice applies across the board to books, plays, dance, music, and all other forms of criticism.

FREDERIC HEATH-RENN

"There's a lot writing a diary has in common with writing a review blog"

Frederic Heath-Renn, a computer programmer who lives in London, writes an excellent blog on popular music called *Radio Ember* (http://radioember.blogspot.com).

Frederic Heath-Renn

Why did you decide to start your blog?
I fell sharply for music at the age of about 15, having not really been interested in it when young, and with a convert's zeal I devoured canonical lists somewhat desperately to tell me what I'd missed, including (because I was aware I liked Britpop) the Mercury Prize [an annul award to the 12 best albums from the UK and Ireland]. So when the Mercury Prize rolled around in 2009, I decided I'd listen to all of the nominees, review them, and rank them. A friend encouraged me to continue, and I found that I really enjoyed trying to think more deeply about the music I listened to, so I carried on.

How do you come up with ideas for blog post topics?
For the most part, my choice of topics is quite undisciplined, and I write about anything that's caught my ear recently. But I try to write about new music that interests me as close to its release as possible—it gives me a sense of entirely undeserved satisfaction that what I'm writing is a new and novel opinion that deserves to be recorded (and I've noticed it tends to provoke a spike in hits, too, which is not a bad thing for my ego). And because I enjoy wordplay and trivia, I enjoy tenuously linking my writing to current events—albums with "bronze," "silver" and "gold" in the name during the 2012 London Olympics, for instance. It adds a satisfying challenge because it constrains my choice of things to write about, stopping me from getting lazy and writing about the same sorts of music all the time.

How frequently do you post to your blog (in an average week) and how many hours each week do you spend working on your blog?
While I was at university I usually managed one or two a week (especially since I was also writing about music for the student newspaper at the time), but since I've graduated and got a job, it's become more of a conscious effort to write, and since I'm quite tired in the evening I average around two posts a month now. But the upside of this is that I feel my writing is more considered now, and even if I usually write each of my blog posts over the course of perhaps three hours in total, I spend lots of my time at work and commuting

listening and re-listening to the albums I write about, so I spend a lot of time thinking about them.

What are the three most important things a new blogger who wants to write reviews needs to know?
One, don't be ashamed of rankings. There are a lot of problems with the standard marks-out-of-ten model and it's easy to feel that assigning artworks some arbitrary rank on a scale cheapens your writing and encourages people to skip over what you actually think. But as a writing tool, ranking is really useful because it forces you to distill your thinking into one bald fact: you have to put your cards on the table and say, well, do I actually like listening to this or not? How does this compare to other things I've listened to recently? And even if you never actually publish the mark, I think drawing connections like that in your head and forcing yourself not to be too wishy-washy is useful to strengthen your writing.

Two, challenge yourself. People are often confused when I talk about listening to things I am sure I'm going to dislike, because it seems perverse, but I feel that if you don't force yourself to pay attention to things you hate—and, more importantly, ask yourself why it is you hate them—you're going to find something lacking when you try to write about things you love. Plus, unleashing your most poetic bile on something you truly hate is great fun. Three, keep a diary. There's a lot writing a diary has in common with writing a review blog. Keeping a diary encourages you to go over your days and think about how you felt about them, and that's exactly the skill that's going to help you writing reviews. Plus, it's an excellent excuse to write every day, and if there's anything that will improve your writing ability it's writing as regularly and often as possible.

DISCUSSION

1. When do you turn to advice blogs? What do you look for in choosing one to follow or read?

2. Discuss in small groups what review blogs, if any, you read regularly. Each of you should explain why you like a particular blog. In the same groups, ask your classmates what topic they'd pick for a review blog and why. This can lead to a discussion about just what makes someone an expert.

EXERCISE

Write three reviews about a topic that interests you. It can be anything you've followed closely—music, art, books, video games, new apps, comics, food, dance, fast cars, whatever. Your first review should be a minimum of 600 words. Then write a 300-word review on a different theme. Your third review must be 150 words or less. All must be substantive. Discuss with classmates which review is hardest to write and why.

200

Building Your Blogging Brand

In 1968, the artist and mega-celebrity Andy Warhol said, "In the future, everyone will be world-famous for 15 minutes." In 2002, the Internet theorist David Weinberger updated Warhol's famous one-liner: "On the Web," he said, "everyone will be famous to 15 people."

We assume that if you take on the hard work of writing a blog, you would like your prose to reach an audience wider than family and friends. It could take a while. Building an audience for your blog takes time, effort, and social media savvy.

Think of building your audience this way: When you publish a blog post, you're "pushing" your writing out at a world of potential readers. Pushing alone isn't enough. You need to "pull" readers to your blog as well. And nothing "pulls" like social media.

You need to be on social media because that's where your readers are. The Pew Research Internet Project, in its report "Social Media Update 2013," found that almost half the American Internet users it surveyed used two or more of the Big Five social media sites: Facebook, Twitter, Instagram, Pinterest, and LinkedIn.

Facebook

The site that pretty much invented social media is still the Big Daddy. In the United States, according to a September 2014 Pew Research Center report, two-thirds of adults use Facebook, and half of those users say they get news from Facebook. "Facebook is an important source of website referrals for many news outlets," the report states.

For drawing readers to your website or blog, "Facebook is definitely the most effective," says Kailani Koenig-Meunster, multimedia editor at msnbc.com. "It isn't my favorite, but it does bring the most traffic. A lot of it has do to with just that's where people are—and that's where normal people are, whereas Twitter can sometimes seem like journalists talking to other journalists. Everyone's on Facebook. My mom is on Facebook."

How can you use it to drive traffic to your blog?

- **Build a separate page for readers of your blog to "like."** When you start your blog, create a new page for it on Facebook. Think of this blog page as your "brand page." First, bring over the friends from your personal account. Then use the Facebook search bar to find bloggers or websites featuring topics similar to yours. If you "like" their pages, and "friend" them, odds are they will "like" your page, too.
- **Link all your blog posts to Facebook**. Every time you publish a new blog post, go to your blog's Facebook brand page and post the link. Make sure you choose "public" from the drop-down menu at the lower right of the status box so that anyone on Facebook can see your status and so search engines can easily find it, too.
- **Post what others will want to share**. Few things build your blog audience faster than people "sharing" the link to your blog post. When you write a line or two about your blog post in Facebook's status box, try to write something that: (1) doesn't give away too much of the story; and (2) people will want to "share" with their Facebook friends. When Sarah Platanitis, a food blogger for masslive.com, put the link to her post about a local chef appearing on the TV show *Top Chef*, she wrote: "Sharing my interview with Stacy Cogswell, the hometown girl on *Top Chef Boston*. She's the most likeable chef I've ever met."

- **Keep your Facebook updated**. Do not neglect your Facebook brand page. Evan Allen covers crime and courts for *The Boston Globe*. She was on the team awarded a Pulitzer Prize in 2014 for coverage of the Boston Marathon bombing. She recommends giving a "clear and simple" explanation of your expertise on your brand page. Include contact information in a way that's easy to find and up to date. "There are dead Facebook pages all over the Internet," Allen says. "If you haven't posted in months, I'm moving on."

Twitter

The pros use Twitter. A 2013 survey of more than 1,000 journalists by two professors at the University of Indiana found that more than 80 percent of the journalists used social media to "pull" readers to their work, and two-thirds of the journalists said social media engage them more with their audience.

Matt Porter, a sports reporter at the *Palm Beach Post* in Florida who covers the University of Miami Hurricanes, writes a blog called the *Canes Watch*. Porter, who has more than 8,000 Twitter followers, says he gets more response from Twitter than Facebook.

By maintaining a consistent presence and interacting regularly, and often casually, with readers on Twitter, Porter said, he has seen the number of people visiting his blog increase.

But as Twitter users know, Twitter often seems an unending stream of noise, trivia, and inanity. It takes hard work to make your Twitter account heard amidst the 140-character din. Here are some tips on how to build an audience of Twitter followers:

- **Give your blog's Twitter account a clear and easily understandable name**. If you're writing a blog about restaurants in Portland, don't name your account @AmandaEatz53. Call it @ThePortland Gourmet. "If your Twitter handle includes a ton of apparently random letters/numbers," says the *Globe*'s Allen, "you're just going to fall through the cracks. Your goal should be to make your expertise clear, obvious, easy, fast."
- **Use a real photo of yourself**. Twitter works best when it creates connections with other people, and few things help others connect with you than seeing your face. The photo (called an "avatar")

205

should be high-quality and tightly cropped to show just your face with a bit of background—a photo of you walking down the beach with your back to the camera or with four of your friends at a party isn't going to make a connection. Twitter automatically resizes all avatars to 73 by 73 pixels on a desktop computer, which is about three-quarters of an inch by three-quarters of an inch. But Twitter allows readers to click on an avatar to make the image larger. When you create your avatar, you should make it about 300 by 300 pixels.

- **Write a profile that describes you and your blog and be sure to include the URL of your blog.** Twitter profiles can only be a maximum of 160 characters, so be precise and concise. That 160 characters, though, can leave you space for just a little bit of personality. If you are @The PortlandGourmet, your profile could read: *Blogging news and reviews about the Portland restaurant scene. Culinary school grad and former chef. Lover of dogs and reality TV shows. http://portlandgourmet.wordpress.com.*

- **Build your list of followers by searching for people with an interest in your topic area and following them.** Twitter has a much better and more precise search capability than Facebook. It is called, simply enough, Advanced Search (twitter.com/search-advanced). Abbey Niezgoda, a reporter at WVIT in West Hartford, Connecticut, said discovering the Advanced Search made Twitter much more useful for her. "You can search tweets in a location (miles of a certain zip code), with certain phrases, etc.," she said. "The options are endless and it's a great way to connect with people on Twitter." Says Koenig-Muenster at MSNBC, "I've gained followers by just following other people. I've developed a rapport with other people around the country because I followed them and they followed me back."

- **Don't clutter your tweet with unnecessary hashtags and mentions.** Three professors (from Carnegie Mellon, MIT, and the Georgia Institute of Technology) asked volunteers to rate 43,000 tweets, and "the overuse of #hashtags and @mentions" was one of the most common complaints. Still, avoiding abuse doesn't mean abandoning all use. "I feel like hashtags get a bad rap because young people use hashtags like #throwbackthursday and #sundayfunday," Niezgoda says. "But hashtagging a city like #Hartford helps the reach of your Tweet because people often search Twitter hashtags to see what's going in their city/town and just the simple hashtag sign (#) can help them find whatever you're tweeting about." Koenig-Muenster agrees, and she says using the right hashtags can help you gain new followers. "I'll still use them for specific topics," she says. "If I'm writing about the New Hampshire Senate race, I'll use #NHSen, and I'll get new followers."

- **Take the time to write an effective tweet**. "The art of writing a tweet is difficult," says Koenig-Muenster. "It can take several minutes." The three professors who studied which kinds of tweets readers responded to most positively found the three "most-liked categories" of tweets were: (1) questions to followers; (2) informational sharing; and (3) self-promotion with a link to the tweeter's work. Just so you know, the professors found the "most strongly disliked categories" were what they called "presence maintenance" tweets (such as "Hello Twitter!" or "I'm here. What's up, guys?"), conversation (discussions between users), and the tweeter's current status ("I'm at the gym!").

Porter has two guidelines for using Twitter: **Self-edit** and **Think hard before you tweet**.

"About half the tweets I write I never post," Porter says. "Self-editing is a huge part of successful Twitter use. Be highly critical of your work. If you think you're being funny or smart or wise, take a second to re-think the tweet. Word choice is so critical when you have 140 characters. Pick the right ones."

Adds Porter, "Not tweeting is often the best move, especially when it comes to controversial topics. How many times have you seen someone (a brand, for example) try to be funny or amusing and completely fall flat, leading to apologies and Twitter mob shaming? If you're unsure about it for a second, don't tweet."

Jenny Li-Fowler, web editor and social media manager for Harvard University's John F. Kennedy School of Government, says, "You want your tweets to be like a nugget of information that people can share at a party, that make them feel smart or clever or witty . . . You want them to say, 'Guess what I read on the Kennedy School Twitter feed?'"

For example, researchers at the Kennedy School found that the cancellation of school days because of snow doesn't harm children's education. Instead of saying something formal in a tweet, Fowler says, it's better to be more conversational. You might say, "'Kids not missing

207

out on learning because of snow days,'" Li-Fowler says. "Tease with something interesting and specific. Give them the nugget instead of something formal."

What does Li-Fowler mean by "formal?" Here are a couple of formal tweets about Harvard scientific studies that Li-Fowler did *not* write.

> Climate change study contradicts IPCC reports & others claiming climate change will cause stronger/more hurricanes & extreme temps.

Not a very interesting tweet, and, by the way, what the heck is IPCC? Are we supposed to know? Twitter is a mass medium. Don't expect your audience to understand obscure abbreviations and references. Nor should you expect them to rush to stories promoted by dull tweets such as the following:

> Harvard concussion study says NCAA needs improvement.

That may very well be what the study says, but surely it contains more specific advice to the NCAA than its concussion policy "needs improvement." (The abbreviation NCAA, by the way, for National Collegiate Athletic Association, is widely enough known in the United States to be acceptable here.)

By the way, both of the above tweets use the formal "A study says . . ." construction. Li-Fowler's tweet about snow days and kids avoided that.

208

SCOTT KLEINBERG

"Be yourself and the audience will be attracted to you"

Scott Kleinberg, who calls himself a "social mediaologist," is Social Media Editor of the *Chicago Tribune*. He writes *So Social*, a social media advice column, and founded the *Tribune*'s blog *iPhone, Therefore I Blog*.

What have you found to be the single most effective social media tool for bringing readers to your website/blog? Twitter? Facebook? Some other tool?

Scott Kleinberg

This will vary depending on audience, but for me it's Twitter. I feel like my Twitter followers are engaged. Facebook certainly helps, but Twitter is my favorite. I also use a scheduling tool for tweets called Buffer (https://bufferapp.com), which helps by allowing me to spread out content yet be consistent. (Using the Buffer app, a tweeter can write tweets and then tell Buffer what day and time you want the tweet posted to Twitter.)

What is the most effective mix of social media tools for bringing readers to your website/blog?

The perfect mix to gain traction/readers involves Facebook and Twitter, but also good engagement. When I do social media, I stand by a tested method that works called The Rule of Thirds.

- One third of the time, you talk about your brand and your thing, and you link back to your content on your website.
- One third of the time, you talk about things related to your brand and your thing, but you link to another website. Not yours.
- One third of the time, you are you. Be personal. Answer questions. Talk about the weather. Show your personality.

This method is what shows people that I am human. And it ensures that I engage in social media versus broadcast. I can't stress enough how important that differentiation is.

[Here's a tweet from Scott, who got held up trying to enter a building because two people kept talking as they went through the entrance's revolving door: *So let's talk about conversations while going through a revolving door. Really? Can you not wait 2 seconds?*]

Are Twitter hashtags still an effective way of getting people to your website/blog?

They can be, but I definitely don't rely on them. A hashtag is really intended to keep a group of tweets about one subject together for easy viewing. It was never intended to be an engagement tactic. But if enough people are using a hashtag about a subject, I will as well. During the World Cup, the use of the #WorldCup hashtag provided a big boost in engagement and numbers.

What are your guidelines for writing an effective Facebook status and an effective tweet?

- They must be entertaining, useful and personal.
- No abbreviations other than main ones like FBI and CIA. No "2" for "to" or anything like that.
- For a tweet, don't use all 140 characters. My tweets are always 121 characters or less to allow room for someone to type RT @scottkleinberg.

What advice would you give a young blogger trying to build an audience using social media?

- You have to be consistent. You can't just tweet once a day or a few times a week and expect it to matter.
- You have to be human. The Rule of Thirds will help your mix, but you have to show that you aren't all about links back to your site. Be yourself and the audience will be attracted to you.
- Have a thick skin. Never, ever delete comments. People are going to say mean things. You have to learn to take it and handle it with poise and grace.
- Know your audience. Learn the demographics. Learn when your audience shares the most so you can time your posts correctly.
- Don't be on a social media platform solely because it exists—be there because your audience is there.

210   Other Valuable Social Networks

Google Plus

When most Internet users log onto social media just to hang out and see what's up, they head for Facebook or Twitter, not Google Plus. A 2014 story in the *New York Times* called Google Plus a "ghost town." But it still can be a valuable way to attract readers to your blog, and it has far more members than you might think.

According to Google, 300 million people visit Google Plus every month. That's just a quarter of the number of people who visit Facebook, but it's more people than visit Twitter.

Here's a little secret that makes Google Plus that much more important: when you copy and paste what you wrote on your blog into a Google Plus post, it will appear higher in Google's search engine results than other blog posts—and it will appear more quickly. The Google search algorithm boosts the ranking of posts on Google Plus. (Can you guess why? Think of who owns it.)

If you don't have a Google Plus account, get one and fill out your profile as you would on Twitter. Add as many of your Facebook friends as you can to your "Circles" (Google Plus allows you to create "Circles" of the people you friend). Google Plus has a "People Find" button that'll help you. Finally, use the search function to add to your Circle other Google Plus members in your area of interest.

When you write a blog post, in whatever blogging software you're using, copy and paste it to your Google Plus page. When readers give your post on Google Plus a "+1" (the rough equivalent of a Facebook like), your post gets bumped up the Google search engine results seen by people searching for your post's keywords (see Chapter 6).

"Google Plus is something nobody goes to, but you can establish a Google Plus author page," says Koenig-Muenster. "I write a blog post, I share it on my Google Plus page, and the Google search jumps those posts to the top."

Instagram

The photo-sharing site Instagram doubled its number of users in one year, going from 100 million in 2013 to 200 million in 2014, according to a press release from the company. Instagram users can take photos, edit photos, and post online using the Instagram app, which includes a camera and photo-editing software.

If you use any other social media site, you'll know enough to navigate Instagram. You can add a comment under the post of a photo, you can "like" a post, you can chat with other users (whose usernames begin with the @ sign), and you can use hashtags. Sound familiar?

Facebook owns Instagram, so when you set up your account, Instagram asks if you want to follow the accounts of all your Facebook friends. Just tap on "Yes."

Instagram, like Twitter, allows you to create a brief (150-character) bio. *Make sure to include the link to your blog in your bio.* You'll need this link because any URL you post in the comment box under your photos is not clickable. (Instagram doesn't want users to leave its site.)

As on Tumblr (see Chapter 7), hashtags are the key to expanding your following on Instagram and driving traffic to your blog. Whenever you create a blog post that includes a photo (and most should), post it to Instagram, write a caption, and add a few hashtags. Don't get carried away with the hashtags; if you put 50 under a photo, you'll look like a spammer.

So, for example, if your blog is about bicycling, you might use the hashtags #bicycle, #cycling, #bike. Though Tumblr and Twitter also use hashtags, those on Instagram are much more effective because

Instagram has no search box, so hashtags are the primary way readers search for content.

"On Instagram, I put hashtags on all the photos I post—and that will quadruple the number of likes you get," says Koenig-Muenster of MSNBC.

Pinterest

You may not think a website on which people "pin"—as on a bulletin board—photos of interesting things they find online would be of much use to a blogger. But you'd be wrong.

Not only is Pinterest the fastest-growing social network, with more than 250 million users, but "when it comes to referral traffic from social networks, there's Facebook and Pinterest—and then there's everyone else," said the tech website Mashable in a 2013 article.

What makes Pinterest so useful to bloggers is this: if you post a photo from your blog on Pinterest, when a user clicks on the photo they'll automatically be taken to the blog page on which the photo appears. And Pinterest users can comment on whatever you pin to your board. It's a good way to build your following.

Not only is Pinterest a blog (in its own way) and a useful tool for increasing traffic to yours, but it's also fun. You can create your own categories. Friends and students of the authors have created such categories as "Bucket List," "Tats I like/want/will get," "Tech gadgets," "Awesome photos," "Books worth reading," "Magazine design," "Heroes," "Album covers," and "Infographics."

Be Johnny Blogseed: Wherever You Go, Spread Your Blog

If you're listening, you've joined new social media sites and updated all your bios to link directly to your blog. What now? Here are a few more ways to promote your blog:

- **Add the Web address of your blog to your email signature**. Any email program allows you to set up a signature that will appear, automatically, at the bottom of every email you send.
- **Invite guest bloggers to write for your blog**. Many blogs today feature more than one blogger. By inviting others to contribute to your blog, you not only add more voices and ideas to your blog,

but you build your audience. Most blogs start off being read primarily by family and friends. If you have guest bloggers, you expand your audience to *their* family and friends, too.

- **Make it easy to subscribe to your blog.** In Chapter 3, we explained how to use RSS readers to build yourself a daily reading list of blogs and other websites. If you want to send emails to a list of people each time you publish a new blog post, you can do it using mailchimp.com. The website allows you, for free, to send emails to a subscriber list of fewer than 2,000.

If you're really ambitious, you can even use your feet. If you write a local blog, you can *meet* your readers in the flesh by creating meet-ups. That's what the *Seattle Post-Intelligencer*, once a print newspaper, did after it launched The Big Blog when the paper went all digital in 2009. The Big Blog set up weekly meet-ups in Seattle coffee shops. Other bloggers were invited, as was anyone who read The Big Blog. Sometimes the *Post-Intelligencer* would bring along a "draw": a weather blogger, for example, or a local person who had appeared on the popular American TV show *Dancing with the Stars*.

"I met so many interesting people," says Koenig-Muenster, a Seattle native who liked to go to these events. "It developed a buzz. It can be important to get out from behind the computer and put a face to the people who comment."

213

Don't Substitute Self-Promotion for Substance

Let's pause a moment to remember something. Your success as a blogger is going to rely on more than social media networks and social meet-ups. Don't forget that discussion of voice (see Chapter 4, "Writing as Rap"), or the notion of the special relationship between a writer and reader.

Or, to put it another way, you're not just a blog, you're a person. You have a purpose. Yes, we have suggested a variety of ways to get curious readers to click on your link and settle down for a moment to read what you have to say.

But if what we have suggested in this chapter can get readers to come to your blog, only you can get them to come back again and again. You have to give readers what they want: helpful information and intelligent opinions, perspectives, and guidance. Posts, in other words, that readers will find both useful and a pleasure to read. You also have to give them something of yourself.

"If you're a person who's overjoyed about your cereal or dismayed at your awful airline experience, that's who you are, but I don't want to read about it," says Matt Porter of the *Palm Beacon Post*. "Said a different way: quality over quantity."

Quality and personality. It's that voice your social media posts can convey, too.

"I would say 90 percent of my [Twitter] use is work-related," Porter says. "[But] I include a couple real-life tweets here and there to remind people I'm a real human and to try to keep things light and amusing. Everything you post comprises your personal brand."

Adds Li-Fowler: "You don't want to sound like a robot or like you have a set pattern for everything . . . not like you're just cutting and pasting the headline. You want to sound like a person who's offering a good nugget of information to people . . . Make every Tweet individual."

214

DISCUSSION

1. Discuss with classmates which social media sites they use the most often, and why.

2. With your classmates, plan a meet-up for the readers of a class blog. Where would you hold the meet-up, and how would you promote it?

EXERCISE

Pick 10 bloggers whose work you enjoy. Find their Twitter name and follow their Twitter accounts. Create a list called "10 Bloggers." (Go to your Twitter profile page and click on "Lists." On the right side of the page that appears, click on "Create New List.") Follow this list (go to your Twitter profile, click "Lists," and then click on "10 Bloggers") for two weeks and keep a record of what each blogger tweets, recording specifically how many times each blogger:

1. tweets a link to his or her own blog;
2. uses a hashtag, and which hashtags are used;
3. tweets a link to someone else's blog or website; and
4. tweets something personal rather than something related to his or her blog.

Using these data, discuss similarities and differences among the bloggers' approaches. Do any apply Scott Kleinberg's Rule of Thirds? Do you believe they should? Why or why not?

Glossary

Analytics—Data gathered by either blogging platform, plug-ins, or third-party services (such as Google Analytics) on visitors to a website or a blog, including such information as number of visitors, number of page views, web addresses from which visitors came to a blog, the amount of time a visitor spends on page or post, and more.

Archive—On a blog, the archive is all the older posts that no longer appear on the main page. A blog *archive* can be featured in a sidebar on the blog's main page, usually organized chronologically (e.g., by month and year) or by topic.

Avatar—An image, usually small, that represents a person or group on a social media site, such as the image that appears on the left in all your posts on Twitter.

Blockquote, Pullquote—A blockquote is a direct quote from a source that appears in a blog post indented on both sides and often in a light gray box. A pullquote is a snippet of text from the blog post that is "pulled" from the run of text and appears in larger type as a design element and is often used to visually break up long blocks of text.

Blog—Short for "weblog." The defining characteristic of a blog is that each piece of new content appears in reverse chronological order, with the newest entry appearing at the top of the web page, the next most recent entry appearing below it, and so on.

Blogging Platform—Software that turns a website into a blog. A blogging platform may be software on a computer or it may be software on the Internet provided by a blogging service such as WordPress or Blogger.

Blogosphere—The universe of all the blogs on the Internet, loosely estimated to be about 250 million blogs.

Blogroll—A list of links to other blogs, usually appearing in a sidebar, that a blogger likes and wants readers to know about. The blogroll usually lists blogs in the same general topic area as the blog.

Bulleted List, Numbered List—A bulleted list is an indented series of words, phrases, sentences or paragraphs that have a small black dot in front of each item in the list. In a numbered list, a number (instead of a dot) appears before each item.

Comment—Any statement written by a reader—or even the blogger—that appears in the "Comments" section beneath a blog post.

Content Management System (CMS)—Software that allows the user to post content to an existing website template. A *blogging platform* is one type of *CMS*.

Copyright—Legal protection against unauthorized reproduction of an author's or a blogger's work. In the United States, copyright is an automatic right: a blogger owns the copyright to anything he or she writes and publishes. No registration of a work with the government is necessary.

Database—A collection of data stored on a computer in a way that makes the data easily accessible and allows users to update, manage, and retrieve the data.

Deck—A second *headline* that appears, usually in a smaller type size, below the main headline and expands on it without repeating words or ideas.

Domain Name—A unique name used as the plain text Internet address for a website or blog (e.g., "slowlanetravel.com"). Domain name suffixes (also known as "top-level domains") indicate the type or origin of a website: ".com" is mostly used by companies, ".org" is mostly used by nonprofit organizations, and ".edu" is used by schools, colleges, and universities. Countries have domain name suffixes, such as ".au" for Australia, "uk" for the United Kingdom, and ".ca" for Canada.

Freelancer—A writer who is paid per article or blog post.

Gallery, Slide Show—A gallery is a group of images appearing on a web page with navigation buttons (next, previous) and captions. A slide show (sometimes known as a slider) is a group of images appearing on a web page that moves from one image to the next automatically.

Graf—Short for "paragraph." Commonly used in journalism.

Hashtag—A word or words preceded by the number sign (#multimedia) that serves as a link to other posts with the same hashtag. It serves as a way for users of social media to search for posts on a topic, and helps posters, with the addition of a hashtag, make their posts easily searchable. On Twitter and Instagram, hashtags must be one word (e.g., #SummerOlympics2016), but on Tumblr they can be multiple words (e.g., #Summer Olympics 2016).

Headline—The words that appear above a blog post. Headlines are set in larger type than body text.

HTML—Abbreviation for Hypertext Markup Language, a standardized set of commands that tell a computer how to display a web page. A helpful introduction to HTML is available at w3schools.com.

Hyperlocal—News that is primarily of interest only to a limited geographic area, such as a village, town, or small city.

Hypertext—A software system that allows users to click on a word or image and be immediately taken to another page on the Internet.

Keyword—Search engine users type in a keyword or keywords when performing a search. Bloggers can increase the chances a search engine will highly rank their posts by including keywords in the HTML *meta tags* of their posts.

Lede—Journalism jargon for the first paragraph of an article. The most common theory for the odd spelling is that it is used to avoid confusion with the word "lead."

Link—A single instance of *hypertext* (a word, a phrase, an image) on which a reader may click to be taken to another website or web page.

Meta Tags—A statement in HTML that describes the content of a web page. Meta tags, such as keywords and descriptions, can be added by a blogger to each blog post.

Microblogging—Creating and publishing short (often constrained by character or image size limit) and usually frequent blog posts on social media platforms such as Twitter and Tumblr.

Mobile—Any small computer device, usually with Internet access, that can be easily carried by the user.

Multimedia—The use of more than one medium—e.g., text, video, audio, and hypertext—to communicate and tell stories.

Page View, Unique Visitor—A page view occurs when any reader accesses any page on your blog. A unique visitor is an individual reader, determined by the reader's IP address, who accesses any page on your blog. If one person visits your blog 25 times in a day, that would be counted as 25 *page views* but only one *unique visitor*.

Permalink—A link that takes the reader not to the front page of a blog, but to a specific blog post.

Pingback—A notification sent by software to Blogger A when Blogger B links to Blogger A's blog. Both bloggers must be using software with an enabled pingback function.

Pixel—Short for "picture element." The smallest element of an image on a computer screen. The size of a pixel depends on the resolution of the computer screen. Pixels are most commonly used to measure image sizes.

Plug-in—A piece of software that enhances an existing application by adding a new function.

Podcast—An audio recording, much like a radio show, that can be downloaded from the Internet.

Post—Any addition to a blog or a microblog. A blog is a *website* and each new article added to the blog is a *post*.

RSS feed—A system that delivers the content from chosen websites or blogs to a user every time the content is updated.

Screenshot—An image capture of the user's computer display or a part of the computer display.

Sidebar—Boxes with text content and links that appear on either side of the main text area of a blog.

Smartphone, Tablet, Phablet—A smartphone is a small, portable computer with Internet access and the capability of making phone calls. A tablet is a small, portable computer—most commonly about 7 inches wide and 10 inches high—roughly the size and thickness of a small pad of paper. A phablet is a portable computer, larger than a smartphone but smaller than a tablet, that combines the functions of the two.

Spam—Unwanted emails or comments, usually trying to sell something, sent to very large numbers of Internet users. Spam is the Internet version of junk mail. In a blog, spam can frequently appear in the *comments* section.

Spambots—A computer program designed to "harvest" email, website, and blog addresses, and automatically send spam to those places.

Stream—To send audio or video content over the Internet so it can be consumed by users in real time. For example, consumers can either download a *podcast*, which will take up memory space on their computers or mobiles, or they can stream the podcast and listen to it without downloading it.

Subhed—Small headlines placed at intervals through the text of an article, often but not always in the same *typeface* and size as the text. Also known as "chapter breaks."

Template—Pre-designed websites and web pages made available to users of *blogging platforms* so users will not have to design their websites and page from scratch.

Tumblelog—Originally, a blog composed of short posts in various media: sentences, quotations, images, videos, and links. Now, tumblelog refers to a blog on the Tumblr platform, and a blog composed of short posts in various media is called a *microblog*.

Tweet—A single post, no more than 140 characters, on Twitter. Twitter automatically shortens long *URLs* to 20 characters.

Twitterverse—Like the *blogosphere*, the *Twitterverse* is the universe of all posts made on Twitter and all Twitter users. According to Twitter, the social network has 284 million "monthly active users."

Typeface, Font—A *typeface* is an entire set of characters—letters of the alphabet, numerals, and symbols—of the same design. Times New Roman, Helvetica, Courier, and Veranda are popular *typefaces*. A font is all the characters of a typeface in one size and one style. For example: Courier is a *typeface*, and Courier Bold 12-point is a *font*.

URL—Abbreviation for uniform resource locator, more commonly known as a "web address." For example, the URL for the University of Alabama is http://www.ua.edu and the URL for the University of Alabama Libraries is http://www.ua.edu/libraries.html.

Vlog—A blog whose content is videos.

APPENDIX A
Legal and Ethical Issues in Blogging

Legal Issues

The United States legislative and legal system usually lags behind advances in technology. The laws and court precedents involving blogging continue to evolve. Legislators and judges, faced with a new communications medium, have begun to consider blogs' similarities and differences to traditional media such as newspapers. In most—but not all—cases, the protections extended to traditional media have been extended to blogs, and the violations of the law for which traditional media may be held liable have also been applied to blogs.

We will touch on four major legal issues every blogger should be aware of, but the laws are complex, and this is by no means an exhaustive summary. The most thorough synopsis of the legal issues involved in blogging is the Electronic Frontier Foundation's "Legal Guide for Bloggers." You can find it at www.eff.org/issues/bloggers/legal.

Copyright

Most of the material on the Internet—text, images, audio files, videos—is owned under copyright law by the people or the corporations who created it. Our advice on copying material from other websites and using it on your blog can be summed up in one word: *don't*.

U.S. law on copyright-protected material is simple: The reproduction and dissemination of copyright-protected material by anyone other than the copyright holder without the agreement of the copyright owner is illegal.

This does not mean that if you download and use an Associated Press photograph on your blog, the police will kick down your front door and slap you in handcuffs. Violation of copyright laws are generally not a criminal offense. But it does mean that the Associated Press can sue you and ask the court to order you to pay it a large sum of money, although in most cases the first action of the copyright owner will be to contact the blogger and demand the copyrighted material be removed from the blog.

You say you've seen other bloggers post copyright-protected material on their blogs and get away with it? No doubt you have. That doesn't make it legal or ethical. It just means they didn't get caught.

There is an exception to copyright law, known as "fair use," that allows you to use a limited amount of material without permission from the copyright owner. For example, if you are writing a blog post that is a book review, you can quote passages from the book to demonstrate to the reader points you are making. How much can you quote? There is no hard and fast rule. The website of the U.S. Copyright Office states: "The distinction between what is fair use and what is infringement in a particular case will not always be clear or easily defined. There is no specific number of words, lines, or notes that may safely be taken without permission." A good rule of thumb is "not too much."

Be aware that the copyright restrictions on music and song lyrics are stringent, and that recording and music publishing companies are among the most zealous of copyright owners in taking violators to court.

The biggest (and best) place on the web to find images and other multimedia for use on a blog is Creative Commons, which is at creativecommons.org. Creative Commons, a nonprofit organization, offers free copyright licenses to a variety of works.

Now for the good news: copyright law works both ways. You own the copyright to everything you create, write, and post on your blog. In the US, copyright is an *automatic* right. Anything you create that is fixed in a tangible form of expression is your property. You don't need to register with the government and there are no forms to fill out; if you create it, you own it.

You may, perhaps in exchange for money or something else of value, transfer the copyright (in writing) to another party. If another blogger or website uses what you have created, your work has been stolen and your copyright has been infringed. If you don't want to pay a lawyer and sue the offending blog, contact the blog that has stolen your material and ask that it be taken down. Most bloggers will comply.

Libel

Libel is the act of publishing a false statement that damages the reputation of and defames an identifiable individual. Bloggers can be—and have been—sued for libel.

People who are "public figures" in the eyes of the court (elected officials, for example) must not only prove that the published material is defamatory, they must also prove that the material was published with "actual malice," meaning that the writer knew the statement was false or published it with a "reckless disregard" for the truth.

A "private figure," someone who has not sought the public spotlight (a neighbor, a classmate, a check-out clerk at the supermarket), needs only to prove falsity and negligence. The standard courts use is whether a "reasonable person" would have published the material.

If a published statement is true and can be proven true, it is libel-proof. Truth is an absolute defense to a libel claim, although, as the Electronic Frontier Foundation points out, "the truth may be difficult and expensive to prove."

The publication of opinion (a review, for example) is also protected from libel charges, but what is and what is not an opinion can be a tricky thing to decide. The courts look at the context of the statement to determine whether it is an opinion or statement of fact.

Under U.S. law, bloggers cannot be held liable for defamatory statements posted by commenters to a blog. But bloggers may be held legally liable if a commenter's statements violate federal law or infringe copyright.

One final thing to remember about libel: to repeat a libel is to commit libel. If another blogger defames someone and you repeat that statement on your blog, you are liable to a defamation claim. So far, U.S. courts have ruled that linking to a website containing a libel is not an actionable offense.

First Amendment Protections

Although the body of law on this issue is still emerging, most U.S. courts have ruled that bloggers are as entitled to the same freedom of the press protections as other news media.

To date, the most important case on the matter was decided in January 2014 by the U.S. 9th Circuit Court of Appeals. In the case, known as *Obsidian Finance Group, LLC v. Cox*, a blogger named Crystal Cox was sued by Obsidian Finance Group after she used her blog to accuse the company and its principals of illegal activities, including fraud and money laundering.

In 2011, an Oregon jury found against Cox and awarded Obsidian Finance Group and its attorney $2.5 million. Cox appealed the decision, and the appeals court overturned the lower court's decision.

"The protections of the First Amendment do not turn on whether the defendant was a trained journalist, formally affiliated with traditional news entities, engaged in conflict-of-interest disclosure, went beyond just assembling others' writings, or tried to get both sides of a story," the Circuit Court of Appeals decision states. "In defamation cases, the public-figure status of a plaintiff and the public importance of the statement at issue—not the identity of the speaker—provide the First Amendment touchstones."

In its decision, the appeals court cited a statement from the 2010 U.S. Supreme Court decision in the *Citizens United v. Federal Election Commission* case: "With the advent of the Internet and the decline of print and broadcast media . . . the line between the media and others who wish to comment on political and social issues becomes far more blurred."

Student Blogs

In addition to the Electronic Frontier Foundation's "Legal Guide for Bloggers" (see above), the Washington, DC-based Student Press Law Center (www.splc.org) provides a useful guide to media law for students.

In determining the First Amendment rights of students in the US, the courts have made a series of distinctions: between public and private schools, between high schools and colleges, and, perhaps most important, between school-supported publications and independent, off-campus publications.

Public high schools have been granted permission by the Supreme Court, in the 1988 *Hazelwood School District v. Kuhlmeier* decision, to censor the content of school-sponsored publications (including online publications). The justices wrote: "A school need not tolerate student speech that is inconsistent with its basic educational mission, even though the government could not censor similar speech outside the school."

Courts have determined that the *Hazelwood* decision applies only to public high schools and *not* to colleges. Publications created by public college students essentially enjoy the same First Amendment protections as professional publications. The exceptions are if content in a college publication "materially disrupts classwork or involves substantial disorder or invades the rights of others."

American courts have also made a distinction between high school-sponsored publications and "public forums for student expression," and they exempt these "public forums" from the *Hazelwood* standards. A public forum is defined, according to the Electronic Frontier Foundation, as "one where the student bloggers, not school administrators, have the authority to determine the content." The EFF advises: "Whether a school-hosted blog would be considered a public forum, and therefore not subject to Hazelwood censorship, is determined on a case-by-case basis, looking at the school's policies and statements. If your school has an Internet Policy or Terms of Use for its site-hosting services, look it over carefully to see if the school has a right to edit or censor content."

Because public high schools and universities are run by government employees and private schools are not, private school students do not enjoy the same First Amendment protections as students in public schools. Many private high schools and colleges have adopted their own free press policies. It is wise to advise student bloggers to find out whether their schools have such policies and what rights the policies grant.

Independent, off-campus blogs—even if they write about the schools the bloggers attend—enjoy strong First Amendment protections, *especially* if the blogs are not hosted on the school's network. We advise student bloggers who may be planning to write controversial material about their schools not to use the schools' blogging software or network; find an off-campus website to host your blog.

This area of the law is still evolving. Some courts have held that off-campus blogs written by high school students can be held to school restrictions. Other courts have ruled in favor of the students.

Students at private high schools have been punished by their schools for what they wrote on their personal, off-campus blogs. One student at a private high school in New York State was expelled by school officials because of a post on his personal blog, and a court upheld the expulsion simply because he attended a private, and not public, school.

Private colleges have much more leeway to regulate and punish students for what they write and post. The state of California has a law on its books that requires all nonreligious private colleges and universities to extend to their students the same First Amendment protections students at public colleges have. No other states have a similar law.

Ethical Issues

Making good ethical decisions demands much more than checking your gut. It's complicated. That's why several dozen books are listed on amazon.com on just the topic of journalism and media ethics. That's why the *New York Times* "Ethical Journalism Guidebook," available online at www.nytco.com/who-we-are/culture/standards-and-ethics/, runs 57 pages.

Mark and Jerry, the authors of this book, don't believe ethical decisions typically can or should be prescribed. Nor do they believe that a handful of lofty generalities—"don't plagiarize" and "don't do PR for your friends"—is terribly helpful in reaching such decisions (in contrast to the *Times*, the Radio Television Digital News Association's Code of Ethics runs fewer than three pages and offers such pearls as "continuously seek the truth").

While the law dictates what you, as citizen and blogger, must do to avoid getting in trouble, ethics tell you how, as citizen and blogger, you should behave in the huge collective known as the blogosphere. A series of questions can help find the right answer, questions such as, "How would I feel if roles were reversed and I was the subject of this blog or its reader instead of the writer? Would I feel misled? Misquoted? Insulted? Or would I feel reasonably well represented?" Another good question might be, "Would I be comfortable—indeed, proud—to tell my mother what I did today and how I did it?"

Though it's hard to either dictate ethical behavior or to arrive at it on the basis of broad-brush guidelines, it is possible to find a balance point that suggests guidelines but also encourages bloggers, like reporters, to think through each case carefully and individually: this is called "applied ethics."

One news organization that took this approach a few years ago in revising its ethics code is NPR, also known as National Public Radio.

In its ethics handbook, found at http://ethics.npr.org/category/a-preamble/#1-about, NPR management writes: "The art of ethical decision-making is as much about the way we make decisions as it is about what we decide. So the handbook should include not just rules about what NPR journalists do and don't do, but more importantly, decision-making frameworks we can apply in different situations to guide us."

We believe this to be a good approach. Like reporters, bloggers have to weigh alternatives, to apply ethics to the case at hand rather than impose those ethics on that case from afar. There's a good example of just that in the "Travel Blogging and Ethics" section toward the end of Chapter 9. There are also a series of questions that can help the blogger reach a good decision.

Sure, it's important to know key professional guidelines and have personal standards or values that provide the underpinnings of your decision-making. But it's equally important, as ethicist Robert Steele, formerly of the Poynter Institute and DePauw University, has written, to "do ethics." This means weighing the pros and cons of a variety of ethical choices, choosing the best one, and testing the approach you choose. Steele is one of a host of ethicists who suggests a list of questions to help make good ethical decisions. Among those you might consider are these:

Are you willing to tell your readers what you've done and explain why? If the answer is "yes," you're probably on the right track. Transparency can go a long way in establishing your ethics, in part because if you err, your readers will tell you. If your answer is "no"— you don't feel comfortable disclosing what you've done and why— then there's a good chance you haven't acted ethically.

Do you know what motivated you to reach the decision you made? If the answer is greed, you've almost certainly made a bad decision.

Have you considered the consequences, short- and long-term, of your actions? Let's say, for example, that you wrote a restaurant review but left out that your friend's veal cacciatore was overcooked because you liked the place's owners and for the most part liked the food. The short-term consequence of your omission might be happy owners. The long-term consequence, however, might be disappointed customers who also happen to feel deceived by your blog and suspicious of your motivation and/or abilities.

Ethics, again, is a big field. Here are a few guidelines that might help you wrestle with your own ethical decision-making:

Don't Steal or Copy

Plagiarism doesn't just mean stealing someone's exact words. It can mean stealing that person's research without attribution or a link to his or her work. It can mean stealing someone else's ideas and passing them off as your own. Once again, let's do ethics: How would you feel if you had written a blog arguing that the Boston Red Sox should bunt more often based on an analysis of the last three season's attempts and then read the same blog, written with slightly different language but the same data, that in no way credited your analysis or linked to your earlier efforts? We bet you'd be both mad and hurt. So why shouldn't someone else feel that way if you did it to them?

Don't Spread Rumor; Do Verify

Good bloggers have rich voices and strong opinions. That's great. But the most interesting opinions are based on facts, not assumptions or, worse yet, rumors that just might prove false. The 24/7 world of social media has led to egregious errors that spread like a prairie fire. At minimum, give a source for the information you are sharing. Better yet, verify the material yourself.

The current shoot-from-the-hip attitude toward information was evident a few years back when the Poynter Institute in St. Petersburg told the story of a *California Watch* senior editor who overheard the cellphone conversation of a woman he was quite sure was a Santa Ana city council member and started tweeting what she was saying. He never identified himself to her. He didn't ask her for a comment. Nor did he bother to verify that she was the person he thought she was. Instead, Poynter wrote in an article headlined "Editor overhears councilwoman's phone conversation, tweets about it," he told his Twitter audience that he was "99 percent sure it was Michele Martinez [the councilwoman]."

Let's do some more ethics. Would you like to have your conversations tweeted around the world without being asked for an explanation of what you said or being given the chance to identify yourself? We rather doubt it.

NPR's new media handbook tells its staff: "Conduct yourself online just as you would in any other public circumstances ... Verify information before passing it on."

We agree.

Don't Be a Paid Mouthpiece; But If You Must Be, at Least 'Fess Up

One of blogging's biggest challenges is to take it beyond a hobby. But to make money, some bloggers resort to being shills—a derogatory term used for generations in journalism to describe those who shamelessly wrote about products or people for pay.

We're former journalists so, no, we don't believe it's OK for you to write about Magnificent Mountain Resorts in your blog when you're on the resort's payroll. But if you must, at least make clear that you are telling about the virtues of the resort because the resort either pays you to or bought an ad on your site.

Journalists, particularly those covering fashion, cars, and other fun things, can be accused of their own share of ethical foibles, as David Weddle wrote a decade ago in a stunning *Los Angeles Times* magazine article titled "Swagland" on the topic of free gifts—known as "swag" —given to journalists. "You might call it a state of mind, a wondrous alternate universe concocted by publicists," Weddle wrote, "funded by corporations eager for media coverage of their wares and frequented by journalists who have cast off concerns about conflicts of interest and embraced a new creed of conspicuous consumption."

Journalists are paid. Most bloggers are not. But that doesn't give bloggers license to hide payments from their readers or make money through deceit. Again, at the very least, be honest with your audience.

Why?

The bottom line: if you're writing about Aunt Bertha's big bagels shop or cousin Bobby's candidacy for the city council, you are in conflict of interest, whether you're being paid or not. The least you can do is disclose your relationship. Better yet, pick a different topic altogether. Even if you believe you can write objectively about things you have a financial or other stake in, the perception of your readers just might be that you can't. Hiding the connection can only make matters worse.

231

Practice Good Blogging Etiquette

In some ways, ethics starts with the Golden Rule: "Do unto others as you would that they should do unto you."

This can be applied in a variety of ways in blogging. For starters, it makes sense if you plan to write about someone by name to identify yourself and let them know your plans before you start an interview. No one likes to be burned by a sneak. Reporters are expected to tell people that they're reporting before they start interviewing people. Bloggers should do the same.

The courtesy of disclosure can be applied in other ways in the blogosphere. If you plan, for example, to reprint someone's work in its entirety on your blog, be good enough to ask permission or, at the very least, to let that individual know. And, of course, use the byline of the person's work you are reprinting.

We could certainly go on; whole libraries of books have been written on ethics. But this appendix, alas, has only the space to whet your appetite for this really important subject.

So we'll leave you with a single last tip. In Steele's "10 questions for ethical decision making," he suggests this final question before pushing the publish button: "Can I clearly and fully justify my thinking?"

Again, ethics is a thought process, not an emotional gut reaction. Then he expands on that question about justification. To paraphrase, ask yourself, "Can I clearly and fully justify my thinking to other bloggers? To the people I'm writing about or have interviewed? To my public?"

By pausing to reflect and to both challenge and stretch your reasoning, you'll likely settle on an approach that serves both your readers and the truth.

APPENDIX B

Two Bloggers and Their Work

By now, we're guessing you've read at least some of our advice on blogging. We thought it had some value to show that we try to practice what we preach.

In this appendix, we've each picked out a half dozen of the many dozens—no, hundreds—of blog posts we've each written. Mark, the specialist who takes his own advice to stay tightly focused on topic, writes about the news media. Jerry, more the dabbler, has blogged on a variety of subjects, most recently travel.

We hope you enjoy our posts and welcome your comments.

234

Jerry Lanson ● Become a fan ✉ 𝕐 👍
Journalism professor, Emerson College

12 Tips on How to Spend 6 Months in France Without Going Broke

Posted: 02/07/2014 1:13 pm EST | Updated: 04/09/2014 5:59 am EDT

From the start, the math didn't add up.

My wife, Kathy, and I were headed to France for a half year. I'd be on a paid sabbatical, but Kathy was retiring, and we weren't ready to tap her Social Security. Even with our house rented at a discount, complete with our golden retriever, the basic addition looked daunting:

Overall income: Down 40 percent.
Basic expenses: Up at least $1,000 a month.
Outlook: A bit scary.

Still, this would be that "trip of a lifetime," so we didn't want to scrimp either. No hostel hopping. No sleeping in a VW van. No diet of sprouts and beans. (Though we may be in our 60s, The '60s ended long ago.)

Instead, we planned early and budgeted about $2,500 a month from retirement to cover what my income wouldn't. It still meant scaling back some plans. But, so far we're living within our means, and not feeling the least bit deprived.

So if daddy didn't leave you a trust fund, you itch to see the world and you favor long-haul travel with a dash of comfort, here are a dozen ways to make it happen:

1. Establish a base:

Travel costs increase in direct proportion to the speed at which one moves. Gas alone in France, for example, costs nearly $9 a gallon. Trains are pricey, too. We chose to live in one place, Aix-en-Provence, a city of about 140,000 in the South of France, for five of our six months here, settling for occasional day trips out of town.

2. Rent with care:

It's one thing to weather a bad night on the road. It's quite another to hate coming home for months at a time. I began scouring rentals on sites such as homeaway.com, vrbo.com, airbnb and sabbaticalhomes.com a year before we left. We wanted someplace in easy walking distance of the old city, with an extra room for guests and work, and an outdoor patio. After carefully reading renter reviews, we choose a three-bedroom apartment on a quiet street (found on homeway.com, which unlike some services, doesn't charge renters).

The apartment isn't cheap -- about $1,775 a month now with a weak dollar. But it's less than smaller apartments in city center, and it comes with morning serenades by the local birds.

3. Avoid big cities:

Everyone loves Paris. We're no exception. But we chose Aix for its slower pace and more reasonable costs. It's a city with just about everything -- daily markets, movies, outdoor cafes, concerts, bookstores, scenic walks, good restaurants, a smattering of museums and squares that positively ooze ambiance. It also, usually, has plenty of sunshine. And all this at a fraction of what will tumble from your wallet every day in that city on the banks of the Seine. We'll spend a week in Paris and love it. But smaller cities are still plenty of fun.

4. Cancel everything you can before you leave home:

We shut down our phones, parked our cars, cancelled Netflix, a French-language TV station, my school parking space and newspapers. It adds up.

5. Get credit and debit cards that don't charge a fee:

Most cards tack on a three percent overseas transaction fee. Not Capitol One.

6. Keep track of daily expenditures:

This allows us to both check ourselves and reward ourselves. It takes little effort. I keep a running tally in a notebook I keep in my back pocket.

7. Eat out at lunch, not dinner:

One of the pleasures of life in France is the food. So although Kathy cooks most of our meals with the riches of the daily marketplace, we treat ourselves to a couple of meals out each week. On those occasions, we usually eat a big mid-day meal. The *formule* at many restaurants -- a main course, entrée or dessert, and a glass of wine -- is perhaps 50 or 60 percent the cost of an evening dinner. The portions are as large and the food just as good.

8. Look for little local places, too:

At Le Brun'ch, on Rue Portalis, the food is fresh and the language of choice French. A slice of quiche -- spinach, mushroom or the special of the day -- costs $3.20 and makes a lovely light lunch. Hungry? The plat du jour is $11. And a bottle of water sits on every table (You can always ask for "*une carafe d'eau*" in France. Don't pay for sparkling water.)

We're finding that the places locals frequent not only have good food but cost less. There are always good alternatives between haute cuisine and fast food. Find them.

9. Leave the driving to others:

Being car-free makes us carefree. We have no parking costs. Pay no insurance or tolls. Buy no gas. We've already taken bus trips with our language school to Nice and the Luberon mountain towns of Provence. We've visited Marseille on our own and will again this weekend. The full-day bus trips cost us $35 each (gas, tolls, parking and rental would have been more). And the roundtrip fare to Marseille costs about $14.

As spring arrives, we'll need a car to do more research for my blog, slowlanetravel.com. We'll probably rent one for a couple of individual weeks and the month of June. But six weeks costs a lot less than six months. And we do not miss driving at all because we can walk everywhere.

235

10. Shut down your smart phone:

We call the States by Facetime or Skype. Email to email calls are free. For a pittance, you can buy a Skype "phone number" that allows friends and family at home to dial a local number to call overseas. For local calls, we've bought cheap phones for less than $40 each, and monthly phone cards that cost $28 each. The overall cost of calling anywhere in France is half of our monthly Verizon Wireless bill at home.

11. Trade off with friends who visit:

We have a simple rule for visitors. We'll house you and feed you if you rent a car. This gives us the chance to see more places off the beaten track when friends come to town.

12. Don't fritter; do reward yourself:

It's the little things that burn a hole in your wallet: The $5 you drop on coffee because you get it with cream, the $3.50 cokes you don't need if you carry a water bottle, the overpriced vendors in the market because you haven't comparison-shopped. Drink wine; it costs so much less. And be selective. For example, we went to a lovely free concert of Bach cantatas, but passed on $55 seats to the Mozart Requiem. I pay $10 for a weekly four-hour bridge game. We walked to the park where Paul Cezanne painted "Mont St. Victoire" for nothing.

But do reward yourself. Every so often, Kathy and I simply have to stop by Bechard for a pastry filled with whipped cream and fresh fruit. Yup. Each one costs $4.50. But you can't buy these in Boston. Anywhere. And without food, without wine, you might as well not be in France.

Follow Jerry Lanson on Twitter: www.twitter.com/jerrylanson

MORE: Living Without a Car, France, Budgeting, Long Haul Travel, Slow Lane Travel, Renting an Apartment, Aix en Provence

Tasting French Bread With A Talented Provence Baker

by Slowlanefrance • May 15, 2014

Benoit Fradette is a master baker, arguably the best in Aix-en-Provence.

He starts his workday shortly after 2 a.m. so that he can make bread with a minimal amount of yeast (meaning it rises more slowly) and the maximum amount of taste. At his bakery, *Le Farinoman Fou*, he uses only flour made from organic wheat. He never refrigerates his bread in the process of making it. And he takes great pride in every detail of its quality.

That quality is evident in the taste and from the line that snakes out his bakery door into the street near Place des Precheurs each market day. That's why I couldn't resist when Fradette invited me by his bakery after work for what he called a "bread taste." I hoped to eat some of his bread as part of the bargain.

But first a bit of context. Bread is part of a bubbling *crise,* or crisis, in French cuisine these days, as more of the French seem willing to sacrifice quality for speed and lower costs. Fradette, in turn, is part of a small but growing number of French bakers, according to an article in *The Provence Post*, who are pushing back, baking their breads in full view of customers and stripping away the pastries and other extras that distract from the art of making the best bread. Call it bakery basics.

Though he's a purist, Fradette isn't even French. Nor did he bake his first loaf of bread until he was 20. Canadian born, he moved to France from Montreal a decade ago. He opened his Aix bakery in 2009. (Its name, by the way, is pretty whimsical: *farine* is flour and *fou* is crazy, so the hybrid French-English name *Farinoman Fou* might be translated "the crazy flour man.")

With his early hours you'd think Fradette would look both bleary-eyed and crazy. But he's extraordinarily fit and youthful looking; his permanent home is at the base of Mount Ventoux, about 75 miles away from Aix. For fun, he likes to bike up and down this 6,300 foot mountain, the highest in Provence.

If biking is one passion, bread is his other; he writes a blog and speaks passionately about bread, too.

"The quality of French bread is awful," he said when I first met him while reporting an article on bread for the *Christian Science Monitor.*

"It's a jungle out there," he added after our bread taste.

But for all his strong words, he's usually smiling, as he was when I showed up with five loaves of bread from different bakeries as he'd asked me to.

"I sold my last loaf at 4 o'clock today," he said. "You've tasted my bread anyway." I had, but .....

And then our bread taste began, or something like that. Because Fradette put nothing in his mouth. As I stood at his shoulder he lined up the five breads he told me to buy on a wooden counter top. I'd bought different types from different places and wrapped them all in his bags in an effort to throw him off course. Not a chance.

First he looked at each bread. Then he touched each bread. Then he smelled each bread. He told me what each one would look like inside and why — how dense, how many air pockets — and what I could expect from their taste. Then he cut them open, horizontally, to make his point.

"C'est impossible, c'est impossible, c'est Impossible," he muttered after looking, from left to right at the first three loaves. But if they were "impossible," the fourth loaf was *"le pire"* — the worst, so loaded with yeast to make it rise fast that it would have no taste, he said.

Only the fifth bread, a $2 *petit compagnes* from an independent bakery called *Jean-Pierre Vignes* sort of passed muster. It had a decent crust and was reasonably well-baked, he said.

For the record, the worst was a baguette *tradition*, a name French law reserves for baguettes cooked without additives. It came from an independent Aix baker. Of the other three, one was from the Aix market and two were from French bread chains — Paul, with 449 outlets in 27 countries, and Joseph, a Marseille-based bread company. But while both of the chains discount their baguettes to draw customers, I had bought their more expensive breads for the taste — a $2.80 six-grain bread in the case of Paul, which pushes three baguettes for $2.80. That's only about 85 cents more than Fradette charges for one.

Fradette had proven his point: France's once-famous bakery bread often doesn't measure up to expectation or reputation anymore. But I, alas, went home with just the one loaf he said was pretty good — and, given his empty shelves, none of his.

Fradette sells about three dozen types of bread in his bakery, baking some of these only once every couple of weeks. We particularly like his baguette; his l'Olympique, sort of an oversized version of the baguette; his raisin and nut bread, and his apricot bread. Most of his breads are sold by the kilogram, and it's possible to ask for a half or quarter of a loaf. The store is at 5 Rue Mignet and is open Tuesday through Saturday.

This blog also appeared in the Huffington Post Travel Section.

f Like 2   **Tweet** 2   **8+1** 0   **✉ 🔊 Follow**

Tags: Aix-en-Provence   bread-making   Farinoman Fou   French baguette   French food   Provence   Provence travel
Slow lane travel   travel news

← Last Call: May in the Luberon   Aix-en-Provence's Best-Kept Entertainment Secret →

News Prints

Home   About   About

← Once in awhile, even true stories have happy endings   Is it goodbye or see you soon? →

Memories of Dad have been passed through the generations

Posted on June 20, 2010

My Dad died on Father's Day 30 years ago. On a beautiful June night, my family walked out of Mary Hitchcock Hospital, then in Dartmouth, N.H., where he had been rushed two weeks earlier after suffering an aortic aneurysm. We were exhausted and dazed.

If Dad wasn't larger than life, he certainly was brimming over with it. Even today, in my mind's eye, I can see him limping onto the tennis court, waving his racquet before the game against a phantom foe, or standing on the deck of my parent's Vermont home, a Marlboro dangling from the corner of his mouth, eyes twinkling.

Dad never met our two daughters, but they've met him, in family stories shared during holiday celebrations. In fact, "Gunther stories" crop up just about everywhere when we see relatives and old family friends. He was just too big a personality to bury and forget.

Gunther Lanson was born Gunther Lichtenstein in Berlin, Germany, on Aug. 19, 1909, the only child of a bank executive and a mother so imperious that we called her "the duchess" as boys. But there was nothing stuck up about Gunther, as all my college friends called him. His was an American story.

He fled Hitler's Germany, hiking over the mountains into Czechoslovakia in 1935. Though he'd earned a doctorate in German law, once he found his way to America, he learned English by working as a movie usher for $14 a week. He joined the U.S. Army in World War II, serving as a staff sergeant for a propaganda unit whose main mission was to break the will of German soldiers by sending broadcasts behind enemy lines.

239

Back home, he took a job as sales promotion manager for his uncle's lighting company in the era of three-martini Madison Avenue lunches. He bought a prefab Levitt house in Carle Place, Long Island, for his family, paying $14,000, and did his best to catch the Penn Station train that got him home at 6:31 for dinner. But if this was a Leave It to Beaver life for my brother Dennis and I, Gunther, I suspect, would have preferred something more exciting, more international, more bohemian.

Still, if he sacrificed to support us all, he never lost his essential self. That is the man I remember, a rotund, white-haired, mostly bald gentleman with a thick German accent who loved to bend the rules (unless he'd set them), could be generous to a fault and periodically left us all trembling when he "blew," family shorthand for his temper tantrums.

Sometimes bending the rules was something as simple as the thrill of sneaking into more expensive seats at the ballpark. Dad seemed to enjoy that challenge as much as he did the game on the field.

Sometimes it was something more serious. So, for example, when in the days of segregation my family took a boat ride across the Chesapeake Bay, he sat us down in the empty "colored" dining section rather than standing in line for the crowded "whites only" one. After a bit of heated fencing, he got served. I'd like to say it was a blow for social justice, but suspect Dad was simply hungry.

Still, having gone to college under the spreading cloud of Nazi law, he didn't hesitate to do what he considered right rather than what was required, a few times taking personal risks to help friends of my brother during the turbulent Vietnam era.

Gunther Lanson prided himself in helping. When I was a kid, he would drive us all over the greater New York area on the weekends to visit the old German ladies — friends, family, his mother. After he'd retired to Vermont, he'd regularly drive two hours to Boston to pick up a neighbor or one of us at the airport. When the Connecticut River overflowed its banks, he won the trust of his reserved Vermont neighbors by helping one of the toughest and poorest families in the community.

It was not that Gunther Lanson was a do-gooder. He'd have shuddered at the mere thought. He was as politically incorrect as they come, openly flirting with waitresses in front of his wife and kids, sometimes talking too loudly or too crudely, embarrassing us with more frequency than I'd like to remember. But he cared about people and would always take them for who they were, not what they were worth or their rank or stature in society.

That, to me, was his greatest gift. On this day, three decades after his death, I miss him still.

Share this:

f Facebook   ♪ StumbleUpon   🐦 Twitter   ⑂ Reddit   ✉ Email   🖶 Print

Jerry Lanson ☙ Become a fan ✉ 🐦 👍
Journalism professor, Emerson College

A Second Take at Parenting After Years on Our Own

Posted: 09/10/2014 10:48 am EDT | Updated: 11/10/2014 5:59 am EST

| 👍 45 | 6 | 9 | 0 | 0 |

🔲 Like   f Share   🐦 Tweet   *Pin it*   Comment

LEXINGTON, Mass. -- Mornings have gotten a lot livelier in the Lanson household this fall.

My day starts with exercises and free-dancing with 7-year-old Devon, usually to Steve Songs' "Marvelous Day" CD.

From there it is time for breakfast, with "MISS Devon," the fifth-grade teacher of my twin sister Kathy and I. Miss Devon bears a striking resemblance to my exercise partner, Devon, but we keep this under wraps.

Fifth grade, Kathy and I are learning, has pretty strict rules. We must raise our hands to ask questions.

"Teacher, may I scratch my nose?" I asked today.

"That's gross," my teacher's pet twin blurted out. (Miss Devon disciplined her for talking out of turn.)

It all gets pretty goofy.

None of this, of course, would be all that unusual except that Kathy and I are card-carrying members of the Medicare generation. And our younger daughter (no, we're not twins) turns 30 this fall.

Devon is our grand-daughter, and she's living here and attending 2nd grade in the marvelous elementary school about a mile from our house.

I can't say we weren't a little worried about having a kid back in the house. Devon is our oldest grand-child and, as I always tell her, my best friend. But parenting full-time again in our mid-60s? Yikes.

As it turns out, it has been a treat and a gift. Devon brings light and laughter to our house just about daily. Watching her learn, being at the receiving end of her curiosity, makes me wish I'd been around more when my daughters were little and I was working long hours as a newspaper editor.

"What's *mezzo-forte*?" she asked me as she got ready to head to school.

"Moderately-loud," I said.

"I didn't know that," Kathy said (she's the artistic one; I sing).

"What's *piano*," asked Devon.

"Quiet."

241

242

Where do kids get these questions? She has a million and one.

Nor is it only Devon who has delighted us as the school year begins. I've gained a new understanding of Lexington's reputation as a terrific school district. The first week, parents walked kids to school in droves with dogs and pre-school siblings in tow. Though Devon's school is the second biggest in town, with more than 550 students, the assistant principal greeted Devon by name when I dropped her off the third day on the blacktop where the kids line up. She bent low so she was at Devon's eye level.

"I bet that's your favorite color," she said, looking at Devon's bright pink outfit.

"One of them," Devon said.

"Well, I can tell that you like bright colors," she told her.

"I like your outfit, too," Devon replied.

This moment of connection was one of many we saw in Devon's first few days. By Tuesday of her second full week she asked me for the "rolling dropoff," a spot at which kids can hop out of cars and head alone to their class lines. She already felt at home in her new school.

Devon has started to read to us, too. Simple books, mind you. But she's excited; she read five yesterday. And as long as school brings a sense of fun and accomplishment rather than fear, I expect she'll have a great year.

Kathy and I are learning, too, or perhaps re-learning. Here's what we're observing: Give children time and positive attention, and the world that they see and share is pure joy. Make learning a pleasure and not a test, and creativity and knowledge both thrive.

Yeah, Kathy and I are plenty tired come the weekend. Seven-year-olds have a whole lot of energy. But we're also rediscovering how amazing the world, real and imaginary, is through the eyes and experiences of young children.

That, as the Master Card ad says, is priceless.

Follow Jerry Lanson on Twitter: www.twitter.com/jerrylanson
MORE: Grandparents Raising Grandchildren, Grandchildren, Elementary School, Imagination, Humor, Play, Grandparenting, Learning

Jerry Lanson ♥ Become a fan ✉ 𝕐 👍
Journalism professor, Emerson College

Media Need to Establish Clear Ethics Codes on Using, Posting Tweets

Posted: 04/11/2012 3:59 pm EDT | Updated: 06/19/2012 5:12 am EDT

👍 0	9	17	0	5

🔁 Like Ⓕ Share 🐦 Tweet Linked in 💬 Comment

Thinkstock

Don't retweet this yet.

Don't post it on your news site. Not until you check to see if I am who I claim.

That I'm a professor and not a charlatan. That my links are real. That I didn't make up this blog -- wholesale -- or attribute it to unnamed sources who thought they overheard something.

Twitter has been praised for helping to break major stories from Arab Spring and the Trayvon Martin shooting to Syria's atrocities. It is a powerful tool.

But along the way, the world of Twitter has led journalism through its own atrocities, or at least train wrecks. And Twitter's use by reputable news sites, professional reporters and opinion writers at times remains about as sophisticated as law enforcement during the days of Wyatt Earp and the O.K. Corral.

The latest big error, as the *New York Times* reported this week, came when "old and venerable media" (CBS News and *The Washington Post*) joined *The Huffington Post* and others in rushing to publish a false rumor that South Carolina Gov. Nikki Haley was about to indicted on charges of tax fraud. Noted the *Times,* the case involved:

> ...a liberal-leaning 25-year-old blogger eager to make a name for his new Web site, and a buzz-seeking political press corps that looks to the real-time, unedited world of Twitter as the first place to break news.
>
> In retrospect, there were clear reasons to doubt the March 29 report, from a blog called the Palmetto Public Record ... The blog's editor, Logan Smith, never asked the governor's office for comment before he posted his report. Later, in an e-mail, Mr. Smith said he could not be sure whether his sources were correct.

Shame on the blogger. But much more shame on news organizations whose professionalism rests -- or should -- on checking facts and publishing only what's true.

That surely didn't happen. A *Times* timeline notes that two minutes after Smith posted under the headline "Haley indictment imminent" -- this based on two unidentified "well-placed legal experts" -- a blogger for the Washington newspaper *The Hill* had tweeted it. Nine minutes later, *The Daily Beast* reposted the piece; 20 minutes later, the *Washington Post* -- and the deluge of calls to Haley's office was underway.

243

Were this some horrible aberration it would be embarrassing enough to journalism, whose very future as a paid profession rests to a significant extent on what of value it can provide readers and viewers beyond the gossip mill of YouTube, Twitter, the blogosphere and "citizen journalism."

But this is anything but a horrible aberration.

Writes the *Times*, "This episode is not the first time that a questionable Twitter report has roiled the 2012 elections."

And national politics has no corner on the market. I teach journalism ethics, and questionable or tasteless uses of Twitter have become a recurring course theme.

1. On Jan. 20, the Poynter Institute told the story of a senior editor for California Watch who tweeted the overheard conversation of a woman he was "99 percent sure" was a Santa Ana City councilwoman. He neither confirmed her identify nor asked for comment.

2. In early February, CNN suspended contributor Roland Martin after he sent homophobic tweets during the Super Bowl, Poynter reported.

3. A week later, Jim Romenesko reported that Fox Sports' Jason Whitlock posted a crass stereotype about Asian-Americans after basketball sensation Jeremy Lin, the remarkable Chinese-American point guard who burst onto the scene this season, led the New York Knicks to victory.

In a letter to Whitlock, the Asian-American Journalists Association wrote: "The attempt at humor ... exposed how some media companies fail to adequately monitor the antics of their high-profile representatives."

The list goes on. Which raises the question: Why?

When it comes to issues such as plagiarism or conflict of interest, most high-profile journalism organizations have clear, blanket policies -- don't. Don't steal other people's work, don't serve on your school board when you're covering education, don't endorse presidential candidates.

But the rules for Twitter are murkier, if articulated at all. For example, the *New York Times'* lengthy ethics code, posted online with 139 separate points, has an entire section on blogs, but nothing on Twitter. Then again, the policy is dated October 2005.

NPR's new Ethics Handbook, unveiled in February, includes a special social media section. It warns reporters to "Conduct yourself online just as you would in any other public circumstances as an NPR journalist. ... Verify information before passing it on."

That seems like good advice. But then NPR seems to suggest it won't always happen:

> One key is to be transparent about what we're doing. We tell readers what has and hasn't been confirmed. We challenge those putting information out on social media to provide evidence. We raise doubts and ask questions when we have concerns ... And we always ask an important question: am I about to spread a thinly-sourced rumor or am I passing on valuable and credible (even if unverified) information in a transparent manner with appropriate caveats.

I, for one, like the emphasis on verification rather than on passing on rumor and saying it may or may not be true. But in an age in which millions of Americans still believe our president is a Muslim born in Kenya -- and no, he's neither -- even the most upstanding news sites can't always ignore what's whirling around on the Internet.

That does not mean, however, that journalists need to contribute to the confusion. Their news organizations need policies that emphasize the importance of being right, no just first. They need to remember that a reporter's first responsibility is to check things out -- before passing things along. They need guidelines on how to check the veracity of tweets.

So. Maybe my name is Ernie and I'm a dentist. Don't believe what you read just because it's in print.

Follow Jerry Lanson on Twitter: www.twitter.com/jerrylanson

MORE: Social Media, Twitter, Journalism Ethics, Ethics Codes, Journalism, Ethics, Social Life, Media Critique

245

Jerry Lanson ♥ Become a fan ✉ 🐦 👍
Journalism professor, Emerson College

It's Time to Push Back Against the Bullies and Bigots

Posted: 03/03/2012 7:50 pm EST | Updated: 05/03/2012 5:12 am EDT

| 16 | 74 | submit | 6 |

f Share   🐦 Tweet   reddit   Comment

The firestorm of rebuke that met Rush Limbaugh's crude characterization of a Georgetown law student who dared to speak in favor of free contraception flashed across the headlines, the blogosphere and Facebook Friday. Such contempt -- he called her a "slut" and a "prostitute" -- appears to have crossed the threshold of what most Americans will tolerate.

But I can't say Limbaugh's words shocked me. This kind of remark is all too familiar in this political season -- or perhaps century -- of dissing and disregard for fact.

It is, after all, less than two weeks since an ESPN producer posted the headline "Chink in the Armor" on the sports network's mobile user platform after Chinese-American basketball phenomenon Jeremy Lin played his first bad game for the New York Knicks. It's only a month since CNN political commentator Roland Martin tweeted anti-gay "jokes" during the Super Bowl.

And the Limbaugh brouhaha broke on the same day my morning *Boston Globe* told of a new round of fraternity hazing at Dartmouth University so crude and degrading that it led Theatre Professor Peter Hackett to ask the paper, "Why do we have a social system that is from the 19th century?"

Yes, why? The answer, perhaps, is that the hazing and Limbaugh incidents are just the latest sign that if we don't live in the 19th century, plenty of people still appear to long for a time when white males from the right families ruled supreme and everyone else could just damn well get used to it.

One doesn't have to look much past the abuse heaped on our first African-American president to realize that. Barack Obama has been called a socialist (repeatedly), a closet Kenyan Muslim (where's the birth certificate, huh?), a liar (before the joint houses of Congress) and lots more.

Wrote Andrew Rosenthal in a *New York Times* commentary, "There has been a racist undertone to many of the Republican attacks leveled against President Obama for the last three years, and in this dawning presidential campaign."

Still, the issue posed here is larger than the president and more wide-ranging than the issue of race alone. At least Barack Obama chose to run for office. Sandra Fluke, the third-year law student Limbaugh savaged, merely had the temerity to speak her mind, to support the Obama Administration's call for greater access to insurance-covered birth control for women. She might think twice before she speaks out again.

What perhaps offers some hope is the response to Limbaugh not only from Democrats but from some members of his own party.

Massachusetts Republican Sen. Scott Brown, was quoted by the *Los Angeles Times* as saying "Rush Limbaugh's comments are reprehensible." (Yes, Brown is up for re-election in a largely blue state, but still.) House Speaker John Boehner's office trotted out a spokesman, who, the LA Times reported, said the speaker "obviously believes the use of those words was inappropriate." And even arch social conservative Rick Santorum reportedly managed to say that Limbaugh was being "absurd."

Incivility is too nice a name for incidents like this and others in recent weeks. They are bullying. They are bigotry. And they will continue to stretch at the country's fragile fabric as long as Americans in positions to say and do something stand back and stay quiet.

In his book *Integrity*, Yale Law Professor Stephen Carter wrote that an integral person can't stand pat after discerning right from wrong. Integrity means owning up to what we believe to be right -- acting on it and then speaking up to explain our actions.

Scrolling the headlines, I'd say on most days we have a way to go before living up to Carter's standard. ESPN fired the producer of that racist headline about Lin and CNN suspended Roland Martin. But neither network said much more about the incidents. It took Republican frontrunner Mitt Romney until Friday night to say anything about Rush Limbaugh's vitriol, and then he managed only "I'll just say... it's not the language I would have used." And Dartmouth President Jim Kim seems to be trying to thread a needle on the hazing incident, suggesting, according to the *Globe*, that any effort to ban the Greek system at the college would merely push the problem underground and off-campus, where drinking and driving would pose greater dangers to students.

Perhaps. But at least the college's message would be clear and the new risks would be to the bulliers, not the bullied.

Bullies, like those hazers, like Limbaugh, can only thrive when others stay mute. Silence tells the haters and hecklers they've got a green light. So let's make some noise.

Follow Jerry Lanson on Twitter: www.twitter.com/jerrylanson

MORE: Sandra Fluke , Rush Limbaugh Sandra Fluke, Rush Limbaugh Slut, Rush Limbaugh, Rush Limbaugh Prostitute

247

Gatekeeper

Mark Leccese watches Boston and the people who report on it

< Back to front page   Text size

What, exactly, did David Ortiz say?

Posted by Mark Leccese April 20, 2010 06:56 PM

| 23 | 0 | 0 | 0 |

Comments ()
E-mail story
Print story

Share   **f** Facebook **⌄** Twitter **⌕** Pinterest **8+** Share **✛** Share

Back in the clubhouse after an 0-for-4 night against the Yankees two weeks ago, David Ortiz was not a happy man. Reporters' questions about his struggles made him less happy. Ortiz was so far from a happy place that his answer contained, by my guess, at least two of the seven dirty words banned from broadcast by the 1978 Supreme Court decision FCC v. Pacifica Foundation.

I read three different stories about Papi's pop-off, and all three had different quotes. Not entirely different, but different enough. So what did he say? No, not the curse words â€" we can all guess those â€" but the direct quote, the words that came out of his mouth.

The *Springfield Republican's* website had him saying this:

> You guys just wait. (Stuff) happens. Two (expletive deleted) games, and you (expletive deleted) guys are going crazy. There's 160 games left. Relax.'

The *Boston Herald* quoted him thus:

> (Bleep) happens. Then you guys talk (bleep). Two (bleeping) games already. (Bleepers) are going crazy. Whatâ€™s up with that, man? (Bleep). Thereâ€™s (bleeping) 160 games left. Yâ€™all (bleepers) go ahead and hit for me.

And ESPN Boston reported this quote:

> You guys wait 'til [expletive] happens, then you can talk [expletive]. Two [expletive] games, and already you [expletives] are going crazy. What's up with that, man? [Expletive]. [Expletive] 160 games left. That's a [expletive]. One of you [expletives] got to go ahead and hit for me.

Let's get rid of all the brackets and parentheses and replace the naughty words with less naughty words so we can get a better look at the differences in the quotes.

Republican: "You guys just wait. Stuff happens. Two darn games, and you darn guys are going crazy. There's 160 games left. Relax."

Herald: "Stuff happens. Then you guys talk stuff. Two darn games already. Chowderheads are going crazy. Whatâ€™s up with that, man? Darn. Thereâ€™s darn 160 games left. Yâ€™all chowderheads go ahead and hit for me."

ESPN: "You guys wait 'til stuff happens, then you can talk stuff. Two darn games, and already you chowderheads are going crazy. What's up with that, man? Darn. Darn 160 games left. That's a darn. One of you chowderheads got to go ahead and hit for me."

So did he say "Stuff happens" or did he say "You guys wait 'til stuff happens" or did he say "You guys just wait. Stuff happens"?

Did he ask *each* reporter to go ahead and hit for him or did he just ask "*one of you*" reporters?

I can understand that having an intimidatingly large man swear at you might make your pen pause over your notebook. But all three reporters wrote down what Ortiz said, and they were probably all using digital voice recorders, too.

It's a credibility issue; if a reporter gets a quote not quite accurately, the reader begins to wonder what other facts in the story aren't quite accurate.

Keep an eye out for this. Different version of the same quote in different media occur more often than you'd think, and when it does, I'm darn puzzled.

249

Gatekeeper

Mark Leccese watches Boston and the people who report on it

< Back to front page   Text size

Speculating — no, not that kind — on the gyrations of the stock market

Posted by Mark Leccese May 24, 2010 03:10 PM   Print | Comments (0)

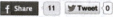 

So why did the stock market dive last Thursday? Let the best business media in the country explain:

Barron's: "European contagion and financial reform continue to weigh on stocks this morning, with the Dow Futures down 95 points at 9,961, and the S&P 500 futures off 9 points at 1,061."

The New York Times: "Fears that the fragile economic recovery in the United States might be threatened by the financial and political crisis in Europe gripped Wall Street on Thursday, sending the stock market into a sharp decline and leaving anxious traders wondering where the pain might stop."

The Associated Press: "Stocks plunged again yesterday as more investors woke up to the possibility that economic problems such as Europe's debt crisis might spread around the world and stop the growing recovery in the United States."

Fox Business: "Wall Street drowned in another sea of worries and U.S. markets suffered their steepest losses in more than a year on Thursday, a reflection of how concerns about Europe's debt crisis have snowballed into fears about the sustainability of the global economic recovery."

OK, I get it: Jitters about Europe's debt crisis caused the stock market to go down.

But hold on. The next day, the stock market went *up*. I read Friday's news carefully and I did not see any stories about Europe's debt crisis being solved while I was sleeping Thursday night. With Europe in the midst of debt crisis, the stock market went down. With Europe still in the midst of debt crisis, the stock market went up. Please explain.

Bloomberg's Friday story takes a shot: "U.S. stocks rose, rebounding from the market's biggest drop in a year, as investors speculated equities may have fallen too much this week on concern about Europe's debt crisis."

Now I'm beginning to think they're just guessing. Journalists who cover the stock market make a common practice of not only reporting whether the stock market went up or down but *why* the stock market went up or down. How can they possibly know why millions of individual and organizational buyers and sellers bought and sold stocks?

The job of people who write the news is to report facts — demonstrable, verifiable facts. It is a fact that on Thursday, May 21, 1) Europe was in the throes of a debt crisis; and 2) the stock market went down. Those two facts are correlated, but it is not a verifiable fact that 1 caused 2. Especially when the stock market went up the next day.

Look again at Friday's Bloomberg story (three paragraphs above). The stock market went up on Friday because "investors speculated equities may have fallen too much this week." What the reporter is doing here is speculating on what investors are speculating. Or, to put it another way, guessing what investors are thinking and reporting it as fact. The story does include one quote from one bullish investments manager who appears, for the purposes of the story, to represent "investors."

At this point we've left verifiable facts far behind.

Here's the beginning of the Globe story from Friday.

> The turbulent stock market took a turn for the better yesterday, but investors still went home bruised by one of the worst trading weeks of the year.
>
> Worries over Europe's financial mess have driven stocks sharply lower around the world.
>
> Key US benchmarks have fallen by more than 10 percent since their late April peak, a so-called market correction. Overall, the Dow lost 427 points, or 4 percent, just this week, with Thursday's 370-point plunge the index's worst one-day setback in a year.
>
> But after three straight days of pounding losses, the Dow Jones industrial average climbed 125.38 to 10,193.39 yesterday, thanks to a late afternoon surge. The Dow did briefly go below the 10,000 mark in the morning before recovering.

251

Cut that second paragraph — the speculation — and you have the beginning of a story built from facts. Shouldn't that be enough?

Gatekeeper

Mark Leccese watches Boston and the people who report on it

< Back to front page

Text size ■ +

Condoms for kids in Provincetown: Three newspapers, three angles

Posted by Mark Leccese June 24, 2010 11:35 AM

Print | Comments (2)

f Share 26   Tweet 8   in Share 0   g +1 0   Share This 122   E-mail

Just a glance at the headlines in the two Boston dailies this morning telegraphs each paper's emphasis in a story about the Provincetown School Committee voting two weeks ago to make condoms available to students in its elementary school and high school.

Herald, top of page 7: P'Town puts condoms in kids' hands

Globe, below the fold on page 1: Condoms, secrecy for Provincetown pupils: Parents, officials criticize policy

The first two paragraphs of each story expand on the headlines.

Here's the top of the Herald story.

> A new policy in Provincetown to make condoms available to even first-graders is being called "absurd" and a frantic overreaction to sex education.
>
> "What's next? Birth control pills?" asked Kris Mineau, head of the conservative group Massachusetts Family Institute.

Here's the top of the Globe story.

> Students in Provincetown — from elementary school to high school — will be able to get free condoms at school under a recently approved policy that takes effect this fall. The rule also requires school officials to keep student requests secret, and ignore parents' objections.

> "The intent is to protect kids," said School Superintendent Beth Singer, who wrote the policy that the Cape Cod town's School Committee unanimously passed two weeks ago. "We know that sexual experimentation is not limited to an age, so how does one put an age on it?"

For comparison's sake, here's the top of the June 11 story on the website of the Provincetown Banner, headlined "School leaders OK condom policy in Provincetown."

> A condom distribution policy at the elementary and high school here was approved by the school committee on Tuesday.
>
> Some committee members were concerned that the policy requires students to speak with a school nurse or other trained counselor before receiving a condom. However, Dr. Beth Singer, school superintendent, argued that since there is no age limit on the distribution policy, she wanted to ensure that younger students requesting condoms receive information on their use.

253

The Banner begins its story by doing no more than stating the Provincetown School Committee took the action. It reports that some School Committee members were "concerned," but immediately follows that up with reassurances from the superintendent of schools. The Banner story, which is only seven paragraphs long, quotes only the superintendent and three school committee members, all of whom were in favor of the policy. No controversy there.

The start of the Globe story only hints that this may be a controversial decision, emphasizing that the Provincetown policy requires school official to "ignore parents' objections." It doesn't *say* the new policy is controversial, but "ignore" is a loaded verb (as opposed to, say, "not consider") guaranteed to plant a thought in the reader's mind that would go something like this: "Ignore the parents? Well, that's going to tick off some people."

The first paragraph of the Herald story — with its "even first-graders" and "'absurd'" and "frantic overreaction" — makes it clear that giving condoms to school children is at least controversial and perhaps, as the British say, barmy.

Despite its beginning, the full 12-paragraph Herald story devotes six of its paragraphs to sources in favor of the policy (the superintendent and the School Committee chair) three paragraphs to reporting neutral information (including a neutral statement from a state Department of Education official). Only three of the paragraphs in the story are devoted to a vocal opponent (the head of the "conservative group" the Massachusetts Family Institute).

But those are the first three paragraphs of the story, and that makes the emphasis of the story clearly hostile to the Provincetown policy.

Counting sources and paragraphs in the Globe story reveals a textbook journalistic balance. There are three sources in favor of the policy (the superintendent, the School Committee chair, and the chair of the Board of Selectmen) and three against (a parent, the town manager, and the head of the Massachusetts Family Institute). Each side gets nine paragraphs. Eight paragraphs are devoted to reporting neutral facts.

Like the Herald story, though, what the reporters and editors chose to put at the top of the story — in the first five paragraphs — reveals an emphasis that appears to support the Provincetown policy.

A news story may be balanced in its distribution of sources and its quotes from the two sides, but it is the top of the story, the first few paragraphs, that signal what is most important in the story, which side gets the most prominent play, and what most readers will come away with.

Yet another reason to be glad we live in a city with two daily newspapers.

AND ANOTHER THING

Today's Mangled Metaphor Of The Day comes from Republican gubernatorial candidate Charlie Baker, quoted in Yvonne Abraham's column in this morning's Globe on the mounting problems with state's finances and what Baker agues is Beacon Hill's inadequate response.

> "I feel like we're just kicking the can," he says. "And eventually, it's going to blow up."

What the heck is *in* that can?

Follow Mark Leccese on Twitter at @mleccese.

Gatekeeper

Mark Leccese watches Boston and the people who report on it

< Back to front page   Text size

Globe, WBUR fail to fully examine Future Boston Alliance's claim of "brain drain"

Posted by Mark Leccese June 11, 2012 09:12 AM   Print | Comments (0)

f Share 5   Tweet 4   in Share 0   +1 2   ShareThis 127   E-mail

There is "no shortage of media buzz surrounding the Future Boston Alliance and its mission to change what it sees as the city's stodgy reputation," the Globe wrote in a June 7 story.

The headline on the piece tells the story: *Can they make over Boston? A group of activists and entrepreneurs are determined to make the city more appealing for young professionals. And they're prepared to step on some toes in the process.*

I have no doubt the Future Boston Alliance has good intentions and sincerely wants to improve life in the Boston area for young professionals. In addition, I am not the guy to ask how that could be done — when I was last a young professional, Tyler Seguin was in diapers, and my night-life generally involves watching the news, reading with a ballgame on, and heading up to bed by 11.

It is the coverage of the Future Boston Alliance I find troublesome. A week before the Globe story, WBUR's "RadioBoston" aired a 22-minute segment about the Future Boston Alliance and its complaints. This is how the segment began:

> About 40 percent of college graduates leave the Boston region a year after they finish school. That's according to research conducted by the Federal Reserve Bank of Boston. In contrast, fewer than 20 percent of recent college graduates leave California. Brain drain represents a real challenge here.

These are trend stories about a trend the data say doesn't exist. The folks running the Future Boston Alliance are smart, articulate and media savvy, but the Globe and WBUR should have done more reporting on the data that exists — about which more shortly — to present fuller representations of whether the region is suffering from a "brain drain" and whether the Boston area is "appealing for young professionals."

255

Both the Globe and WBUR did contact Boston Mayor Thomas Menino's office for comment, and both news outlets featured the mayor's office's refutation of the Future Boston Alliance's claim in their stories.

In the Globe story, Dot Joyce, Mayor Menino's spokeswoman, made these points:

- Boston is gaining, not losing, young professionals and the 2010 U.S. Census data show that Boston has the highest population of 20- to 34-year-olds of any of the nation's biggest cities.

- The 20- to 34-year-old population of Boston increased 11 percent from 2000 to 2010.

- One of the complaints of the Future Boston Alliance is the city's closing times for bars and restaurants and other late-night establishments; Joyce points out that closing times are the same in San Francisco, Seattle, Austin, and Denver.

In the Globe story, Joyce gets four paragraphs in a 32-paragraph story. In the WBUR segment, she gets one minute of the 22 minutes the station devoted to its story. Neither the Globe nor WBUR quotes any other sources in their stories who might provide data about the retention of recent college graduates in the Boston area and the region.

I could not find a Federal Reserve Bank of Boston report that states a much higher percentage of college graduates leave the Boston area a year after they finish school than leave California, as WBUR reported. That doesn't mean the report does not exist, just that WBUR found it and I did not.

When I heard it, though, it made intuitive sense to me: California is a much bigger state and Massachusetts must have far more college students who come from out-of-state for education than California does.

I checked the numbers at the National Center for Education Statistics and the U.S. Census Bureau and this is what I found: California has 200 colleges that grant bachelor's degrees and a population of 37 million. That's one four-year college for every 1,850,000 residents. Massachusetts has 88 colleges that grant bachelor's degrees and a population of 6.5 million — one four-year college for every 74,000 residents.

The Federal Reserve Bank of Boston's New England Public Policy Center addressed this in a 2009 report titled "Retention of Recent College Gradates in New England."

> Typical migration rates for New England often show net out-migration among recent college graduates — meaning that more individuals appear to be leaving than entering the region. However, such rates reflect only moves made upon graduation from region of institution to region of adult residence, failing to capture the earlier in-migration of students to attend college.

> Why is that important? New England attracts a relatively high share of students from outside the region, with more students arriving to attend college than leaving to attend college elsewhere. Even though the region holds onto only a fraction of those incoming students after they graduate, they more than offset the number of graduates who do leave, so the region comes out ahead for a given class.

The same group, in its 2007 report "Is New England Experiencing a brain drain?," decided the answer is "no."

> While it is true that fewer people between 25 and 39 live in New England today than at any time during the past 15 years, the number of those in the specific category of young professionals has not declined, thanks to steady increases in the share of young people who complete college. Additionally, while this decline in young people is often attributed to out-migration, it is due, at least in part, to a large number of individuals who are aging out of the cohort, rather than leaving the region.
>
> In short, a careful analysis of the data indicates that reports of a major "brain drain" from the region are overstated.

257

"The brain drain of recent college graduates and thirtysomethings leaving Boston" is one of the major problems cited by the Future Boston Alliance in its video mission statement. It does not appear to be true, but the Globe and WBUR both report the claim.

There's more data. A November 2011 analysis of 2010 Census data by the Boston Redevelopment Authority ("Demographic and Socio-Economic Trends in Boston") reports 44.3 percent of Boston's adult population has at least a bachelor's degree, ranking Boston it fourth amongst the 25 largest cities in the U.S.

Still, there are some worrisome data. The Boston Fed's 2009 report looks at college graduate retention in the region by field and finds New England lags the rest of the country in retaining college graduates in some fields while outpacing the nation in retaining college graduates in others.

> New England ranks near the bottom in retaining graduates in most fields. However, health care is an exception: more than 90 percent of this field's graduates remain in New England. Graduates in some other fields also had retention rates above the country's overall average. ...
>
> For example, nearly 77 percent of education majors and 73 percent of business majors stayed in the region after graduation — likely reflecting the strength of the region's academic and professional services sectors. In contrast, only 64 percent of science/technology/engineering/and mathematics majors remained in New England after graduating. Although this is certainly a concern, it is perhaps not surprising, as these individuals are in high demand throughout the country.

We all have anecdotes about young professionals — friends or coworkers — who found Boston not the place they wanted to live and work, for whatever reasons, and moved on. But anecdotes are not data, and the Globe and WBUR could have done a better job balancing their stories by seeking out more data.

Follow @mleccese on Twitter.

Mark Leccese watches Boston and the people who report on it

< Back to front page   Text size − +

Manti Te'o hoax a failure by major media

Posted by Mark Leccese January 22, 2013 08:48 AM   Print | Comments (7)

f Share 33   Tweet 6   in Share 0   +1 2   ShareThis 288   E-mail

In all the media ruckus over the story of Notre Dame star linebacker Manti Te'o, who made up a story about the death of his girlfriend, one obvious fact has been little remarked upon: the complete failure of a surprisingly large number of elite reporters and editors to do basic journalism.

What we have here are two failures: It starts with *Sports Illustrated* — a magazine legendary for tight editing — looking into the face of the hoax and turning away. Once the hoax had been published and thus validated by *Sports Illustrated*, the rest of the American media felt no need to check *Sports Illustrated's* reporting.

Then Timothy Burke, an editor at the irreverent sports website Deadspin, got an anonymous email suggesting he "check out" the story of Manti Te'o's dead girlfriend.
If you read the Deadspin story of Jan. 16, you won't have much doubt who is behind the hoax — Manti Te'o and a young man he knows named Ronaiah Tuiasosopo. Read it and you'll come to the same conclusion.

The day after Deadspin broke the hoax story, the bosses at *Sports Illustrated* asked the reporter and writer of its October 1 cover story, Pete Thamel, to "to give an account of his reporting" which he did in a blog post that runs to nearly 5,000 words and includes a transcript of his interviews with Manti Te'o.

It is an astonishing document. Thamel describes checking the story after his interviews in the Notre Dame campus, finding "red flags," and then solving the red flag problem by making minor changes to his copy.

These are the three big flags and what *Sports Illustrated* did about them.

259

1. Thamel checked the LexisNexis database for information about Lennay Kekua, the name of Te'o's hoax girlfriend. He found nothing. He looked online for an obituary or a death notice. He found nothing. "But," he writes, "that might be explained by the fact that she had three recent places she called home, or by her family not wanting publicity."
2. Te'o had told Thamel that his girlfriend had graduated from Stanford University in either 2010 or 2011 – he couldn't remember which. Thamel called a friend in the athletic department at Stanford University, who told Thamel he could not find anyone with the name Kekua in the Stanford alumni directory and added that he "thought it was odd that, on such a small campus, he'd never heard of a student dating Te'o." Thamel, while admitting "this was the most glaring sign I missed," simply removed any mention of Stanford University from the article.
3. Manti Te'o told Thamel that his girlfriend had been injured in an automobile accident with a drunk driver, and it was at the hospital after the accident that doctors discovered her fatal leukemia. Thamel and the magazine's fact-checker searched the Internet for details of this drunken driving accident and could not find a word about it. So Thamel "took the drunk driving reference out. It was just a car accident."

Why did Thamel ignore three solid pieces of evidence that Lennay Kekua did not exist and had never existed?

Well, who wants to believe that the young man you are writing about would make up a story about a dead girlfriend? Michael Rosenberg, a college football reporter at SportsIllustrated.com, wrote on the night the hoax was revealed:

> We're all supposed to have b.s. detectors in this business, but mine would not have gone off there. Evidently, I'm not alone, because dozens of media outlets mentioned the girlfriend without wondering if she existed. In that situation, a reporter tries to talk to her family, other people who knew her -- you fill in the edges of the story. But if you don't get a hold of those people, would you really think "Hey, this is probably just a hoax, and this girlfriend doesn't exist"? Be honest.

Honestly, no – after the interview with the young athlete, I would not have begun to think he made up a dead girlfriend.

But, honestly, after I could find no obituary, no evidence of an auto accident, and no evidence any such person ever attended Stanford? At the very least – the very least – any responsible journalist would tell his or her editors to hold the story back until more reporting could be done.

The sports website SBNation quickly compiled a list — with links to stories — of 21 media organizations who fell for the hoax, including SBNation itself, *The Boston Globe*, ESPN, *The Chicago Tribune*, *USA Today*, CBS Sports, The Associated Press and *The Los Angeles Times*.

The Chicago Tribune, in a story the day after Deadspin revealed the hoax, saw a "black mark on sports journalism."

> The scam does more than shatter a college football fairy tale. It also leaves a black mark on sports journalism, as many news outlets — including the *Tribune* — ran stories about Kekua's passing without verifying her death. There was no published obituary for Kekua and no California driver's license issued to anyone with that name. The Social Security Administration database had no record of anyone with the surname Kekua dying in 2012.
>
> Yet respected national publications such as *Sports Illustrated*, *The Los Angeles Times* and *The New York Times* all ran stories about Te'o's heartbreak. *The Chicago Tribune* published 15 articles mentioning her death in the past four months.

So many reporters and editors at so many respectable news outlets fell for the hoax for a simple reason: because *Sports Illustrated* and ESPN and The Associated Press fell for the hoax.

Eric Wemple, the media blogger at the Washington Post, agrees.

> Critics simply cannot believe that so many reporters fell for it, though the history of the Internet yields one clue: Once a big-name news outlet reports something, the rest of the media is free to repeat without confirming.

Wemple blames all sportswriters in the world.

> The colossal embarrassment will prompt a whole lot of soul-searching among sports-news outlets about their addiction to treacly human interest stories on big-time athletes. The outcome will be nil. There's no way that a single story, even one as astonishing as this one, will tweak the collective instinct of generations and generations of sports reporters. These are people, after all, who will never be content to simply let sporting events speak for themselves. They must *add* something, and it's all too often this sort of garbage.

Nah. I'm still convinced the best sportswriters tell stories as solidly reported and as affective as any journalist in any area.

More importantly, you're naïve if you think the casual disregard of the huge holes in the Manti Te'o story is a sportswriter thing. The *Chicago Tribune* is wrong: this doesn't leave a black mark on sports journalism, it leaves a black mark on all journalism. Bad journalism is bad journalism on any beat.

Follow @mleccese on Twitter.

COGNOSCENTI Thinking That Matters

LATEST   CONTRIBUTORS   ABOUT

MEDIA

'Callous And Crass': Some Thoughts On Rolling Stone's Cover

Thu, Jul 18, 2013 | by **Mark Leccese**

Mark Leccese: The sub-headline says "monster," but the photo of Dzhokhar Tsarnaev on the cover of the Aug. 1, 2013 issue of Rolling Stone says "teen idol." (Wenner Media/AP)

🖶 PRINT

✉ EMAIL

👍 Like ⟨ 1 ⟩

🐦 Tweet ⟨ 3 ⟩

➕ Share ⟨ 1 ⟩

I have no objection to Rolling Stone putting a photo of alleged Marathon bomber Dzhokhar Tsarnaev on its cover. My objection is to the photo the editors chose.

I'm looking at this week's cover ("The Bomber") alongside a cover the magazine ran in 2011 featuring pop icon Justin Bieber ("Super Boy"). The similarities are striking. The Bomber and Super Boy look directly into the camera — and at you. Both of them have artfully tousled hair. Neither smiles; their faces are smokily expressionless.

263

To some extent, that's just the format of Rolling Stone covers. Do a Google Image search of "Rolling Stone covers" and your screen will fill with faces. The cover of Rolling Stone cover has always been about portrait photography.

Dzhokhar Tsarnaev and Justin Bieber. (Rolling Stone)

But not just portrait photography — high-quality portrait photography of pop stars, from John Lennon to Johnny Depp, in which each portrait chosen for the cover reveals something about the subject. That's what good portrait photography does.

Rolling Stone chose a photo of Tsarnaev that makes him look like just another wide-eyed teenage boy. That is part of the story about Tsarnaev inside the magazine. The other part of the story, of course, is that Tsarnaev is a cold-blooded murderer and a monster. But do you see that in the cover photo?

Some people have argued, that it says "monster" and "bomber" right there on the cover of Rolling Stone, so there's no need to get all worked up about the photo. Those people lack an understanding of the power of images.

> " [Rolling Stone editors] knew their choice would generate controversy, and, not incidentally, publicity. They got both.

Enter "Dzhokhar Tsarnaev" into Google Image Search and you'll find, at most, seven or eight different photos of Tsarnaev. You've seen them all many times before.

These few photos are the ones the editors at Rolling Stone had to select from to illustrate its story with the cover line: "The Bomber: How a Popular, Promising Student was Failed by his Family, Fell Into Radical Islam and Became a Monster."

Editors could have selected the photo of Tsarnaev, white baseball cap turned backward, standing with his brother, coolly surveying the happy crowd at the finish line of the Boston Marathon. The backward baseball cap, shaggy hair and casually opened jacket says "student," and the dead look on his face says "monster."

Dzhokhar and Tamerlan Tsarnaev pictured moments before the blasts that struck the Boston Marathon, April 15, 2013. (Bob Leonard/AP)

The photo Rolling Stone chose was an old self-shot that Tsarnaev used on his Twitter account; it is a photo that has been used in many publications, including on the front page of The New York Times. But Rolling Stone could have chosen the self-shot that Tsarnaev used on the Russian social media site VKontakte.

It's a black-and-white photo in which Tsarnaev, with puffy and narrowed eyes, looks into the camera. He does not look friendly or cute. He looks — or is trying to look — menacing but doesn't quite pull it off. To me, having read the Rolling Stone story, it looks like a photo of someone in the middle of a transition from "popular, promising student" to "monster." And a black-and-white photo on the cover of the usually colorful Rolling Stone would have really made a visual statement.

The editors of Rolling Stone knew what they were doing when they placed the most innocuous image of Tsarnaev they could find into the slot that, for the past 45 years, has come to coronate pop idols.

They knew their choice would generate controversy, and, not incidentally, publicity. They got both.

This undated photo provided by the vkontakte website shows Dzhokhar Tsarnaev. (vk.com/AP)

The story, which has been lost in this brouhaha, is a solid recap of what has already been published in other places with some new quotes and anecdotes. But the cover is callous and crass.

265

Related:

- Outcry, Boycotts After Rolling Stone Puts Bomb Suspect On Its Cover
- Rolling Stone's Tsarnaev Cover: What's Stirring Such Passion?

Index

267

269